People and the Competitive Advantage of Place

MAXINE GOODMAN LEVIN
COLLEGE OF URBAN AFFAIRS

Cleveland State University

Cities and Contemporary Society

Series Editors: Richard D. Bingham and Larry C. Ledebur,
Cleveland State University

Sponsored by the
Maxine Goodman Levin College of Urban Affairs
Cleveland State University

This new series focuses on key topics and emerging trends in urban policy. Each volume is specially prepared for academic use, as well as for specialists in the field.

SUBURBAN SPRAWL
Private Decisions and Public Policy
Wim Wiewel and Joseph J. Persky, Editors

THE INFRASTRUCTURE OF PLAY
Building the Tourist City
Dennis R. Judd, Editor

THE ADAPTED CITY
Institutional Dynamics and Structural Change
H. George Frederickson, Gary A. Johnson, and Curtis H. Wood

CREDIT TO THE COMMUNITY
Community Reinvestment and Fair Lending Policy
in the United States
Dan Immergluck

PARTNERSHIPS FOR SMART GROWTH
University-Community Collaboration for Better Public Places
Wim Wiewel and Gerrit-Jan Knaap, Editors

REVITALIZING THE CITY
Strategies to Contain Sprawl and Revive the Core
*Fritz W. Wagner, Timothy E. Joder, Anthony J. Mumphrey, Jr.,
Krishna M. Akundi, and Alan F.J. Artibise, Editors*

THE UNIVERSITY AS URBAN DEVELOPER
Case Studies and Analysis
David C. Perry and Wim Wiewel, Editors

PEOPLE AND THE COMPETITIVE ADVANTAGE OF PLACE
Building a Workforce for the 21st Century
Shari Garmise

People and the Competitive Advantage of Place

Building a Workforce for the 21st Century

Shari Garmise

CITIES AND
CONTEMPORARY
SOCIETY

M.E.Sharpe
Armonk, New York
London, England

Library of Congress Cataloging-in-Publication Data

Garmise, Shari.
 People and the competitive advantage of place : building a workforce for
the 21st century / by Shari Garmise.
  p. cm. — (Cities and contemporary society)
 Includes bibliographical references and index.
 ISBN 0-7656-1071-X (cloth : alk. paper) — 0-7656-1072-8 (pbk. : alk. paper)
 1. Intellectual capital. 2. Knowledge workers. 3. Knowledge workers—Training of.
4. Labor supply—Effect of technological innovations on. I. Title. II. Series.

HD53.G37 2006
331.11'09'051—dc22   2005017677

Printed in the United States of America

The paper used in this publication meets the minimum requirements of
American National Standard for Information Sciences
Permanence of Paper for Printed Library Materials,
ANSI Z 39.48-1984.

| BM (c) | 10 | 9 | 8 | 7 | 6 | 5 | 4 | 3 | 2 | 1 |
| BM (p) | 10 | 9 | 8 | 7 | 6 | 5 | 4 | 3 | 2 | 1 |

To my parents
Adrienne and David Garmise
For their love and support
And to my daughter
Heidi
Simply because . . .

Contents

List of Tables, Figures, and Exhibits   ix

Acknowledgments   xi

Introduction   xiii

1. The Emergence of People-Centered Places   3

2. Mapping the Maze: Charting the Workforce System   22

3. Establishing System Entrepreneurs: Intermediaries   47

4. Enhancing Mobility: Skill Standards, Certification,
   and Credentials   66

5. Increasing the Pool: Talent Expansion Strategies   87

6. Bringing the System to Scale: Engaging Employers   110

7. Instituting a Lifelong Learning Culture: Connecting
   Services to Support Advancement   126

8. Conclusions: People-Centered Economic Development   146

References   167

Program Interview List   177

Index   179

List of Tables, Figures, and Exhibits

Tables

1.1 Economic Development Models   10

3.1 Summary of [Employer] Brand Attributes by Intermediary Type   56

3.2 Wisconsin Regional Training Partnership (WRTP) Benchmark Data   60

7.1 The Differences Between Education and Training Programs   130

Figures

1.1 Skill Requirements Are Increasing   15

1.2 Without a High School Education, Workers Are Far More Likely to Be Unemployed and in Poverty   20

8.1 Foundations of a Regional Workforce System   150

Exhibits

1.1 Summary of Skill Need Forecasts   14

2.1 Key Players in the Workforce System   23

2.2 Mandatory One-Stop Partner Agencies   38

6.1 Summary of High-Road Partnerships   119

7.1 Six Lessons for Delivering Effective Incumbent Training   144

Acknowledgments

I am indebted to many individuals who have contributed to this book, each in his or her own way. Seth Beattie, my graduate research assistant, did superb work researching case studies and copyediting and formatting the manuscript. His insights, suggestions, and reflections on the materials enriched and deepened this book in significant ways. His contribution was well beyond the call of duty and more than I could have expected.

When developing this book, I drew on the expertise of many professional colleagues. They all gave of their time, sharing insights, resource materials, and suggestions for further exploration. I am fortunate to have had access to them and am even luckier to call some of them friends. They include Jeff Finkle, John Foster-Bey, Robert Giloth, Tim Henderson, Tom Kingsley, Robert Knight, Stephanie Powers, Roy Priest, Tom Lindsley, Elaine Scott, Ruth Schimel, Tracy Schmidt, Mark Troppe, Marc Weiss, and Dan Cudaback, whose loss is still felt.

The book also benefited from the experiences, stories, and lessons shared by the many dedicated people who work daily to enhance workforce and economic development. Their voices also are heard in this book, although they are too numerous to thank individually. Many are listed in the interview bibliography found at the end of this book. Many others I have been fortunate enough to meet throughout my professional life.

In addition, I am grateful to Richard Bingham, the series editor, for reviewing and commenting on the book, and providing overall support through the project. Harry Briggs and the rest of the M.E. Sharpe staff were a pleasure to work with. They responded rapidly and cheerfully to my questions and concerns throughout the long process of developing the manuscript. Larry Ledebur also generously read and commented on several chapters and provided helpful encouragement.

Finally, I would like to express my appreciation to several individuals who were highly influential in how I think about economic development. Their ideas, their friendship, and their overall support for my professional development still stamp my approach to this field. Kevin Morgan and Gareth

Rees convinced me early on that education and training were integral to dynamic, innovative economies. Robert Leonardi taught me the value of networks, regional economic development, and learning from a multitude of countries and places.

Any errors either of fact or interpretation in this book are entirely my own.

Introduction

Hospitals are places of epiphany.

Lying in the emergency room, I was confused and scared but conscious of my surroundings. Coping with the closure of another nearby city hospital, the hospital staff remained in motion, trying to manage an overflow of patients. The examining rooms were full, so the staff stuffed new arrivals in every empty nook and cranny they could find. Beds were everywhere in the ER, behind desks, next to the lavatories, and in the hallways. It was not a scene that inspired confidence to those of us confined to those beds. When I left the hospital, however, I was smiling.

During the six hours I spent wrapped in hospital gowns and bed sheets, the nurses, the technicians, and the registrar calmed my fears, took my blood, and monitored my life signs while navigating the chaos of the emergency room and completing the paperwork (no small feat nowadays). Of those six hours, I spent a total of only five minutes with the attending physician.

Needless to say, in spending six hours on my back, I had plenty of time to observe my environment and to think about it. This book was born during those six hours. My epiphany was a simple one: for a complex environment to work effectively, people matter. And not just the leadership (e.g., the doctor); every individual involved impacted not only my experience, but the health and welfare of everyone in the hospital. That people matter is such a simple insight it seems obvious and almost trivial. But for someone who has been involved in the world of economic development for fifteen years, the idea that the talents of people determine the state of the economy is almost revolutionary.

In communities and nations, as in hospitals, people must be at their best. For that to happen, we need to make people the center of our understanding of what makes economies work. Everything connects. The employees who wash the laundry and empty the toxic waste ensure the safety and smooth functioning of that hospital and are as vital to a safe, successful stay in the hospital as are the nurses, doctors, technicians, and administrators. People work best when they are committed to their jobs, receive living wages, are respected for their contribution, have clear opportunities to advance and acquire new skills, and believe in the work they are doing. The technician, who held my hand and kept me laughing while he stuck several needles in my arm, was just days away from starting training to advance to a nursing position. He already had several levels of technical certification and a positive attitude that infused all around him. He kept stopping by to make sure I was still smiling throughout the long wait to see the doctor. He loved what he did, he loved where he was, and he understood how to advance in that work environment. To him, I credit an overall positive experience, considering I was in an emergency room in chaos and had been brought there by ambulance.

The second epiphany that drove this book is peripherally related to hospitals, for it emerged from the birth of my daughter, Heidi. Her arrival, although most welcome, delayed the book's completion by over a year. But watching her grow has renewed my belief in its importance. Anyone who has spent significant time with babies and toddlers will discover quite quickly that people are indeed wired to learn. Aside from eating and sleeping, their whole purpose is to figure out their world—to explore, experiment, and problem solve. Children focus on self-mastery to achieve their goals. Learning, creating, and moving forward is what we are born to do. There is more than enough research out there to support this mother's insights (Acredolo and Goodwyn 2000; Gopnick, Meltzoff, and Kuhl 1999). But it really comes down to this: the people, the economies, and the communities that thrive in the information era are those that recognize and nurture people's natural spirit—their innate need to learn and to create around that learning.

Intellectual epiphanies are all well and good, but they hold little meaning if they are not backed up with solid research. The epiphany started the journey of rethinking the paradigm of economic development by reviewing new literature and new data, working with communities as a consultant trying to help them manage human capital issues as a stimulus to economic development, and doing case study research. I also gathered a variety of information on workforce development while I was vice president of research for the Council for Urban Economic Development, now the International Economic Development Council, and as assistant professor at Cleveland State University, Maxine Goodman Levin College of Urban Affairs. Throughout my career, I have been fortunate enough to talk with many people involved in the field, both in informal conversations and through formal, structured interviews. I searched for answers to the questions:

- What does the transformation to a knowledge economy mean for the theory and practice of economic development?

- What institutions and strategies provide the infrastructure for economic development in the knowledge economy?
- What have we learned from existing efforts that can help communities create and sustain a human capital strategy?

This book represents the accumulation of the knowledge and experience gleaned from the journey. It is the epiphany investigated and found convincing.

While people have always mattered, they matter differently today. Historically, people were viewed as labor to be used and discarded, not as assets that could be developed. According to classical economics, labor is subject to a phenomenon known as diminishing returns, which means that its contribution to the productivity of a firm decreases over time. Investing in people, therefore, was not considered a logical course of action. In the knowledge economy, knowledge overcomes the problem of diminishing returns. People, when conceived of as human capital assets defined by the knowledge and skills they bring to a job, become the source of growth. Knowledge spurs innovation and can be recycled and reused. Knowledge creates knowledge. Therefore, the emergence of a networked world, integrated through information technologies, in which knowledge development drives competition, has moved people to the position of primacy when one is trying to understand what factors make a city, state, region, or nation economically strong and socially just. Our institutions, however, are just catching up to this reality. The discussion of people as economic assets is vastly different from the discussion of people simply as labor. When we place people first, then education and training institutions, which develop and disseminate knowledge, become the critical infrastructure of the information age.

While innovations and inventions can be patented and thus limited for use by individual firms (for a certain amount of time), the use of knowledge vested in people cannot be limited so cleanly. Thus, knowledge spills over for use in the wider economy. As Isaac Newton is credited with saying, "I stand on the shoulders of giants." The root of new knowledge is creating from, and reconceptualizing, the knowledge that already exists. While information can be shared internationally within the blink of an eye in this Internet-connected world, the socialization and exchange of information needed to create knowledge is a much more local phenomenon. Even if all regions have access to the same information, those with a stronger human capital base (people with high levels of training and education) will be able to produce more knowledge from it and thus experience a higher rate of development (Mathur 1999).

This book will make the case that emergence of people-centered places means that investments in human capital assets are the most effective and the most desirable approach for economic development in the twenty-first century. This approach is based on the following assumptions:

- Creative, innovative workers are the infrastructure of the knowledge economy. How they are educated and networked determines the levels of innovation, technology development, and entrepreneurship in an economy.
- Economic development that fully incorporates workforce development into its mission will create both a wealthier and more just society because a people focus provides greater opportunities to a wider range of individuals. By linking skill attainment to economic growth, we recognize that for a city or region to prosper, all of its people must have access to wide opportunity sets. Thus, economic development needs to focus simultaneously on creating higher-wage jobs and preparing individuals for them.
- Knowledge is reusable and recyclable and thus provides the foundation for sustainable development. This model assumes that we can find ways to renew resources because it is not built on physical resources that will diminish over time.
- Finally, this new model puts humanity back into technology, recognizing that technology itself is not the end or the answer. Rather, it is the human application of technology that determines its use and its potential.

Once I have made the case for the new model of economic development, the rest of the book will identify the institutions and strategies that communities should consider if they want to strengthen their human capital base and enhance their competitiveness. To achieve this purpose, the book is informally divided into two sections: (1) the emergence of human capital–based economic development; and (2) the infrastructure for human capital development.

Two chapters comprise the first section. Chapter 1, "The Emergence of People-Centered Places," explains how the transformation to the knowledge economy has changed the assumptions underlying economic development, and points out the trends that make people-centered strategies critical for managing economic challenges of today and tomorrow. Chapter 2, "Mapping the Maze: Charting the Workforce System," discusses how the labor market has changed in the new economy, categorizes the current institutions involved in shaping the labor market, and identifies the existing and emergent institutions that are critical to facilitating labor market flows in an increasingly networked world.

The second section contains the remaining chapters. Chapter 3, "Establishing System Entrepreneurs: Intermediaries," discusses the emergence of intermediaries who serve as labor market entrepreneurs that both enhance the overall skill base of a community and improve the flow between supply and demand regionally by brokering information and relationships. Chapter 4, "Enhancing Mobility: Skill Standards, Certification, and Credentials," points out the need to create recognizable, portable, and transferable skills to assist individuals and businesses in navigating the labor market and in better facilitating a community's ability to manage current and future workforce demands. Chapter 5, "Increasing the Pool: Talent Expansion Strategies," summarizes the programs, policies, and approaches that communities use to increase the skill and educational attainment of their residents. An in-depth look at Cleveland is included.

Chapter 6, "Bringing the System to Scale: Engaging Employers," looks at challenges to, and opportunities for, better engaging employers in the workforce system. The chapter also explains why employer engagement is an essential precondition for the emergence of a lifelong learning culture. Chapter 7, "Instituting a Lifelong Learning Culture: Connecting Services to Support Advancement," outlines the type and scope of services needed within a region to support career advancement, which is the second precondition to establishing a lifelong learning culture. Finally, chapter 8, "Conclusions: People-Centered Economic Development," concludes the book with recommendations for building a first-class workforce system.

The ideas on which this book was founded have been gelling for many years. Cases and examples have come from academic and applied case study research in both the United States and Europe. The research is of a descriptive and partially theoretical nature: its role is to demonstrate how things are working in the field and to illustrate why this new model is the most powerful one around for communities seeking to compete effectively in a networked, knowledge-driven, global economy.

My objective is to contribute to the conversation about what regions can do to improve the quality of lives of their people. The main premise is that, ultimately, our priority needs to be to expand the overall pool of talent. We do this first by recognizing that all people are born talented. Regions provide the educational, political, social, economic, and cultural resources that influence how that talent is developed. We can do better. We must do better. Read on and see.

People and the Competitive Advantage of Place

MAXINE GOODMAN LEVIN
COLLEGE OF URBAN AFFAIRS

Cleveland State University

— 1 —

The Emergence of
People-Centered Places

In the knowledge economy, the economic vitality of places depends on the skills of the workforce, making workforce development our economic priority. Competitive places in the twenty-first century will be people centered, investing in and nurturing the skills and talents of their populations. Economic development, consequently, is in the throes of a paradigm change. It is moving from a focus on the assets of place to recognizing the assets of people. Like all paradigm changes, it means rethinking policies, strategies, and assumptions.

Notably, while this paradigm shift has been driven by changes in the economy, demographic, social, and economic trends promise to make our need for people-centered policies more urgent. This chapter, then, will first review the economic changes associated with the emergence of the knowledge economy, outline the impact of those changes on the practice of economic development, and finally look at the trends to understand the urgency of increasing our investment in human capital.

The Knowledge Economy: Competitiveness and People

Our need to develop the potential of our population is the result of the restructuring of our economy from one based on resources to one based on knowledge. In the United States and abroad, these structural transformations, including the expansion of information technologies into all economic sectors, globalization of product and labor markets, rapid technological change, shortened production and product cycles, and emerging new economic sectors and occupational needs, have led to fundamental changes in the economic environment, particularly the acceleration of the innovation process. In short, the application of new knowledge and information furthers and quickens knowledge development (Castells 1996). Accelerated innovation, in turn,

3

- drives fierce competition between firms and regions, leading to heightened mobility and insecurity for firms and workers as well as the rapid churning of small firms;
- heightens our dependence on knowledge as the primary input into innovation and new product and service development to compete in these faster, shorter cycles; and
- increases our reliance on training and education to keep skills and knowledge up-to-date and competitive. Competition is not based on cutting prices (although cost issues are not eliminated) but is founded on improving products or creating new ones, putting a premium on the human propensity for innovation (Cortright 2001). Ideas and innovations rather than raw materials are the primary inputs into products, services, and processes.

Knowledge, and people and their skills by extension, has become the source of personal, business, and community wealth leading to the empowerment of the human mind. The human mind, therefore, has become a direct productive force rather just one element of the productive system (Castells 1996).

What Is Knowledge and How Does It Drive Growth?

Knowledge includes everything we know from high-level science such as the laws of thermodynamics to everyday routines such as baking a cake (Cortright 2001). Knowledge can be straightforward and transferable, such as a recipe, or it might be tacit—knowledge that is synthesized through learning and experience but may not be easily transferred. Tacit knowledge provides people, thus businesses, with their competitive advantage. The knowledge economy, therefore, puts a premium on highly skilled people because they generate, disseminate, and apply knowledge through their labor.

In a knowledge economy, ideas drive economic growth. Joseph Cortright explains:

> The non-rival quality of ideas is the attribute that drives economic growth. We can all share and reuse ideas at zero, or nearly zero costs. As we accumulate more and more ideas, knowledge about how the world works, and to extract greater use out of the finite set of resources with which the world is endowed, we enable the economy to develop further. (Cortright 2001: 6)

As a result, growth, according to Cortright, may be limitless. Rather than eventually running out of natural resources, knowledge can improve our ability to shift and rearrange physical resources to provide higher value. In other words, we will be able to produce more with smaller physical inputs. However, this assumes that we prioritize knowledge (as opposed to information) development as a core economic development principle. Knowledge development centers on two interrelated strategies: investing in new knowledge production (stimulating research, technology transfer, and restructuring business and workplace organizations) and investing in human capital development (skills, education, and workforce systems).

Among scholars and practitioners alike, there is no agreement and research is insufficient to determine whether communities should target their resources on the institutions that foster commercializable innovations and create new jobs or on the people that generate ideas, apply them, and could assume those jobs. The truth is both are necessary and both are critical parts of the emerging new-economy model of economic development. Communities need chickens and eggs. In practice, it seems as if there is much more activity in the realm of knowledge development than in that of human capital development. Surveying activities in the field, many state and local governments are starting to find ways to invest in knowledge development, defined as research, discovery, and adaptation. Actions include:

- creating new knowledge by stimulating university and other research and then providing ways to commercialize those discoveries. Examples include Michigan's Life Science Corridor, Georgia's Research Alliance, Pittsburgh's Greenhouse Initiative, and St. Louis's Bio Belt Effort as well as more traditional efforts to encourage research parks and incubators;
- fostering innovative businesses by supporting business-to-business networks such as Arizona's industrial clusters initiative or Pennsylvania's Lightning Manufacturing; and
- applying new ideas and innovations into new products, services, or processes such as Manufacturing Extension Programs or E-Commerce Ohio.

While states and cities are moving forward in the area of knowledge development, often by focusing on their university resources, human capital investment has not made much progress. Although much lip service is given to human capital investment, it is in this area that places are least clear on how to invest and least clear on the return to investment. Thus, rather than implementing well-thought-out, comprehensive plans, cities tend to implement piecemeal approaches. The purpose of this book, therefore, is to lay out a more strategic approach to human capital investment. I am not ignoring the broader field of knowledge development, which is critical, but my purpose is to hone in on and develop our understanding of the human capital piece of this equation.

With the recognition that knowledge and skills are the source of wealth creation in the new-economy model, the nature of competitiveness, at every unit of analysis, has changed. For individuals to earn living wages, they need skills beyond those learned in high school, and to advance, they will need to keep upgrading those skills. For businesses to compete, they need top-class talent that innovates rapidly, increases productivity, and adds value to product and service development. For communities to compete, they need substantial pools of talented workers that are available today as well as in the pipeline (in education and training venues) for tomorrow. They also need local workforce systems that can help their populations adapt and upgrade skills as new knowledge and new occupational requirements emerge.

Communities that build systems that invest in people as their core asset, therefore, will have a competitive advantage. Investing in people is multifaceted, including developing them through education, retraining them to meet new challenges, retaining them by offering them a desirable place to live, and supporting them through transitions to higher levels on the knowledge chain. Investing in people also provides cities with economic sustainability over the long term, because people and businesses can adapt more readily to economic upheaval. But perhaps most important, accepting that people are the source of community wealth finally will allow us to deliver on the promise of equality. Equality is founded on the upgrading of skills, hence opportunities. No longer can a community attract a manufacturing plant that can provide family-sustaining wages to individuals with minimal education. No longer can a community afford to lose large segments of its population—its core asset.

A community's economic potential is diminished if a significant proportion of its population does not graduate high school well-trained or have the ability or opportunity to build up knowledge and skills. Places with fewer skilled people will find it difficult to generate wealth or sustain a tax base (Gottlieb 2004). If people rather than businesses are the source of wealth, then the conclusion that communities must make about their economic future is clear: invest in people, albeit within a business framework. In other words, the skills we create must match the skills competitive businesses need. So businesses have not been taken off the table, but building a skilled workforce equitably (in other words, providing skill development and advancement opportunities for all individuals) must begin to take priority on the economic development agenda of all communities.

What Does All of This Mean for Economic Development?

By identifying knowledge and the skills of people rather than the development of businesses, land, capital, or other components of physical infrastructure as the heart of competitiveness, our understanding of how to promote and nurture our economies fundamentally shifts. To understand what the transition to the knowledge economy means for economic development, it will be useful to briefly review a history of economic development.

In the beginning, from the late 1930s until the 1960s, governors, county councilors, and city mayors wanting to strengthen their economies offered incentives such as tax breaks, expansion loans, site acquisition, and zoning assistance to attract or retain businesses to build individual and community wealth. The rationale: capital assets provided the competitive advantage of business, and therefore of place. By lowering the costs of those assets, a city or state gained a competitive advantage as a business location.

Known as smokestack chasing, these location strategies focused on attracting large manufacturing companies that promised numerous jobs to a community. Cities would provide the companies with physical assets, especially facilities, land, infrastructure, and financing for development. Economic development as initially practiced, was a land-centered phenomenon. Supplementing these activities, communities looked to building a supportive business climate, by focusing on tax policy, easing permitting and regulatory activities, and, where possible, lessening the power of trade unions, all with the intent of lowering business costs and becoming more attractive to business. Within this framework, economic developers viewed low labor costs as a recruitment incentive, and a vital part of a good business climate. There was neither any reason to significantly invest in the development of human capital nor any recognition that it might contribute to the long-term competitiveness of regional businesses.

In the next phase, the 1970s and 1980s, the federal agencies, including the Economic Development Administration and the Department of Housing and Urban Development, emerged as the dominant sources of local economic development finance. Consequently, federal programs structured the character and content of local economic development practice. Although economic development practitioners started to experiment with more entrepreneurial, generative approaches to development during this period, especially new business creation, those innovations remained linked to new local uses of federal funds and remained grounded in property development. Notably, federal programs focused on redistributive issues, allocating funding to the economically disadvantaged areas during this period.

In the late 1980s and early 1990s, economic development practitioners continued to expand and diversify their activities. This was due in large part to the globalization of the economy, the retrenchment of federal government financing, and the recognition that past location and property-driven strategies were not successful, especially in this new globalizing world. Many of

7

the manufacturing firms that had readily responded to incentives and reduced labor costs were the first to relocate to even cheaper locations abroad. Communities, facing serious issues of unemployment and downsizing, responded with a range of new economic development practices targeted to creating conditions for the development of successful local businesses. In this period, economic development became more local in content and character.

Examples of new strategies include revolving loan funds to provide low interest business financing, tax increment financing to support redevelopment efforts, enterprise zones, and the start of metropolitan and regional cooperation (Clarke and Gaile 1998). Other approaches included import substitution, business retention, technical assistance, and venture capital development. While these programs are hard to categorize, as they are quite varied, Clark and Gaile (1998) note that they share several features.

- They focus on the ability of government to shape market structure rather than influence individual businesses.
- They use market criteria to set priorities and leverage public and private financing.
- They are managed jointly by the public and private sectors.
- They tend to be easier to manage administratively.
- They are based on contracts rather than rights or entitlements, which are often negotiated on a case-by-case basis.
- They tolerate higher levels of risk.

But perhaps more important, these initiatives still focused on ways to support hard business development, attraction, and retention by providing physical business infrastructure, especially financing and property. While workforce training programs had begun to emerge during this period, especially at the state level, those programs focused on incumbent worker training, upgrading the skills of workers in existing or attracted businesses, not an overall strategy to build community skills. Similarly, community- or neighborhood-based strategies looked to build skills of some of their residents, but many of these programs failed because they did not account for business demand for skills. Although workforce development approaches were in play, they were marginal and viewed as supplementary strategies, not core economic development activities.

From the late 1990s through our entry into the twenty-first century, the foundation of economic development changed. As globalization progressed and the economy heated up, knowledge creation and the lack of skilled workers became core economic development concerns. We have moved from the era of people as labor to the era of people as human capital. Knowledge, skills, training, and academic preparedness are now an essential part of business strategy and competitive advantage. Economic development practitioners were thrown into new places, where they have to deal with more complex issues, work with new partners, and focus on the various soft elements of business, including workforce development and workplace organization. Making deals to increase physical assets was no longer the core need (although it remains important): finding ways to build knowledge, influence human behavior, and develop human assets now came to the forefront. In fact, many economic developers use land development to increase regional knowledge assets such as building research parks to encourage commercialization of new ideas and inventions or revitalizing downtowns to increase their attractiveness to young professionals.

Even with a new focus on people and skills, place still matters. As Waits (2000) points out, it matters differently. Past location strategies aimed to minimize differences between places to make certain areas more attractive to investors. New entrepreneurial strategies try to differentiate places, creating niches and specializations that shape local markets and brand their unique characteristics. Place needs to be attractive to attract and retain a diverse range of professional and technical talent, marked by large pools of talent and competitive workforce systems to build and rebuild core skills. Cities now need to create good people climates in addition to good business climates. If once the presence of a large pool of cheap, unskilled workers helped attract manufacturing companies, now it will discourage rather than attract businesses. Moreover, places dominated by a low-skilled workforce are the most vulnerable to economic change (Conway 2002).

In reaction to the growing business demand for skilled labor, communities began to chase talent in the same way they pursued businesses, using marketing campaigns to sell their environment and cost of living, and building new recreational and cultural amenities. In effect, they simply transferred the focus of their marketing strategies, without rethinking the implications of what these trends might actually mean. The talent chase, however, does little to support the long-term strength of the U.S. economy. It steals from Peter to pay Paul, when the real need is to expand the pool of talent.

This approach is shortsighted and does little to address our long-term skill shortages. Instead, cities need to embrace a new set of local policy choices—to build knowledge and human capital rather than more traditional fixed factors of production to fuel an economy based on talent and innovation (Clarke and Gaile 1998). Skill creation processes are local processes (Porter 1990). Local institutions need to focus on those policies that maximize people's skills (education, training) and their ability to build and contribute those skills (e.g., day care, health care, transportation, financing). People are the new

Table 1.1

Economic Development Models

Classic economic development model	New-economy model
Physical and capital assets	Human capital and knowledge assets
Job creation	Wealth creation
Business-centered climates	People-centered climates
Making deals	Facilitating connections
Tight networks	Loose, wide networks
Government	Governance through partnership
Tax incentives to business	Incentives to stimulate individual choice
Proprietary information within departments, separate databases	Information sharing, shared databases
Zero-sum game	Positive-sum game
Manufacturing	Technology/value-added services
Standardization	Diversity and customization

infrastructure of the knowledge economy. Each place will find its own set of policies to build the local workforce.

Making workforce the focus of economic development efforts turns the field on its head. Old tools such as tax incentives now may, in many places, negatively influence economic development success since certain tax incentives reduce available resources for education and training efforts. In some places, such as northern Virginia, the technology industry has voiced loud opposition to state tax cuts and supported the implementation of a specific local tax for their region for enhancing the education and transportation infrastructure.

Table 1.1 summarizes the changes in the practice of economic development wrought by the information age.

These changes not only reorient the focus of economic development but also have important implications for how economic development is designed and implemented. Core changes include:

- the resurgence of a government role;
- the decline of jurisdictions; and
- the need for adaptive public institutions.

Resurgence of a Government Role

Over past decades, the United States as a whole has looked to increase private sector involvement and private sector leadership in the management and steerage of the economy. While the private sector has a key role to play in skills development, public leadership remains vital.

New-economy analysts note that the private sector tends to underinvest in knowledge and skills development (Atkinson 2001; Mathur 1999). From the business point of view, there is a high level of uncertainty as to whether they can capture the value created through an investment in ideas or in people. Because ideas and people are mobile and nonproprietary, businesses, especially smaller ones, do not have much incentive to pay for skills training. In fact, it is often easier to poach from others than to invest. Even though businesses are significant investors in training, it is not sufficient to meet the wide-ranging needs of the new knowledge economy. In fact, a large talent pool can be viewed as a public good. Thus, places where state and city government are willing take on a substantial role with respect to investing in knowledge (research, technology transfer, and business and workplace organization) and human capital development (skills, education, and workforce systems) gain an economic competitive advantage.

The Decline of Jurisdictions

The labor market, commuting zones, and the cachement areas of training providers (e.g., community colleges) are usually regional in scope, and have traditionally crossed political boundaries. Workforce Investment Boards (see chapter 2), which represent a federally driven strategic approach to workforce development, are also regional in nature, and look to build skills in a more integrative fashion. From a workforce perspective, jurisdictions can be a hindrance.

Even more to the point, one of the more fundamental changes in the nature of the new economy is a growing inability to define the local labor force. Increasingly, a significant percentage of the local workforce may not work locally. Telecommuting, for example, is changing the nature of the local labor force. While what this means is still unclear, it points to emerging challenges and opportunities for human capital investment strategies. For example, Boston-based Putnam investments has set up home-based jobs in Vermont, funding workstations, high-speed Internet access, and training to Vermonters who work for Putnam from home. According to Carol Conway, "The bottom line is there is a growing disconnect between a state's education and training system and the people who work for the firms in that state" (2002: 18). The educational attainment of the workforce, therefore, is not solely a function of the local education system (Gottlieb and Fogarty 2003). Grabbing a hold of the workforce challenge will mean working across jurisdictions. It is not resolvable within a solely local framework.

Institutions Must Adapt

For many public institutions, moving into a new role will be difficult. Many of our institutions are being challenged by the information revolution: key among them are government and schools. According to Romer (1992):

> As the world becomes more and more closely integrated, the features that will increasingly differentiate one geographic area (city or country) from another will be the quality of public institutions. The most successful areas will be the ones with the most competent and effective mechanisms for supporting collective interests, especially in the production of new ideas. (cited in Cortright 2001: 19)

Not only will public institutions have to find new ways of working, and begin to share information in uncommon ways, they will have to promote experimentation and learning as critical to continued competitiveness. Public institutions will need to become learning institutions. That learning and adaptation must occur at both the formal level through changes in laws, regulations, the structure and function of governmental agencies, and the informal level in terms of culture and workplace organization. The need to "reinvent government" is not new (Osborne and Gaebler 1992), but it remains important as local areas look to build a new system to keep their economy sustainable and to open up new economic opportunities.

Our school systems will be particularly challenged. In this new, technology-driven economy, where we do not know what skills and talents will be required five or ten years down the road, all individuals must be academically prepared and technologically savvy. As Hicks noted about Texas, "the vast majority of the employers and employment on which Texans will depend in the year 2026—or even 2006—do not yet exist" (cited in Kelly 1998: 109). Thus, we may be unable to provide the information individuals can use to survive over the coming decades, but we can provide them the skills. It is not what we know that will determine our success, but how we learn. Skills are the basis of new knowledge acquisition. One of the hardest lessons communities must learn is that the size of the talent pool and the quality of its workforce system will be an essential determinant of competitiveness.

Emerging Trends and Challenges

Even if the reader remains skeptical about the underlying changes in the economy and their significance for economic development strategies, there are other pressing challenges that insist that workforce development become a community priority.

To summarize the challenges in brief, there are not enough skilled people around. Nor do the forecasters and statisticians expect there to be for some time to come. Economic, demographic, and income trends, taken cumulatively, indicate that: (1) businesses are not finding people with the skills they need; (2) current and future workers will not have those skills; and (3) since skills determine a person's income potential, income disparities will increase, thus increasing social instability. These challenges make the need for aggressive, well-resourced human capital investment essential. Although we have done much to improve national skill levels, the following trends demand more attention to, investment in, and innovation toward building higher skills. The rest of this chapter lays out those challenges, which include:

- forecasted skill shortages;
- changing demographics;
- an increasing gap between richest and poorest; and
- service sector dominance.

Forecasted Skill Shortages

When we talk of skill shortages, we are actually referring to four separate but interrelated problems. The first challenge refers to a shortage of highly skilled professionals such as engineers, designers, physicists, sales representatives, and physicians. These workers, also referred to as talent, design, develop, and create. They are the frontline workers of the knowledge economy. Workers at this level usually possess at least a B.A. and often a higher degree. These individuals are trained and recruited from national markets but the ability to grow them locally provides a community with a large advantage. Forecasters from numerous research institutions agree that the jobs that will continue to grow fastest are in the professional and high-skill sectors (see Exhibit 1.1). But the number of students choosing career paths based in math, science, and technology is declining, signaling that our talent gap will continue.

The second challenge is the lack of certified technicians and other skilled workers. Technicians produce, modify, repair, care, and maintain. Members of this workforce receive education and training post–high school but do not necessarily need a four-year degree. They will, however, require regular training and certification to keep their skills up-to-date throughout the course of their careers. Examples might include welders, electricians, respiratory therapists, or phlebotomists. This workforce is predominantly trained and recruited from the regional labor market, although, in times of shortage, recruiters may expand that search area. Some evidence suggests that jobs requiring some postsecondary education are growing at a much faster rate than workers with available skills. One forecast notes that by 2028, demand for work-

Exhibit 1.1

Summary of Skill Need Forecasts

National Science Foundation (NSF)
Between 2000 and 2010, the NSF estimates a 47 percent job growth of science and engineering occupations. All others will grow at about 15 percent (NSB 2004).

Employment Policy Foundation (EPF)
According to Robert Byrd, chief economist at the EPF, "In 30 years, if current trends continue, management and professionals will make up most of the workforce, followed by mid-skilled workers, then manual laborers" (cited in NAB 2001: 3).

National Alliance of Business (NAB)
By 2028, there will be up to 18 million skilled positions unfilled, predominantly in six areas: information technology, engineering, teaching, health care, business, and medical and engineering technology (NAB 2001).

ers with at least some postsecondary education will outpace supply, with up to 18 million skilled jobs left unfilled (National Alliance of Business 2001).

The third challenge refers to enhancing the skills of those who have only a high school diploma or below. Often, this population lacks the important basic academic skills that provide the foundation on which to advance. As Figure 1.1 shows, to compete in the labor market and earn family-sustaining wages, most individuals will need training beyond high school. These workers, who may be employed in areas such as retail and hospitality, are usually recruited from a local job market.

Finally, the overall community population, even those in entry-level jobs, will need to be well skilled and savvy on the technological and global scale. They will have strong science and math skills, be academically prepared, entrepreneurial, flexible, and creative as well as eager and able to learn new skills throughout life. In other words, having a strong education system is a precondition of a good workforce system.

On the positive side, we have witnessed improvements in the numbers of students finishing high school. Data show that in 1960, only 10 percent of U.S residents had a bachelor's degree and over half the population of the prime-age workforce had not finished high school, while today, only 12 percent have not graduated from high school (Van Opstal 2001). Between 1973 and 1998, the proportion of workers who were high school dropouts fell by 50 percent among less skilled blue-collar and service professionals, while the proportion of workers in this category with some college or more trebled (ibid.).

However, increased high school graduation rates do not guarantee that businesses are finding the skills they need in the new labor force. For example,

14

Figure 1.1 **Skill Requirements Are Increasing**

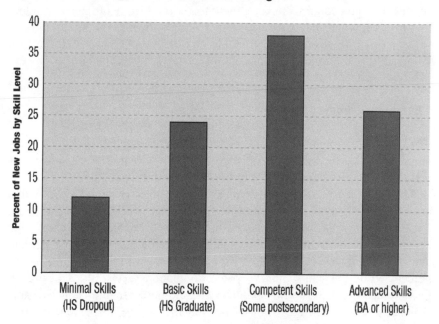

Source: Council on Competitiveness. Data Central. U.S. Competitiveness 2001a.

about one-third of companies have to provide remedial education to their workforce (Council on Competitiveness 2005). This makes current problems with literacy more significant than ever. Literacy must be recognized as a community priority and not left in the realm of social services or charity work.

What are the implications of these skill shortages? Cities and states with a strong human capital foundation will grow most rapidly and be more prosperous. In their analysis of the 2000 Census, Glaeser and Shapiro (2001) found that cities with a strong human capital base, measured by the percentage of college graduates, grew faster than cities lacking that skill base. The cities with the least-educated populations tended to be the poorest cities measured by per capita income. Notably, poverty and unemployment negatively predicted growth, which Glaeser and Shapiro interpret as additional evidence supporting the importance of skills. Another study, conducted by Gottlieb and Fogarty (2003), also found a significant relationship between cities with a highly educated population, defined by attainment of bachelor's degrees, and the growth rates of income and employment between 1980 and 1997.

Glaeser and Shapiro's research sheds more light on the changes in economic development models. They found that cities growing fastest also tended to have more young people and were situated in warmer climates suggesting that economic development has shifted from a focus on production needs (cool climates for manufacturing plants, natural resources) to a focus on consumption needs (lifestyle opportunities). This evidence provides additional support that competitiveness is no longer business centered but people centered.

Changing Demographics

Changing demographics may profoundly influence the quality, management, and availability of our labor force. Key factors will be the significant increase of minority populations and the graying of the population.

The 2000 Census revealed that substantial changes in the U.S. population are leading to increased racial and ethnic diversity. According to the report, *Investing in People*, which assessed the census data results, Hispanic and Asian Americans dominated the population increase, growing 58 percent and 50 percent, respectively. The African-American population rose by 16 percent while the white, non-Hispanic population grew only 3.4 percent. Given these trends, the study predicts that the percentage of non-Hispanic white population will fall from 74 percent in 1995 to 53 percent in 2050 (Business-Higher Education Forum 2001).

Immigration also adds to the diversity of the population. One in every ten people in the population is foreign born, and in cities that ratio may be higher, perhaps one in six. This has meant substantial efforts at adapting local cultures, school systems, business cultures, and language capacities and creates substantial challenges for human capital investment (Conway 2002).

Different racial and ethnic groups have different relationships to education and training. According to *Investing in People*, in 1998, about 90 percent of whites and African Americans graduated from high school, while only two-thirds of the Hispanic population did so (Business-Higher Education Forum 2001). In their investigation of new-economy metropolitan areas, Atkinson and Gottlieb (2001) found that cities with high levels of immigration from developing countries (Miami, Los Angeles, San Antonio) had lower percentages of individuals who had obtained some degree of post–high school education.

Disparities increase among groups as we move up the education ladder. In 2000, 28 percent of whites finished their B.A., compared to 17 percent of African Americans and 11 percent of Hispanics. Given the increasing need for higher skills training, this trend clearly threatens our economic future (Business-Higher Education Forum 2001).

Equally ominous is the potential impact of these demographic changes on the future science and technology workforce. Professional and technical jobs are growing most rapidly, and they are critical to the growth of knowledge businesses and industries. Traditionally non-Hispanic white males have formed the bulk of the science and technology workforce (65 percent in 1997), while the labor force of the future will be predominantly women and minorities (National Science and Technology Council 2000). According to data from the White House Office of Science and Technology Policy, in 2050, 74 percent of the labor force will be women and minorities (Valdez 1998, cited in Council for Urban Economic Development 1998). If current patterns of career choices continue, the expected impact will be a 9 percent drop in the science and technology workforce by 2050 (National Science and Technology Council 2000).

Better adjusting to our diverse workforce will have a profound impact on national wealth. If Hispanics and African Americans received equivalent education and earnings as whites, national wealth would increase by about $113 billion annually for African Americans and $118 billion for Hispanics (Carnevale and Fry 2000, cited in Business-Higher Education Forum 2001: 15). This brings us to one of the core arguments of this book—investing in equality, defined as access to skill development, will lead to the prosperity of our community and our nation.

In addition to the increasing diversity of the population, the graying of the labor force also poses significant challenges and opportunities with respect to our economic strength. To understand these changes, we first need to review the demographics of aging. Since World War II, there have been three distinct demographic periods: the baby boom (1946 to 1964), the baby bust (1965 to 1976) where birth rates dropped precipitously, and then the echo boom (1977–1997), where birth rates rose again.

From the point of view of workforce availability, this indicates that as the baby boomers age, the pool of workers following in their footsteps will be smaller, predicting a period of labor shortages, which will add to the skill shortages we already experience. The predicted gap between the number of retired baby boomers and workers is unprecedented in U.S. history. By 2030, there will be less than three workers for every retiree. In other words, about 30 percent of the population will be over age sixty-five. As a comparison, in 1950, there were seven workers per retiree (Committee for Economic Development 1999).

Although the echo boomers will be following quickly behind to enter the job market, they will be younger and have less experience and maturity. In other words, the middle tier of the workforce—the critical tier with tacit knowledge gained from experience—will be missing. In many communities, business concerns about a future pipeline to skilled workers have been the catalyst for the development of future workforce programs. The impacts of these demographic changes will be more dramatic in specific sectors. Particularly hard hit will be the public sector and education and health services.

What will be the overall impact of the aging of the population on the economy?

The answer to that question depends on many things but several scenarios are possible, with very different outcomes. Some examples are offered below, but there are other possibilities for the future as well.

Scenario 1

National savings will be reduced to pay for spiraling costs of old-age support programs. This may encourage or even compel mature citizens to keep working, thus helping communities to deal with increased costs and providing access to needed skills. Former retirement patterns may be replaced with alternative work arrangements such as an increased number of part-time older workers, and also older workers who take on consulting and free-agent positions to deal with demand levels. However, for this to come about, we will have to enact substantial changes in the culture of work (e.g., eliminating discrimination against older workers), pension and other financial arrangements (some private pensions, social security, and Medicare benefits involve barriers to work that revolve around earnings), and training (while older workers provide dedication, stability, and flexibility, they also often have not kept their skills up and may not adapt quickly to new technologies and new workplace cultures).

Scenario 2

As the aging population exits the workforce, fewer workers will be working fewer hours, thereby producing less in the economy. The decline in the size of the labor force (and tax base) means we will need to increase productivity, which will inevitably lead to technological solutions (in turn increasing skill needs), increase immigration, and increase outsourcing abroad.

Whatever scenario emerges, we need to address many of these issues today. The older population is part of the core of assets our communities have available. We will continue to need their knowledge and labor in some form, albeit in new or innovative ways. How we integrate their knowledge and skills into the economy will be important for the long-term sustainability of our cities, states, and the nation.

An Increasing Gap Between Richest and Poorest

One of the most profound and disturbing implications of a knowledge-based economy is its impact upon the fortune of individuals. The gap between the richest and poorest is increasing significantly. Lester Thurow explains:

> In the global economy where employers arbitrage the world looking for the lowest wages, people's pay is not based on whether they live in a rich or a poor country but upon their individual skills. The well-educated living in India make something that looks like American wages, while the uneducated living in America make something that looks like Indian wages. If unskilled first world workers don't want to be in competition with equally unskilled but lower wage third world workers, they will need much better skills. With globalization and a skill intensive technological shift, much better skills must be delivered to the bottom two-thirds of the labor force in the developed world if their wages are not to fall. (1999: 132–33)

Globalization and a knowledge-based economy have led to increasing wage inequality, a situation determined predominantly by skill-level acquisition. According to Council of Competitiveness data, U.S. wage inequality has grown considerably between the late 1970s and the late 1990s. The average college graduate earned 38 percent more than the average high school graduate in 1979. In 1998, that differential had jumped to 71 percent. Without the minimum of a high school diploma, an individual is likely to be unemployed and in poverty (see Figure 1.2).

Lower-skilled individuals also are more vulnerable in the face of an economic downturn. Research by the Employment Policy Foundation (2001) shows that during the recent economic slowdown (September 2000 through October 2001), job losses most heavily affected individuals with no postsecondary training while 1.2 million jobs were created for individuals with postsecondary training. Since September 11, 2001, that impact has been exacerbated as jobs for individuals with postsecondary training have grown while those with the least amount of education have faced job losses. Put in another way, during the recent slowdown period, the unemployment rate was 2.1 percent for individuals with a B.A. and above, 3.7 percent for persons with vocational degrees, and 9.8 percent for individuals with less than a high school diploma.

The growing income disparities point to an economic reality that has not yet been sufficiently addressed: the continuing dominance of service sector jobs in the economy, which produces a large proportion of low-paying jobs.

Service Sector Dominance

While new job growth in skilled positions is outpacing now job growth in low-skilled positions, replacement jobs (jobs opened when an employee

Figure 1.2 **Without a High School Education, Workers Are Far More Likely to Be Unemployed and in Poverty**

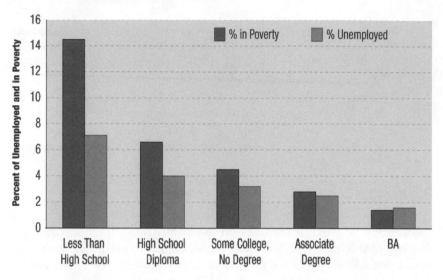

Source: Council on Competitiveness. Data Central. U.S. Competitiveness 2001b.

leaves) available in the economy are expected to be greater in low-skilled jobs paying $10.60 and less per hour (Bennici, Mangum, and Sum 2000). Since these jobs are marked by high turnover, they may comprise a larger percentage of available jobs within the economy than does new job growth. Moreover, although most labor market projections indicate slow growth in low-paying entry-level jobs, these sectors remain substantial employers. For example, the retail trade, which is the largest employer in the country, is projected to have slow growth (1 percent per year) but will remain the dominant economic sector through 2010. As another example, the eating and drinking industry, another source of lower-skilled jobs, is projected to increase about 2.9 percent in the same period, adding about 1.5 million jobs to the economy (Berman 2001). Low-skill, low-wage jobs will remain a core component of the economy. In fact, dynamic economies are marked by a range of recreational amenities that include retail, food, and drink. The creation of high-wage knowledge jobs seems intimately tied to the generation of low-wage service jobs. This may represent a dark underside to the knowledge economy.

So we have a dilemma. If we focus on increasing the skills and capabilities and thus the ambitions of our population, will it undermine core components of the local economy? Will we have insufficient workers for the service sector? The answer is no, it does not have to. It will take us a long time to comprehensively approach human capital development. But more than that, these types of jobs can be important entry-level positions, stepping-stones in a career path for those entering or reentering the workforce. With alternative-style work arrangements, the labor force can be supplied with students, mature workers, transitional workers, immigrants, and the disabled who can use these positions as part-time, supplementary, or training opportunities. With a few exceptions, these jobs should not be seen as end-points in anyone's career path, but developmental points. The challenge is not to allocate these jobs to the low skilled, but rethink how to integrate them into full-scale human capital development strategies in a way that benefits the individual, the business, and the community. Later chapters will take this issue up in more detail.

Conclusion

Herein lies the paradigm change. Economic development is about people. Equality of opportunity, whereby all people have access to skill development and career advancement, is the surest way to prosperity. For communities, the challenge is to create a workforce system that serves as a driver of economic development by expanding and enhancing the regional pool of talent. The ability of a community to nurture the talents of its residents from birth through alternative work arrangements in retirement will determine a community's competitiveness in the years to come.

On the flip side, the lack of top skills condemns individuals, and, increasingly, communities, to second-class status in a global economy. The knowledge economy, which holds great promise as the foundation of sustainable development, also suggests emergent new definitions of disparity and exclusion that need to be addressed. Fortunately, improving opportunities for individuals translates into improved opportunities for regions and businesses. The answer to improved competitiveness is to create a strong workforce system that builds talent. This book is part of the conversation about how we can learn to do this. Government activity will be an important part of the answer, but only part of the answer. The future will be a function of solid partnerships among the public, private, and community sectors.

The next chapter examines the impact of the new economy on public, private, and community institutions that bolster the labor market. It identifies the institutions that need to be in place to build and maintain a twenty-first-century workforce system.

— 2 —

Mapping the Maze: Charting the Workforce System

Although investing in people is a straightforward answer to current and emerging economic challenges, its implementation is anything but simple. Workforce development is comprised of a bewildering array of agents and institutions serving different populations at different levels of skill development. Creating even greater complexity, this labyrinthine world is bifurcated into a supply side (those serving individuals) and a demand side (those serving business needs), which have historically worked in isolation. This chapter will introduce these institutions and start addressing the question that makes up the heart of this book: what institutions and strategies help communities to maximize their human capital potential, in order to foster an environment that nurtures the creative talents of all citizens? The goal of regional efforts to build talent should not focus simply on transferring a defined set of skills but on enhancing the ability and desire of individuals, businesses, and organizations to learn and develop further, in order to create a culture of lifelong learning.

Yet, too many programs and institutions related to the labor market were established in response to assumptions and exigencies of an industrial economy. Given the emergence of the knowledge-based economy, communities need updated labor market institutions and economic development strategies in tune with new demands. This chapter looks at how labor markets have changed and what our institutions need to be if we want to meet the challenges of the twenty-first century and strengthen the competitive advantage of places.

Changes in the Organization of the Labor Market

It is always useful to readers when an author elaborates her assumptions about how the world works because these assumptions influence the conclusions generated. In this case, the world is the labor market, and this author

---

Exhibit 2.1

Key Players in the Workforce System

- Workforce investment boards
- City, state, and federal agencies
- Business and labor associations
- Neighborhood and community-based organizations
- Public-private partnerships
- Educational institutions (kindergarten through graduate school, including community colleges and other higher education alternatives)
- Foundations, religious, and charitable organizations
- Individuals who influence career choices, such as parents and guidance counselors

---

starts with an institutional perspective. An institutional perspective assumes the labor market is essentially stratified, whereby different subpopulations have differential access to the opportunities in it. More specifically, an institutionalist perspective assumes that institutions (which are composed of organizations, e.g., firms, training agencies and employment services, rules and regulations, such as those determined by the government, and informal and formal practices as in workplaces and unions) are influential in the allocation of jobs and wages. An institutionalist does not ignore the impact of market competition, but assumes that institutions and social relations give the market its shape, and structure the labor market incentives to which people and businesses respond.

Many of the institutions influencing the functioning of the labor market, however, have evolved in the industrial age and have been weak because, overall, they were not needed. The academic education system, which prepares individuals for work, has functioned well for the majority of the population. In the industrial era, individuals did not need more than a high school education to find a job that could provide them with family-sustaining wages. Moreover, there was less mobility in the labor market. Once hired, it was common practice to stay with a firm through retirement (Osterman 1999).

For those who did not receive an appropriate education, a second-chance system, the public training regime, was available. However, the programs in the second-chance system were relatively small and only available to a narrow band of low-income or disadvantaged populations. Consequently, these programs were implemented outside the main labor market, meaning that people were provided training with no reference to actual labor market needs. On average, neither companies nor individuals used many of the available programs (Osterman 1999).

The information age has transformed the character of the labor market, with substantial implications for the working of labor market institutions. Osterman (1999) identified three critical changes. First, job mobility has increased, which creates a demand for institutions that can help individuals navigate multiple job transitions throughout their lives. Second, the balance of power between labor and management is shifting toward management, with consequences for job security and wage stagnation. Career ladders have historically been tied to a person's place of occupation. Increased mobility now places the onus of career advancement on individuals, who will be responsible for developing new skills, obtaining credentials, and navigating a volatile labor market on a more regular basis. Third, new institutions, such as temporary-staffing firms and private-training providers, have emerged and are redrawing the labor market in ways we do not yet understand.

In addition to these three changes, a fourth change requires our attention: the pace of knowledge development. Given that we do not know what problems, industries, or technologies our children will need to manage, in good part because they do not exist, we need education, training, and other labor market institutions that can continuously adapt to meet yet unrecognized needs.

With globalization and the ability to transfer information in real time, companies can buy skills at the cheapest price wherever they may be found. Communities that have institutions that can respond quickly to new skill and knowledge needs may have an advantage in the global search for talent. Communities must learn to build lifelong learning opportunities into the core design and philosophy of the workforce system.

For most communities, developing a workforce system that meets the needs of the knowledge age will be a significant challenge. Many current programs offer training to meet highly defined tasks or government regulations or solve only a current issue, and do not address building a competitive business or person over the long term. Moreover, the workforce landscape is marked by multiple programs, providers, and participants that are competitive, disconnected, and duplicative.

The challenge is to look at the system in a way that truly integrates competitive skill building into it—not as a last resort to solve a specific problem at a specific point in time. Thus our education and training institutions need to be linked through career pathways that allow individuals to pick up additional training at different points in time from different institutions, and that cumulatively provide advanced credentials.

In sum, the emergence of the knowledge economy has created a demand for new institutions and new approaches that can facilitate job transitions, help individuals improve their overall marketability, and meet business's continuously changing demands (Osterman 1999).

In response to these emerging needs, what has happened in the past decade or so has been: the proliferation of a wide variety of workforce-related institutions; increased dissatisfaction with existing institutions (e.g., schools); increased expectations regarding the economic-development contribution of existing institutions (universities, community colleges); research clearly indicating that past approaches to training have been generally unsuccessful; and a growing consciousness that the workforce matters, although with no common understanding of what that means nor what we should do about it. These trends are pushing communities to reflect on what the purpose and design of a competitive workforce-development system should look like.

To address these questions, this chapter first lays out the range of players involved in the workforce system, then reviews recent attempts by the federal government to create a new institutional foundation for managing regional workforce systems, and finally offers a framework communities can use to develop the institutional infrastructure demanded by the exigencies of the knowledge economy.

Who Are the Key Players in the System and What Role Do They Play?

A fully functioning workforce system will provide a framework that creates linkages and career pathways for critical careers, helps institutions, businesses, and individuals adapt in order to meet changing needs, innovates and pools new resources for changing objectives, and maximizes the potential of individuals, businesses, and regions. To put that system together, communities need to understand the roles of the multitude of players involved in workforce development and where they fit in the system.

Primary Schools (K–12)

When discussing the education and training of the workforce, the discussion must start with schools, although it is beyond the scope of this book to make specific recommendations on how to reform schools. From an economic development perspective, schools' main roles are: (1) the academic preparation of students, and (2) the development of transparent, articulated connections to the world of work and secondary education.

First, as expressed recently by the federal No Child Left Behind Act, and as acknowledged by businesses now for many years, students' academic achievement is a troublesome issue. Maintaining high academic standards for all students, not just those who are college bound, is a critical principle for schools. No matter what path students take past high school (work, two-year school, four-year school), they must first and foremost be prepared academically. At one time, vocational or technical tracks were (and in many places still are) considered the place for less-talented students. Students did not require the same academic rigor nor were they believed to be able to handle it. Because of the increasing technological requirements of many occupations, many two-year curricula are no longer an easy route to a job. Community colleges, for example, are starting to find that students cannot handle some of the more science- or technology-based curricula (e.g., nursing, environmental sciences).

Thus, communities wanting to compete in the new economy must ensure that all students stay in school and graduate with a high level of academic skills, no matter what career path they choose to follow. Neighborhoods experiencing 50 percent dropout rates and high levels of illiteracy—and they exist in many inner-city neighborhoods—should be considered a national emergency.

Second, communities also need to find ways to create more formal career pathways by building connections between high school and work and high school and institutions of higher education. Example strategies include: dual enrollment classes whereby students receive high school and college credit and are exposed to the college environment; tech prep, which sponsors articulation agreements with community colleges along occupational pathways; school-to-work programs, which build career preparation directly into the curriculum, such as internships, mentorships, and other activities that increase student exposure to the world of work; and academic pathways that move students into math and science, as well as other, careers.

In sum, the workforce development role of K–12 is to:

- build core academic and technical skills for the entire student population;
- ensure that all students graduate with those skills;
- provide career planning and education, with a focus on the need for lifelong learning and adaptability;
- expose students to the world of work through internships, mentors, experiential learning, and other efforts; and
- create clear pathways for different types of students to follow different career/education tracks via articulation agreements with two- and four-year schools.

Community and Technical Colleges

Community and technical colleges and other two-year institutions are core players in the local/regional workforce development system. They are essential institutions for marrying supply-and-demand considerations in a regional economy, supplying technicians to the workforce, and creating bridges between the first-chance and the second-chance workforce systems. They perform their workforce development role in two ways. First, they often have a workforce development arm, which provides customized training to meet specific and well-defined skill needs as expressed by businesses, usually to upgrade the skills of the incumbent workforce. Second, they provide well-developed certification and curricula to provide more general training for industrial or occupational categories. In many states, these courses are overseen by business advisory councils that meet regularly to ensure the relevance of the curricula to current business needs. Community colleges can usually develop or borrow a curriculum much more quickly than universities. Although they are still bureaucracies, they tend to be more flexible and can change course more easily than other secondary educational institutions.

While some community colleges have excelled in this area, in practice, many two-year institutions have not necessarily built up their capacity to meet regional workforce needs. Rather, they serve as transfer institutions, meaning that the majority of their students attend school as a strategy to move on to an advanced academic degree, not directly into the labor market. This is not to say that the transfer component is not important. In fact, when looking at talent expansion broadly it is quite critical and this will be discussed later on in the book. Rather, the problem is that the workforce component of their work is minimized, often by state regulations and funding structures.

State laws determine the degree to which community colleges can develop their workforce. Traditionally, community colleges have received funding based on full-time credit students, thus serving as a disincentive to provide workforce training, which usually consists of noncredit courses. In Texas, for example, they changed these laws in conjunction with offering large workforce grants, providing incentives for colleges to build up these activities.

Two-year colleges also are core institutions for helping individuals to transition into new career fields or advance in their current field because they: provide more flexible course hours; have advanced in the area of distance learning, which provides greater flexibility and access, especially for adult students; are more attuned to the needs of the regional economy; are more affordable than four-year universities; and have experience providing remediation for students with poorer skills.

Finally, two-year schools can help communities to dig deeper into the labor pool in order to build talent. Some have well-developed programs to support former welfare recipients entering the workforce or to help at-risk youth to stay in school and receive career training and preparation. Others provide training opportunities directly to prisons, to make prisoners more employable when they reenter society.

In sum, two-year schools:

- educate the technical workforce for the region;
- provide customized training to improve the skills of incumbent workers;
- offer continuing education, certification, and customized workforce programs to local residents;
- have faculty members who work with local businesses to solve problems and to develop intellectual property, adding workforce power to local industry;
- improve the academic standing of students;
- help older workers transition into new career fields;
- provide training for harder-to-serve populations (former welfare recipients, prisoners, ex-offenders, at-risk youth);
- are more attuned to curriculum needs of regional businesses;
- link the second-chance training system back into the first-chance education system; and
- can use local business leaders as adjunct faculty to inject practical, real-life approaches to learning, which better prepares the workforce for the real-life challenges and opportunities they will face.

Universities

Four-year colleges and beyond are the core institutions for building professional talent. While state schools are important feeders for state markets, private institutions serve a national and increasingly international customer base (Tournatzky et al. 1998, 2001). Cities and regions with top-tier universities, such as Pittsburgh, struggle to find ways to keep the top-level talent in the region after graduation. States have also looked at ways to better ensure that state schools feed the state labor market. Georgia and Oklahoma, for example, have developed sophisticated Web-based labor recruitment vehicles to match their state university graduates with state-based businesses.

While a university's education mission often is not focused on serving the local economy, some are increasingly willing to work with the community, in particular local businesses, to ensure their curricula serve business skill needs. For example, Greater Philadelphia First, a business-led economic development agency, has worked with the University of Pennsylvania to upgrade some of its information technology curricula. The purpose was to make the university graduates more directly business ready.

Besides their direct education mission, universities contribute to the workforce in the following ways:

- They train professional workers.
- They can provide continuing education, certification, and customized workforce programs to local residents.
- Faculty and students work with local businesses to solve problems and to develop intellectual property, adding workforce power to local industry.
- Universities attract talented students from outside the region, which potentially can add to the region's talent pool and can help market the region as an attractive place to live.
- Universities can work with business groups to ensure that they are teaching the appropriate skill sets in relevant curricula, or they can even develop relevant curricula for new and emerging needs.
- Universities can offer internships, mentorships, cooperative programs, and experiential learning as well as hold local job fairs to help feed their students into their local community.
- Universities can support entrepreneurship initiatives to identify and support entrepreneurial talent.

Neighborhood and Community-Based Organizations

Community-based organizations (CBOs), including religious institutions and some social service organizations, are important intermediaries in the workforce system for the low-income, disadvantaged, or dislocated jobseekers and the underemployed. CBOs recruit, place, train, and provide pre- and post-training services to local residents to help them access, retain, and advance in work.

However, for many individuals, getting and keeping a first job is only the first step on the long road to self-sufficiency. Often, once placed in a job, these individuals may need extensive assistance in overcoming barriers that impede their ability to retain the job. Additionally, placement into the first job usually does not eliminate poverty. First jobs tend to provide low wages. Individuals must learn how to use that entry-level position as a stepping-stone to advancement. Research has shown that these individuals often need to switch jobs several times to build their skills and earn a salary that provides economic self-sufficiency (Giloth 2000). In other words, for these individuals to advance, they must learn to navigate through the labor market.

CBOs can be important support institutions to help individuals through this process. They provide a range of services including case management, child care, transportation, legal aid, and counseling, which help these individuals overcome many barriers to job retention.

Even when CBOs do not directly furnish workforce placement or retention services, they can be key intermediaries between workforce programs and community residents who would benefit from them. Because they have the knowledge and trust of those residents, CBOs can help recruit individuals into training courses and other services that can support their entry into, and growth in, the workforce.

Successful CBOs directly involved in training, placement, and retention usually have well-developed relationships with regional businesses that help them with placement of their clients. In some cases, such as the Philadelphia-based Campus Boulevard Corporation (CBC), the organization represented a consortium of businesses seeking ways to build the neighborhood workforce as both a contribution to the neighborhood in which they work and as a means of obtaining a trained workforce. In the case of CBC, the nonprofit represented ten medical and educational institutions in northwest Philadelphia and trained people for careers in health-related industries.

In sum, CBOs provide the following contributions to workforce development:

- training, placement, retention, and career development services to help low-skilled, low-income individuals enter the job market and stay in it;
- recruitment channels to reach the lower-skilled population;
- a well-developed understanding of the assets and barriers facing the disadvantaged in the labor force; and
- they can serve as an effective intermediary between the business community and neighborhood residents regarding job training, placement, retention, and advancement.

Federal, State, and City Agencies

There are numerous public agencies involved in the workforce system. To summarize their roles, they design, fund, regulate, and monitor workforce development policies and programs.

The core agencies at the federal level are the Department of Labor, which oversees the Workforce Investment Act that governs the public training system, the Department of Education, and the Department of Health and Human Services. Agencies such as the Department of Commerce, the Department of Agriculture, the Veterans Administration, the Department of Housing and Urban Development, and others, also provide programs and resources for training initiatives. Even the Immigration and Naturalization Service enters the picture for the recruitment of international workers to manage skill shortages in certain industries.

At the state level, the management of labor issues differs from state to state. Like the federal government, in most cases, functions are divided and overlap among various agencies. As a result of the Workforce Investment Act, all states have state workforce investment boards tasked with overseeing and thinking through the state approach to workforce development (see below for details). States also provide funding and regulatory oversight for the state universities, community colleges, and other public postsecondary institutions.

Similarly, at the city level, each community has a different institutional map of public agencies involved in workforce-related issues, as well as education institutions, CBOs, and business and labor groups. Economic developers increasingly enter the mix as well. Each city has a different map of institutions with varying strengths and weaknesses.

In sum, public agencies serve the workforce system in the following ways:

- They develop, regulate, and monitor workforce, education, and training policies and programs.
- They provide resources to support federal, state, and local efforts.
- They collect, interpret, and disseminate information on the labor market, available resources, effective training agencies, and industry and occupational trends.
- They find ways to work across jurisdictions and borders to meet common goals.
- They provide leadership and serve as catalysts to bring different groups together to collectively coordinate and integrate efforts to: (1) meet short-term goals; and (2) work together to build a better workforce system to address the challenges of the future.

Workforce Investment Boards

As part of the Workforce Investment ACT (WIA), each state and local area must create a Workforce Investment Board (WIB), a public-private entity, to oversee strategic and policy issues related to the workforce development system. WIBs were envisioned to be central players in the oversight and management of a holistic workforce system that included initiatives in the public, private, and community sectors. As discussed above, WIBs were given the unprecedented opportunity to provide strategic leadership and policy development for the entire workforce system. While initial evidence suggests that most workforce boards have had difficulty achieving this vision, the opportunity to provide leadership and build a functioning workforce system lies dormant in each of the WIBs.

WIBs offer:

- leadership for the workforce system;
- a forum where various players get together to manage workforce concerns;
- access to, and allocation of, federal training resources; and
- the creation of links that better marry labor market supply and demand.

Business, Labor, and Their Representative Associations

Business, labor, and their representative organizations (such as chambers of commerce, industry groups, trade associations, and labor unions) are heavily involved in workforce development. Not only are they key customers in the workforce system, they can be primary providers of training and skill upgrades.

For communities, business and labor organizations serve as important intermediaries between the demand side and the supply side. Not only can they help articulate specific training needs to support training programs and curriculum development but also they can take a leadership role in the community. For example, the Greater Tulsa Chamber of Commerce has engaged in the development, implementation, and management of nationally recognized school-to-work and welfare-to-work programs.

These organizations contribute to workforce development by:

- directly providing training services;
- articulating the demand for training;
- providing leadership and resource development in the workforce field;
- developing training and advancement opportunities within the workplace;
- providing resources to the workforce system;
- recruiting business participation in the workforce system;
- educating businesses on the importance of training investments; and
- bringing the demand-side perspective directly to the table.

Public-Private Organizations

Other public-private partnerships have emerged to take on workforce issues, especially on the regional level. Regional organizations may better reflect the labor market than do the political jurisdictions that have direct responsibility for managing programs. These bodies can have a strong business flavor, such as Greater Philadelphia First, or they can be created as an intermediary for nonprofits involved in regional workforce concerns, such as Workforce Organizations for Regional Collaboration in the Washington, DC, region.

Public-private organizations can help a community to:

- work together across political jurisdictions;
- work across sectors (public, private, community), which builds understanding, creates a dialogue, develops assets, and helps to prioritize and allocate scarce resources;
- coordinate and create synergies across a range of resources;
- bring industries together to articulate skill demands; and
- address cross-cutting issues, such as transportation.

Foundations and Other Charitable Organizations

Some communities benefit from the presence of community and national foundations that invest heavily in the needs of their local communities. The Indianapolis-based Lilly Endowment, for example, a national foundation, has supported Indianapolis and Indiana in many of their attempts to address workforce challenges. It even takes the lead in this area.

These groups furnish the following assets for human capital development:

- resources, especially financial;
- leadership to achieve key objectives;
- the ability to bring together groups across jurisdictions and sectors; and
- intellectual capital (lessons learned from other areas, projects, and programs) for program development and improvement.

Private Training and Staffing Agents

The past decade has been marked by the emergence of a diverse range of private education and training institutions (such as the University of Phoenix online approach or ITT Technical Institute), and the increasing size and reach of temporary staffing agencies (such as Manpower) and large Internet-based job search intermediaries (such as Monster.com). While we know little about this population within the workforce system, and cannot say what their impact will be, they are a presence in most communities.

Individuals Who Influence Career Choices Such as Parents, Parents' Organizations, and Guidance Counselors

Certain adults influence students' academic and career choices and are often overlooked when discussing workforce and economic issues. Increasingly, programs are looking to work with and educate these key adults, especially parents, guidance counselors, and teachers, who often favor academic tracks over technical ones, irrespective of the economic opportunities available. These individuals are highly influential on the skill choices of the emerging workforce and must be considered stakeholders when strategically considering workforce and economic development decisions.

The Governance Structure of the Workforce System

The purpose of a workforce system is to match labor supply with demand. Education and community institutions tend to serve as the intermediaries that translate the need for skills into the supply of skills. In practice, the governance structure on the ground is complex because of the sheer numbers of actors, the diverse areas of policy activity, and the constraints established by federal rules and regulations.

One of the challenges of developing an effective strategy to human capital development is the recognition that there are four target policy areas:

- The emerging workforce, including K–12 and youth-based initiatives. Key actors include schools, nonprofits, foundations, community groups, and government youth programs. More recently, businesses and their representative groups have begun to get involved in this area. This system struggles with the question of how to create the workforce of the future: how do we ensure that they have the core skills that businesses will need?
- The transitional workforce, including the unemployed, lower-income, disabled, former welfare recipients, mature workers, dislocated workers, and others who are moving into the labor force but who face a range of barriers to doing so. Government policies and agencies, with community groups and foundations, are the key players. In this area, policies grapple with the question: how can we better use our resources to solve current workforce challenges? The traditional lack of business involvement has been a key weakness in these programs.
- Lifelong learning, which includes programs and policies related to upskilling the incumbent workforce, supporting upward mobility, and helping individuals to navigate the labor market. Key players are busi-

nesses, community colleges, and state workforce programs. The non-profit sector is beginning to enter this field. These policies center on the question: how can we keep our existing resources competitive in order to increase and distribute wealth throughout the community?

• Talent development, retention, and attraction, which includes programs that help communities to expand the college-educated population, particularly in science and technology fields. Key players are schools, universities, civic groups, and state and local governments. The focus is on obtaining a higher percentage of college-educated residents, with an emphasis on those trained in science and engineering. This area should also include entrepreneurship.

The above categorization is organizationally useful but, in practice, programs and players may overlap. For example, a former welfare recipient or dislocated worker may attend community college, sponsored by a local business, under a public program supported by welfare dollars to build new skills to enter a new career area. Such individuals are upskilling as well as transitioning.

A second challenge to devising comprehensive human capital strategies lies in overcoming the existing institutional structure that has emerged from federal rules and regulations. Most workforce-related programs have historically been managed by federal government agencies, especially Labor, Education, and Health and Human Services (although others are involved). Each has its own regulatory and resource framework, separate benchmarks for defining success, and different constituent groups that orbit around these individual programs. Because it is resource and rule driven, the state and local players have tended to be competitive within their own regions as they fight for access to limited resources. This has led to an inadequate merging of resources and inefficiencies in packaging resources. These programs have been highly regulated and marked by restrictive frameworks comprised of rigid rules of what can and cannot be done, which has made them unrelated and unresponsive to market needs.

Our task now is to look beyond the traditional approaches to workforce and economic development and to begin to think about a systems approach to human capital development. That approach needs to integrate all four components: building a future workforce; solving current problems of workforce readiness; establishing a learning continuum; and finding ways to expand the talent pool. Such a system, according to Giloth (2000), must include high levels of employer engagement, extensive connections deep within the community, methods of career advancement, and integrative social services; contextual and industry-driven education and training, a stronger community college system, and wide-ranging networks that connect the range of stakeholders and resources. The system must also have multiple entry points and funding options, clearly articulated career and skill development pathways that start from K–12 education, engaged leadership of the public, private, and community sectors with a supportive media, commonly held stories about place that support innovation and change, and a high level of flexibility so institutions can adapt to changing skill needs.

The Promise and the Limitations of the Workforce Investment Act

In the 1990s, the federal government decided to make sweeping reforms in the governance of the public training regime in response to changing economic conditions and recognition of the limitations of the old system. Even before changes in the economy, the evidence was pretty clear that the public training system, while making minimal improvements in job and wage conditions for some people, overall did not meet its objectives (Grubb 1996; Harrison and Weiss 1998). In particular, the system was guilty of:

- Training individuals for jobs that did not exist. Although the goal of the program was to provide individuals with tools for successfully navigating the labor market, there was no attempt to organize training in response to the demands of the labor market.
- Being overly rule driven and stovepiped around different target populations. Overall, the system responded to federal regulations, rather than the expressed needs of its constituencies.
- A limited view of its constituency. It viewed only the individuals it assisted as its constituents and did not recognize that businesses that hired those individuals also required a voice in determining the relevancy of the program if they were going to use these services.
- Stigmatization of its participations. Businesses view individuals coming from public programs in negative terms and as undesirable employees, whether or not they have the appropriate skills (Laufer and Winship 2004). Inability to address these concerns will stymie even the best-run programs.

The reform, known as the Workforce Investment Act of 1998, aims to resolve problems with the prior region known as the Job Training Partnership Act (JTPA) and to transform the system from the inside out. From a theoretical point of view, the WIA was well conceived in terms of new economic realities and the potential to create a public training system of utility to individuals and businesses alike. The WIA promises to establish the infrastructure for a comprehensive approach to human capital management. Overall, however, it has not lived up to its promise. This section will discuss that promise, explain why it thus far is not being met, and then assess whether or not it could be developed sufficiently to anchor a new workforce system.

The federal government developed the WIA to address two different but interrelated concerns. On one hand, it needed to resolve legitimate complaints that the public training system was not meeting its mission. It neither prepared trainees for available jobs nor met the skill demands of business. On the other hand, the government wanted to streamline the complicated labyrinth of public workforce programs (Buck 2002). The new system was designed not only to marry supply and demand and better coordinate the multitude of programs but also to put into place an institutional framework, which, if developed appropriately, could become the local foundation for a comprehensive approach to human capital development, far beyond the past limitations of the targeted federal program.

The new system was based on six principles: one-stop delivery, system-level strategic planning, universal access, customer choice, accountability, and flexibility.

One-stop Service Delivery

To better coordinate the plethora of programs and to help users navigate through the red tape, the WIA mandated that the agencies involved in delivering workforce services be co-located at one-stop centers, which could be operated by either government entities or community-based organizations (see Exhibit 2.2). In addition, the WIA emphasized partnering with Temporary Assistance to Needy Families, Food Stamp Employment and Training, and National and Community Service Act programs.

System-Level Strategic Planning

The act mandated the creation of public-private Workforce Investment Boards at the state and local/regional levels to provide strategic direction to the regional workforce system. Business leaders would comprise the majority on state and local Workforce Investment Boards. Although Private Investment Councils (PICs), which preceded the WIBs under the JTPA, were also supposed to have a majority of business representatives on the board, the PICs focused on managing contracts with training providers. The new WIBs would oversee policy development and strategic planning that could meet the short- and long-term skill needs of businesses. In some cases, the WIBs have been able to design in-depth sectoral strategies, especially in high-demand fields

Exhibit 2.2

Mandatory One-Stop Partner Agencies

- Adult, dislocated worker, and youth activities
- Employment Service (Wagner-Peyser)
- Adult Education and Literacy
- Postsecondary vocational education (Perkins)
- Vocational Rehabilitation
- Welfare-to-Work
- Senior Community Service Employment Program
- Trade Adjustment Assistance (TAA, NAFTA)
- Veterans employment and training programs
- Community Services Block Grant
- Housing and Urban Development (HUD) employment and training activities
- Unemployment insurance
- Migrant and Seasonal Farmworker Program
- Native American Program
- Job Corps

Source: General Accounting Office (2001b).

such as information technology and health, which suggests the potential of the WIBs to become the true center of a comprehensive approach to workforce and economic development.

With the creation of the WIB as a strategic leader, the WIA created an institutional player that could theoretically provide leadership in the building of a new workforce system. By prioritizing business participation, the structure had the means to marry supply and demand over both the short and medium terms.

Universal Access

To make the WIB and the one-stop true centers of a comprehensive workforce system, the WIA now would provide services to all businesses and individuals, instead of just target population groups supported by the JTPA. This innovation promised to make the program the coordinating center of the local workforce system by identifying one place in which both jobseekers and employers could interact. Initial evidence suggests some progress in this area. A review of several one-stops found that about one-third of one-stop customers were employed in jobs requiring high skill levels and were using the resources to improve their career prospects (Buck 2002).

Services provided by the one-stop are tiered. This structure allows the one-stops to be both universal workforce service providers and also to cater to the specialized needs of the target populations served directly by the program partners. It also imposes a new set of requirements on certain target populations because participants must use the services in one tier before being allowed access to the next tier of services.

Tier 1, Core services, are available to all users of the one-stop. Services include job search and placement assistance, labor market information, job banks, and information on training providers. Tier 2, Intensive services, are available only to those unable to obtain employment after using the core services or those in employment but unable to obtain self-sufficiency without additional support. Initial evidence suggests that sites are not using the latter criteria to move people through the system (Buck 2002). Intensive services include skill assessment, individual employment plans, case management, and short-term prevocational services. Tier 3, Training services, are available only to those unable to find employment after Tier 2 services have been expended. These services include occupational and on-the-job training, skills upgrading, and job readiness training. This represents an important and threatening challenge to the ability of the WIA to meet its promise: it reduces skill training and replaces preparation with placement. The strong economy at the inception of the WIA meant it was relatively easy to place individuals.

Customer Choice

The WIA mandated the creation of consumer reports on training providers and individual training accounts to empower individuals to make their own training choices. One-stops are required to provide information on the local labor market, including the local jobs in demand. Training funds are to be used for these jobs. These activities, it was believed, would make the system more market driven because it would encourage training providers to compete for customers, based on placement rates (a core statistic in the consumer reports), thus serving economic needs as well. The local Workforce Investment Boards certify individual programs not providers. Within eighteen months of inception, all providers must meet performance criteria to receive funds and be certified providers.

Accountability

The system would be based on performance measures that would help to ensure that it met individual and business needs. Core performance measures for adults from the age of nineteen are employment rates, retention rates (after six months), earning gains, and skill attainment rates. For youth ages fourteen to eighteen, measures include skill attainment rate, secondary school diploma/GED rate, and retention rates.

Flexibility

Since the system is designed to meet the needs of a diverse customer base and must be responsive to the needs of local businesses, state and local agencies have a high level of flexibility to adapt local programs to meet the training needs of the local/regional marketplace.

Limitations of the Workforce Investment Act

The WIA, overall, has not lived up to its promise, and at this writing, Congress was in the process of reauthorizing the legislation with reforms that address some of the limitations cited in the system. A look at proposed reforms will be cited at the end of this section.

While the WIA has been criticized for a number of shortcomings, such as a limited integration of programs and lack of city and state leadership (General Accounting Office 2001a; Buck 2002), there are two particularly troublesome elements of the legislation from the point of view of long-term human capital development: inadequate responsiveness to business needs and strong pressures that reduce training options. If the reform is to work, these issues must be addressed deeply and completely.

Limited Value to Business

Although the WIA recognizes businesses as a primary customer, in practice, many WIBs have struggled to meet their needs. Although a wider population of jobseekers is using the one-stops, which provides an increase in the skill levels of this applicant pool, overall that pool remains narrowly centered on no- to low-skill employees (Buck 2002). Placement is the one-stop service most used by businesses and serves as a bellwether for business engagement. A 2003 study by Kazis, Prince, and Rubin showed that the insufficient screening of job applicants resulted in businesses' dissatisfaction with the quality of referrals. An earlier study of business involvement in welfare-to-work, by Mills and Kazis (1999), echoed some of these conclusions. They found that employers were similarly challenged by the inability of the workforce system to customize activities to meet employer demand, the poor quality of job referrals, insufficient screening mechanisms, and the inflexibility of public agencies. Hence, the one-stop remains a center for program delivery, not a center that can respond to market demand.

In addition, although WIBs must have 51 percent business representation, this has not resulted in improving business voice in the programs. Many boards are just too big to provide strategic direction and policy leadership. Since the boards have mandated partners and are recommended to include representatives of education, labor, community, and economic development agencies, requiring a business majority means that boards tend to be very large. Every time a new community member is added, a business member must be found to balance it. For example, the Houston, Texas, WIB has sixty-three board members, while Orlando, Florida, has fifty-nine (Buck 2002).

The large boards may be discouraging the business involvement required for the WIBs. A General Accounting Office study (2001a) noted that private sector representatives believed that the boards were too large and unable to address business concerns. This made it hard to recruit participation, set up meetings, and run those meetings efficiently. Moreover, the smaller committees and staff provided to manage specific program components are even less responsive to business needs. The subcommittees are not required to be business led and many do not have a sufficient business voice. The board staff members report to their various agencies and often have seemed dismissive of business concerns and unfamiliar with the nature of the business environment. While businesses are sticking with many WIBs at the moment, frustration levels are rising, and this threatens the potential to meet the long-term needs of the system.

Finally, businesses surveyed in a study by Kazis, Prince, and Rubin (2003) have noted that the performance measures required by the federal government and the reforms to the measures being proposed as part of reauthorization do not measure the value of the system to business but rather reflect the needs of the federal government. Although the federal government notes that it wants a system responsive to business, it is not monitored from this perspective.

Reduction in Training Opportunities

The reforms implemented by the WIA favor a "work first" approach, making it harder to access the training dollars that had been at the heart of the prior public regime. As a result, there has been an overall reduction in the number of individuals demanding and receiving training, further reducing the ability of the one-stops to provide higher skills (Buck 2002). This hurts both individuals, who lose access to training that could lead to higher wages, and businesses, which have been dissatisfied with the quality of the skills available through the public system. Businesses have voiced their need for potential employees to be better trained to ensure a certain standard of skill (Kazis,

Prince, and Rubin 2003). Employers have noted that the one-stops provide insufficient access to training resources that would increase the value of the applicants to business clients. The employers interviewed for the Mills and Kazis study (1999) similarly found that the focus on work first was not always in their best interest. They wanted policies that better married the need for placement with the need for skills training, including preemployment skills and skill advancement strategies for incumbent workers.

Reducing investment in training is even more of a problem when we consider that low-skilled workers generally have less access to work-based training opportunities, especially those that lead to skill advancement. The Department of Labor's 1995 Survey of Employer-Provided Training indicated that over 80 percent of employees in management, professional, and technical fields receive some type of formal training while a little less than 50 percent of service employees do. As another comparison, the survey found that about 90 percent of employees holding a B.A. receive some type of formal training while about 60 percent of those with a high school diploma or less do (Frazis et al. 1998).

The focus on placement instead of training also means that wider issues of career management are being ignored. If the public system really aims to serve as the core intermediary in the labor market, then one of its roles must be to help no- to low-skilled individuals advance their skills and opportunities in the job market.

Decline in training has also had an impact on local training institutions. In some cases, the decline in training candidates has challenged many of the nonprofits that provide training, which may be leading to their closure or downsizing (Buck 2002). The WIA imposes performance monitoring on training providers, a requirement that may be forcing some, especially community colleges, to pull out of the system. Providers are required to undertake the monitoring requirement even if they have only one WIA-funded student in their classes. Given that fewer individuals are being referred to providers due to the reduction of training opportunities, many providers are reducing the courses they make available under the WIA, rather than instituting the burdensome reporting regime required of them (General Accounting Office 2001a).

The WIA reauthorization has attempted to address some of these limitations, but overall, both the Senate and House proposals fall short on the core issues. First, proposed changes to performance measures move in the wrong direction. While changes are indeed required, removing the credential rate measure, which the House Bill proposes, takes out the only performance standard that provides some gauge of quality. Moreover, as noted earlier, no attempt has been made to determine measures that gauge business needs. The measures continue to reflect only the federal agenda.

Second, the House and Senate have both proffered proposals to improve the nature of business representation on the board. The House bill requires board members to be from leading industries and the Senate bill requires representation from high-growth firms, emerging industries, and small business (Patel et al. 2004). In either case, this suggests a growing awareness of the need to segment markets and develop a range of business voices.

Finally, both the House and the Senate propose allowing the one-stops to offer business services as core services and include financing for incumbent training. The Senate bill goes further, supporting the creation of dedicated business liaisons, the development of fee-for-service products, and financing for the establishment of skill certification pilot projects (Patel et al. 2004). These actions form the basis for developing relationships with businesses that can be used as leverage for business engagement in other ways and to open the door for improving the ability of the WIBs to better anchor a workforce system.

Although the WIA was envisioned as the guiding center of a regional workforce system, it does not have the political or institutional scope to achieve that goal, even with the reforms. Businesses are wary of it, regulations inhibit it, and the environment in which it works is complicated, crowded, and complex—issues that the reforms do not sufficiently address. Moreover, none of these reforms address the core concern voiced by business—improving the quality of the individuals available for work. Thus, the core mission of a human capital system in the twenty-first century must be to improve the skills and training available for its people. A competitive workforce system in the knowledge economy, therefore, does not just marry supply and demand but continuously expands and enhances the skills, competences, and knowledge of the regional labor pool.

The WIA's destiny at present is to be one institution in a wide field of institutions that shape the functioning of the labor market. How central it is depends on what it allows itself to do.

This chapter has identified the actors and the main federal program that shape the rules of the current workforce system. The final section spells out the elements needed for a good workforce system, and then identifies the institutions and strategies that comprise a human capital development approach to economic development.

A Human Capital Approach to Economic Development:
The Basics

In a knowledge economy, where skills translate into opportunity labor markets are highly volatile; workforce-related organizations are numerous and

43

disconnected; and demographics, industry knowledge, educational requirements, economic sectors, and our sense of place are changing rapidly, what
do our institutions and strategies need to do to manage this complex, change-
able environment?

In an information society, the driving element of change is to find effective and efficient methods to filter, reduce, and channel the vast information
flows of modern life related to the labor market. This means institutions and
strategies that:

- bridge the information gap between employers and job seekers to create opportunity;
- clarify and consolidate skill obtainment and portability in an era of
  mobility;
- expand the pool of talented, skilled individuals;
- increase the voice and needs of business into a workforce system historically composed of predominantly supply-side institutions;
- promote lifelong learning by providing a spectrum of linked services to
  support upward mobility; and
- create new personal and institutional understandings of place and
  opportunity.

Many communities are working to address some or all of these issues. From
years of research experience in the field, a review of the multitude of approaches,
and an understanding of what seems to be working (at least at a local level),
five areas have emerged as critical targets for city and regional action.

First, a community needs institutions that can serve as system entrepreneurs. Entrepreneurs are social entities that create new opportunities and offer new understandings by assembling dispersed resources, coordinating
networks, and intermediating among diverse players involved in the various
stages of production (or, in this case, the various stages of skill attainment).
Entrepreneurs are not necessarily the inventors or the innovators or the investors (although they may be), but rather the entrepreneur mobilizes and
merges resources, negotiates new understandings and new expectations, and,
in the end, is the entity that gets the job done (Casson 1995; Schumpeter
1976). In the knowledge economy, the workforce intermediary has stepped
in to play this role. Ensuring that a region has intermediaries to bridge supply
and demand and manage the diverse networks involved in workforce and
economic development is a critical precondition for human capital development strategies. Chapter 3 considers who intermediaries are, what they do,
and what makes them effective.

Second, in an era of high job mobility, numerous training providers, and an increasing cry for skills, we need to establish reliable indicators that a certain skill standard has been achieved and to provide the infrastructure for lifelong learning. Historically, educational degrees have played this role, but in the knowledge economy, where new industries and new technologies can change required skill sets rapidly, new mechanisms will be required. Skill standards and the credentials that mark their achievement are core assets that enable jobseekers and employers as well as education, training, and other workforce intermediaries to know what skills are needed; clarify the relationship between skills and wages; and articulate methods for advancement. Chapter 4 examines issues and efforts relevant to the emergence of skill standards and credentialing.

Third, expanding the pool of talent requires regions to implement strategies that increase the number of individuals attaining college degrees and create new understandings of place and opportunity that encourage the development, attraction, and retention of talent. Regions need to rethink their identity and redesign their stories, images, and structures in a way that engages workers and businesses in the economic, cultural, and social vitality of place. Chapter 5 discusses talent expansion strategies, which recognize that in a world of high worker mobility, communities and businesses need to work hand in hand to find ways to expand, retain, and attract talent by providing a wide range of opportunities in conjunction with a new understanding of place in the new economy.

Fourth, workforce development approaches have been marked by their centeredness in supply-side institutions and their lack of engagement with demand-side entities. The WIA's emphasis on business involvement highlights this historic limitation. The challenge confronted in engaging business voice is that different industries and occupations have differing skill needs and those needs change over time. Targeting sectors or clusters creates formal and informal mechanisms for better engaging business voice and for more directly inserting workforce needs into business strategy and competitive planning. Chapter 6 considers the challenge of engaging employers and methods to overcome these challenges.

Finally, to nurture individual skill building and create a culture that stresses lifelong learning, regions must provide a continuum of services that support individual career development. These services range from literacy to Ph.D. acquisition and cover individuals in pre-kindergarten through retirement. These services will be based on articulated career paths that connect the maze of education and training providers, changing occupational categories, and enlarging physical spaces. Labor market volatility, increasing returns to education, accelerating technology, and globalization, and the inability of training alone to alleviate poverty in the knowledge economy requires regular infusions of more education and/or training for most individuals at different points in their working lives. Articulating career paths within firms and across firms and across education and training institutions increases and clarifies opportunity structures for individuals. It also provides businesses with strategies for attracting and retaining workers and increasing their competitiveness in a global economy. Chapter 7 considers lifelong learning strategies and their relationship to upward mobility. Finally, Chapter 8 ties all these strings together to recommend a strategic approach to people-centered economic development.

A community looking to compete in the knowledge economy will need to inventory its institutions, strategies, and capabilities to determine whether it has a complete workforce toolbox. In what follows, how different communities have innovated with different facets of the workforce challenges will be explored. It is an interesting journey, although possibly an unsatisfying one. There are many good examples of effective programs and responsible learning; but most cities and regions remain at the start of what will continue to be a challenging ride.

— 3 —

Establishing System Entrepreneurs: Intermediaries

This book argues that human capital strategies meeting the needs of the knowledge economy require entrepreneurial institutions that facilitate the transfer of reliable, trustworthy information to enable the functioning of a more volatile, less stable labor market. These institutions, known as intermediaries, act as bridges that connect the needs of employers with the choices of training providers and individuals. Intermediaries represent an institutional response to the fragmented workforce environment, changing skill needs in the workplace, and the difficulties of labor-market fluidity in a period of economic restructuring.

This chapter introduces intermediaries and fleshes out how they work. The first section outlines what intermediaries do. The second section identifies the characteristics of effective intermediaries, defined by their ability to create economic development assets and opportunities in the new economy. The third section outlines some of the challenges intermediaries face. The fourth section presents the case studies of two intermediaries: the Wisconsin Regional Training Partnership and the Gulf Coast Workforce Board and its service network, The WorkSource. These cases were chosen because they are nationally recognized as top performers in their respective environments.

What Are Intermediaries?

At the most basic level, intermediaries are information brokers that match supply and demand in the marketplace. While intermediaries have always existed, they have typically been limited in scope, serving simply as marriage brokers who refer jobseekers to employers. While intermediary use is still a young research subject, initial evidence suggests that, in the knowledge economy, more people are using intermediaries to navigate the labor market. In a study comparing intermediary use in high-tech Silicon Valley and manufacturing-based Milwaukee, Leete and colleagues (2004) found an increase in intermediary use in both regions. Notably, the Silicon Valley users of intermediary services tended to be more highly educated than users in Milwaukee, suggesting a growing use of intermediaries by new-economy jobseekers. Intermediaries are more commonly associated with disadvantaged populations. Increased use by those with higher education indicates changes in the nature of information flows within the labor market.

Not only is intermediary use increasing, but new types of intermediaries have mushroomed across the U.S. landscape in response to the needs of different occupational and regional labor markets (Giloth 2004a; Fitzgerald 2004). Many intermediaries in the knowledge-based economy, however, do significantly more than mere matchmaking. The map of intermediaries can be divided into three functional categories: traditional, customized, and labor-market negotiators (Osterman 1999). The following discussion builds upon Osterman's categorizations.

Traditional one-on-one intermediaries focus on matching jobseekers and positions by taking advantage of economies of scale in information collection. Examples include the Department of Labor's America's Job Bank, Monster.com, and temporary and staffing agencies such as Manpower USA. The importance of information, however, means that even these so-called traditional intermediaries do more than the marriage brokering that they did in the 1960s, 1970s, 1980s, and even 1990s. While the study by Leete and colleagues (2004) found that traditional intermediaries were the most often used intermediaries in both Silicon Valley and Milwaukee, many have added a range of services that strengthen their information brokerage function with interesting, although still unclear, impacts on the human capital base. For example, some temporary and staffing agencies furnish free skills training, usually office-based skills, to their workers. According to Autor (2000), providing training furnishes temp firms, which accounted for 10 percent of national job creation between 1990 and 2000, with private information about the individual. In other words, training serves as a screening technique, which gives temp firms an advantage in the marketplace. That advantage is information. Modern temp agencies do not just refer individuals to jobs, according to Autor; they also sell information on worker quality in the marketplace. The growth of temp firms and their new role as a skills filter provide additional evidence of increased employer demand for skills and reliable screening of those skills. Even the federal job bank has had a face-lift. As the Internet arm of the network of workforce investment boards, America's Job Bank provides a potential feeder to wider services and support.

The second type of intermediary, customized intermediaries, interacts to a much higher degree with jobseekers and employers within the labor market. They aggressively recruit, train, and place employees after working with employers to identify specific skill requirements and industry trends. They not only broker skill-based information but also are important institutions for crafting local definitions and understandings of skill needs. Community colleges are representative. In this case, intermediaries often provide or broker a range of services including labor recruitment, training, and pretraining and post-training or retention support.

The third type, labor-market negotiators, function the same way as a customized intermediary but then go one step further; they try to change the terms of trade in the market by bargaining with firms or using power to alter firm behavior to better support the prospects of employees. The Wisconsin Regional Training Partnership (discussed below) is an example of this type of intermediary. In this case, intermediaries fulfill organizing and planning roles by creating partnerships and mobilizing stakeholders to improve labor-market outcomes. Their activities include aggregating employer demand, collecting and interpreting labor-market data, negotiating with providers, conducting research on new approaches, and advocating for new public policies (Kazis 2004). Not only do they broker information concerning skill needs—they create new frameworks to redefine what those skill needs are, who has them, and how the community can get them. By changing the terms of the labor market through their information brokerage role, they open up new opportunities that were not there before.

What is unique about the intermediary role in the knowledge economy, especially as it is clear that different organizations serve as intermediaries? It is the recognition that intermediaries do not just broker the information that underpins labor market flows, they are able to manage and interpret that information in a way that may shape market forces and opportunities. In particular, they are proving to be the institutions that are most adept in helping low-skilled and disadvantaged workers to reach self-sufficiency (Giloth 2004a). For communities, then, the goal is to ensure that sufficient and appropriate intermediaries exist that can help shape labor-market forces in a way that meets their economic development goals.

Intermediaries are able to broker and edit information because they serve as key nodes in the labor-market networks that link the various demand- and supply-side institutions. The image of a node within a network is an important one for understanding the critical role of intermediaries for economic development in the new-economy labor market. Imai's[1] work on networking among businesses provides an important framework for understanding this role. According to Imai, networking refers to a process in which economic agents act in relation to each other:

> A dynamic market process is a process in which inconsistent expectations of economic agents are adjusted through interactive relations among them.

> Markets and organizations interpenetrate each other. . . . "Information exchange" is a key variable in our network view. . . . In the network industrial organization, information is created through interaction, and the creation of information has become the driving force of business activity. (1989: 123)

Networks therefore organize expectations, create common languages and frameworks, and develop rules of the game that are formed and reformed as networks shift. The information developed and disseminated within those networks forms the basis of labor-market interactions. Entrepreneurial entities will work to create new information that reshapes the networks to support their objectives. The discussion of temporary firms above illustrates this process: they provide training as a means to gather private information on skills they sell to the marketplace. They are creating information that gives them a competitive edge when placing individuals. For communities to use workforce policies to create opportunities, they will need intermediaries that can reshape and redefine the quality, and understanding, of their human capital base.

In the new knowledge-economy labor market, intermediaries serve as system entrepreneurs, who adjust inconsistent expectations via information exchange, building the social and economic context for continued relations that can lead ultimately to economic growth. Intermediaries therefore must be at the center of information networks if they are to succeed. Chuck Thomas, executive director of the William F. Goodling Regional Advanced Skills Center (ASC) in York, Pennsylvania, an employer-initiated training organization, explains the challenges:

> keeping up with business trends and how the region itself changes. Companies close and start up everyday. You also have to keep up with technology change. You have to make sure that the directions and information you are getting focus on staying in tune with those organizations and companies that are changing.

Characteristics of Knowledge-Economy Intermediaries

New-economy intermediaries share a number of characteristics enabling them to provide and craft information that meets workforce and economic development objectives. The discussion below draws, and expands, upon recent work by Giloth (2004b).

First, intermediaries recognize that they serve a dual customer base and measure the outcomes of their activities from both employee and employer perspectives. They gather and transmit information from both sides of the labor market. They are bilingual entities that effectively speak the languages of both business and the public sectors (Kazis 2004).

Second, intermediaries integrate funding streams and information from public, private, and community sources. The various intermediaries interviewed for this book uniformly agreed that funding was their greatest challenge and funding diversification the greatest mark of their success. Varied funding not only provides financial sustainability but also helps in better brokering between supply and demand. For example, the York County Economic Development Organization helped launch ASC with business support in response to a business outcry for skilled workers. As ASC evolved, it found it necessary to move into the public funding world to effectively serve the needs of local industries and now is a WIB training provider. ASC expanded its operations not only to increase its access to funding but also to better manage the recruitment side of training and placement. As an intermediary, it needed a pipeline to potential workers and the ability to screen and command information on their skills.

Third, new-economy intermediaries add to the local knowledge base. They not only generate new ideas and innovations but also work to advocate them, whether internal to the organization or external to the political, economic, and social environment. These organizations are learning, entrepreneurial entities that can respond to new opportunities and shifts in the market and even create opportunities. For example, the Wisconsin Regional Training Partnership convinced state legislators to set aside $20 million in funds from Temporary Assistance to Needy Families for a Workforce Attachment and Advancement Fund that supports incumbent training for low-wage workers (Kazis 2004).

Fourth, intermediaries are accountable to their mission and goals, not rules and regulations, making them highly flexible and adaptive. It also means that they assume the risks involved. To cope with the fragmentation of the workforce system, they are not single-purpose organizations. Even if they do not deliver all the services required themselves, they take responsibility for ensuring their delivery. Assuming these responsibilities and the risks involved with them is particularly important when working with disadvantaged and transitional jobseekers, who have been traditionally excluded from mainstream job-finding networks. The segregated nature of the networks surrounding many disadvantaged workers means that employers have rarely been exposed to certain groups of workers, which generates negative stereotypes about them as a group. Consequently, employers may be averse to hiring anyone from that particular group, regardless of the individual's skills (Harrison and Weiss 1998). By assuming the risk for the individual, intermediaries open new opportunities not formerly available to the disadvantaged worker while providing businesses with a safer environment to break down stereotypes. This is further evidence of the intermediary's core role of using information to manage and revise assumptions and expectations.

Fifth, as noted earlier, intermediaries are highly networked to other workforce and economic development players. Mike Jefferson, executive director of the Crispus Attucks Center for Employment and Training in York, Pennsylvania, noted that: "Workforce development can't be done in a vacuum. You must go out there and know what's going on. Get involved in different boards and initiatives to find out what they are doing." Networks allow intermediaries to:

- take on higher risk projects or programs;
- increase internal capacity;
- acquire tacit information from other organizations;
- do business in another organization's jurisdiction;
- increase their size and market power; and
- enhance legitimacy in the eyes of other regional players (Harrison and Weiss 1998: 40).

To be networked means to be politically savvy, to understand how to manage across and among the various stakeholders involved in workforce development. Networked intermediaries also offer disadvantaged or transitional jobseekers entry into wider networks, the power to open doors, to negotiate with organizations, and to demand quality service. They offer businesses access to a wider pool of labor, screened to meet particular needs, and an ability to oversee quality service and access to a wide range of expertise and information.

Sixth, intermediaries have networks that are organizational in character but grounded in personal relationships. Granovetter (1995), who has written a seminal work on job-finding networks, conjectures that formal intermediaries rarely succeed if they have only impersonal relationships with businesses and jobseekers. He suggests that good intermediaries are in fact a hybrid system in which the staff of the intermediary has long-term relationships with businesses and a way to get to know the jobseekers (Granovetter 1995). Those informal relationships form the basis of trust, which is grounded in reputation and an understanding of each other's needs and expectations. They also ground the information in social as well as economic exchanges, enhancing the role of the intermediary to broker information effectively. As we shall see later on in this book, employers expect and value personal relationships of this nature.

These types of personal relationships among staff can proxy for social relations in the business-recruitment process that research shows provides positive returns to businesses. A study by Fernandez, Castilla, and Moore (2000) on employers' use of social networks to support their hiring methods finds that these networks indeed lead to better outcomes. They found that the use of social contacts enriches the pool of available applicants, providing a 67 percent rate of return to businesses in terms of recruiting costs, and eases the transition for new hires by providing an informal mentoring system. Granovetter (1995) finds that jobs acquired through social networks have lower turnover rates, predominately because such networks integrate individuals into the culture of business through collegial circles, more so than formal placements. Common training programs that serve as a group feeder into the same company can also play this role of providing entrants with built-in social support.

Seventh, the activities of new-economy intermediaries go beyond job matching. As noted above, even traditional intermediaries provide additional services to complement their job-matching function. As the cases in this book will demonstrate, intermediaries that have adapted to their role in this economy have been particularly effective at moving disadvantaged people into jobs with higher wages and promotion potential. This element is particularly important in helping to remove significant barriers to finding, retaining, and advancing in the workplace. In the case of transitional workers, the barriers are diverse, wide-ranging, and often multiple in nature. Those barriers include:

- *Finance.* In many cases, the immediate need for money serves as a major barrier to job placement and training. Economically disadvantaged individuals may not have sufficient funds for appropriate clothing for an interview or to pay for transportation the first few weeks on the job in the absence of the first paychecks. In other instances, individuals choose low-wage jobs rather than training that leads to better-wage jobs because they have an immediate need, such as rent, to receive a paycheck. Many intermediaries have had to adapt their programs to these local realities. For example, the Crispus Attucks Center for Employment found it had to reduce the length of its training programs because its participants could not afford to stay in training and receive no wages. Empower Baltimore found ways to subsidize trainees during training to enable them to stay in a longer training course.
- *Geography.* One of the most often-cited barriers to work is geography or spatial mismatch. This argument is a simple one—jobs are being created in locations (usually the suburbs) that are physically distant from those who need jobs (usually inner-city residents), and transportation

options between the job and jobseeker are not available, affordable, or efficient.

- *Race and ethnicity.* Skills and geographic mismatch only partially explain why certain populations have trouble finding good jobs. African-American unemployment rates, for example, are over two times higher at all education levels (Fitzgerald and Patton 1997). Discrimination on the basis of race and ethnicity remains a very real issue in cracking the workforce problem. For example, in the Red Hook neighborhood of Brooklyn, black and Hispanic residents rarely held any of the 3,600 local private-sector jobs available because local employers did not view them as reliable. Rather, employers recruited through the social networks of their existing employees, tapping into Irish, Polish, and Spanish (from Spain) ethnic networks outside the neighborhood (Kasinitz and Rosenberg 1993, cited in Giloth 1998). Historically, certain ethnic groups have practiced closure of recruitment channels and access to informal on-the-job training, denying access and/or advancement to other groups. The continued labor-market impact of institutionalized racism emphasizes the critical need for intermediaries that can use and edit information to change assumptions.
- *Child care and health care.* Available child care and health care, including mental health care that addresses psychological challenges such as substance abuse, affect whether people are able to retain a job. From the point of view of competitive communities, these issues can no longer be considered simply social services but are very much part of the economic climate that makes places people-friendly. It is part of the infrastructure of the new economy. For example, multiple stakeholders I interviewed in a western region perceived that the inability of smaller businesses to provide benefits, especially health benefits, made their region unattractive to many skilled workers.

  Child-care provision is also a part of retaining individuals in education and training. Some school districts in urban and rural areas provide child care to young mothers to allow them to finish high school. Community colleges, key providers of adult education, may be located far away from public transportation or lack child care, which prohibits individuals from pursuing training. Some cities, such as Boise, Idaho, have worked to locate new schools, community colleges, and other educational institutions downtown, making commuting and access to services more available. Not only do such actions enhance the skill base of urban areas, they also improve the quality of place, an important component for attracting and retaining a diverse, skilled workforce.
- *Language and culture.* Many immigrants face linguistic barriers to ob-

taining good jobs, quality education, and promotion opportunities. While language difficulties are most commonly associated with Hispanic and Asian populations due in large part to substantial populations of first- and second-generation immigrants, these challenges are not restricted to them. In different regions, various immigrant groups may be the source of linguistic and cultural challenges. For example, New York City has a large population of Russian Jews with limited English skills. However, group statistics hide the wide variation within groups, as individuals arrive with large differences in both their existing proficiency levels and their ability to learn a new language (Crawford and Romero with Barnow 1991).

This section has identified the key characteristics of effective intermediaries in the new economy. The next section outlines ongoing challenges that intermediaries face in the current environment.

Ongoing Challenges Intermediaries Face

One of the biggest challenges experienced by intermediaries, especially those that serve disadvantaged populations, has been the creation and stickiness of brands associated with different workers. In their study on employer attitudes on the workforce program, Laufer and Winship found that "*the facts of a program's success matter less to employers than the attitudes employers have about the program, what type of institution is running it, and the workers it serves*" (2004: 216, emphasis in original). In other words, employers brand intermediaries based on biased assumptions that they have about the workers they serve.

According to Laufer and Winship, a brand is a relationship that is based on a set of assets and emotional connections between the consumer and the product, with the result that the consumer uses emotional rather than rational processes of evaluation of it and other goods and services. This is a trust-based phenomenon. Brand images can be positive or negative. Laufer and Winship's research reveals that employers hold the following assumptions.

- They associate low-income workers with crime and substance abuse problems.
- They associate former welfare recipients with problems of work ethic, loyalty, and motivation for work.
- They display a preference for immigrants from Asia and Eastern Europe/Russia, whom they assumed were more skilled, willing to work hard, and less picky about the job.

Table 3.1

Summary of [Employer] Brand Attributes by Intermediary Type

Type of intermediary	Positive brand attributes	Negative brand attributes
Community-based nonprofits	1) Low-cost 2) Good community relations	1) Insufficient screening 2) Transitory 3) Slow 4) Lack of accountability/ professionalism
Community colleges/ vocational colleges	1) More professional 2) Training expertise 3) Local to company/facility	1) No pool of unskilled labor
Trade organizations	1) Industry knowledge	1) Lack of training expertise/curricula
For-profit companies/ employment agencies	1) Fast turnaround 2) Ability to try before hiring 3) Well known	1) Expensive
State or federal agencies	1) Large pool of applicants 2) Tax credits 3) Bureaucratic	1) Not discriminating; no match w/employer needs 2) Inefficient
Unions		1) Cost escalation at company 2) Loss of employer control

Source: Jessica K. Laufer and Sian Winship, "Summary of Brand Attributes by Intermediary Type," in *Workforce Intermediaries for the Twenty-first Century,* ed. Robert P. Giloth, p. 230. © 2004 by the American Assembly, Columbia University. Reprinted with permission.

Perhaps more important, their study revealed that employers identified particular brand attributes associated with different types of intermediaries and that the trainees carry the same brand. Table 3.1 demonstrates the brand attributes associated with different types of intermediaries.

Employers were more likely to use community-based organizations when the economy was tight. Overall, employers preferred intermediaries with close ties to their particular industry.

The second challenge that new-economy intermediaries face is organizational capacity to manage networks, to gather and interpret larger amounts of information, to be able to diversify funding streams, and to be accountable. Developing that level of organizational capability will challenge many nonprofit organizations. As networks expand, activity only gets more complex, which may serve as a hindrance to many groups wishing to strategically expand their networks. In some cases, we see the development of supra-intermediaries, whose job is to manage the networks of intermediaries and support smaller intermediaries in doing their jobs in this new, more complex environment. For example, in the Washington, DC, area, the Workforce Organizations for Regional Collaboration helps nonprofits involved in workforce development activities to build staff capacity of the workforce intermediaries to expand work in the regional framework. It also facilitates links between more local nonprofit workforce development organizations and employers with available jobs at a regional level (Workforce Organizations for Regional Collaboration 2005).

Case Studies

In this section, we present two different types of intermediaries, the Wisconsin Regional Training Partnership and The Gulf Coast Workforce Development Board and its service network, The WorkSource, to gain an understanding of how the intermediary brokers and crafts information and relationships to meet economic development goals.

The Wisconsin Regional Training Partnership

The Wisconsin Regional Training Partnership (WRTP) was selected as a case study because it highlights the range of characteristics of an effective new-economy intermediary and demonstrates how workforce training serves as an integral component of regional economic development. The WRTP had an impact on economic development because it:

- implemented a strategy that prioritized firm competitiveness by targeting process or product innovations within the firm that would maximize the human capital investment;
- used its position as information broker to create opportunities for businesses and individuals that previously did not exist; and
- changed the interactions of the labor market by generating and disseminating new information and creating new relationships.

The WRTP was established in 1992 in response to the downturn in manufacturing. Labor leaders approached the Center on Wisconsin Strategy (COWS), a think tank located at the University of Wisconsin-Madison, to find ways to stabilize this sector. COWS, working with business and labor, developed WRTP as a nonprofit membership organization governed by business, labor, and public workforce agents. Each partner made substantial commitments to make the program work. Member businesses would invest in workforce training, offer good wages, and implement new production processes to leverage the benefits from higher-skilled workers. Labor would develop worker skills and agree to new responsibilities within the new production processes. Workforce agencies would coordinate training and manufacturing extension efforts and form a regional infrastructure for workforce activities. Thus, the program itself created a natural network for information exchange among the various stakeholders to shape new understandings of labor market interaction.

WRTP developed three core services that were delivered sequentially: firm modernization, incumbent training, and the recruiting and training of new workers. WRTP works with one firm at a time. In almost all cases, it starts by facilitating a new management-labor agreement and assessing firm needs. It then provides the three services sequentially in manageable bites that allow firms to absorb the changes over time.

In the first phase, WRTP would help a company to modernize its workplace by implementing new technologies and/or new work processes. At the project's inception, the state lacked institutions capable of providing modernization services. So WRTP spearheaded the establishment of the Wisconsin Manufacturing Extension Partnership to deliver them.

In the second phase, WRTP would deliver incumbent training to improve the productivity of the workforce. Finding the best way to deliver those services required learning and adaptation. WRTP's original vision was to link training agents directly to firms but this proved unsatisfactory. In response to new information about the nature of the local training providers, WRTP assumed a more direct role as a contractor to the training agents, in order to ensure the quality, applicability, and cost effectiveness of the training.

WRTP also took a lead role in curriculum development. They worked with technical colleges to develop three modules: basic skills, process skills, and technical skills that could be applied throughout the industry and customized when necessary. The end result was the development of a training process attached to a series of new job classifications that are ordered to form a recognized career ladder for industry employees, created specifically to increase the competitive position of the business.

In the third phase, WRTP would recruit and train individuals for new entry-level jobs. Thus, the program not only retained the industry but was a significant job creator as well. New worker training consists of a fourteen-week employment-linked training course in which all participants are guaranteed jobs on completion. To ensure that the program met community needs as well as worker and employer needs, it recruited low-income, displaced workers, and other disadvantaged individuals for these placements.

Businesses, however, would need to be convinced to use this service. Tying into its knowledge of and links to the industry, WRTP was able to devise incentives to attract business use. The first incentive was in the actual design of the service: it focused on managing the problem of workforce poaching. If a business gave WRTP four months' notice, it would be guaranteed new workers who had been prescreened according to established and trusted criteria. The ability to rapidly access workers reduces the need to poach the workforce of others and also manages the problems of turnover and wage increases that result from too much poaching. WRTP recruits individuals for training only when good jobs are available. The second incentive was WRTP's ability to demonstrate the financial value of their service. They offered the service as an alternative to temporary staffing agencies, which businesses often used because they did not trust public training agencies. WRTP could show that investing in trained workers was a more cost-effective strategy than using temporary staff.

Of all its activities, recruiting disadvantaged individuals proved to be one of WRTP's largest challenges. At the inception of the third phase, WRTP believed that training agents and community-based organizations would provide a pipeline to disadvantaged populations. These groups did not prove effective. WRTP needed to mobilize community resources themselves to find new workers, especially in tight labor markets. Once they entered this realm, they also learned that they would have to find ways to support the retention of these workers, given the range of barriers they face. WRTP formed an in-firm mentorship program to achieve this goal.

WRTP took full responsibility for all facets of the process, and like an entrepreneur, absorbed the risks. Its role at the center of workforce networks gave it the ability to gather, interpret, and disseminate information in a way that both allowed it to adapt its actions and convince others of the efficacy of their approach. The success of this approach is evident in the numbers (see Table 3.2).

As a result of its success, WRTP is expanding to cover more sectors. As of 2004, they have had some successes in health care and construction, limited success in hospitality and technology, and no movement at all in transportation.

Eric Parker, WRTP's executive director, attributes its success to a combination of factors. We can divide those factors into programmatic and systemic categories. Programmatic factors are those important to a workforce development program design, while systemic factors refer to what needs to exist in the system to help workforce entities be effective.

Table 3.2

Wisconsin Regional Training Partnership (WRTP) Benchmark Data

Benchmark	Measures
Membership growth (1992–2002)	6 to 125 members
Manufacturing members, 1992	100%
Manufacturing members, 2002	70%
Member investment in training, 1995–2000	Over $100 million
Jobs generated in member firms, 1995–2000	6,000
Number of WRTP placements, 1995–2000	1,500
Average retention rates, new workers, 1996–2001	75%
Average earnings, new workers, preplacement	$8,500
Average earnings, new workers, postplacement	$22,500
Average earnings increase, postplacement	165%
Average hourly wage, postplacement	$10/hour

Source: Telephone interview with Eric Parker, Wisconsin Regional Training Partnership 2003.

On the programmatic level, WRTP was able to generate both workforce and economic goals by:

- Focusing on job quality. WRTP set standards that encouraged entry into high-paying jobs with established, articulated career paths. While this approach is harder than placing people in low-skilled, low-paying jobs, it benefited the worker, the employer, and the community.
- Concentrating their efforts on large firms. WRTP worked with large companies that could bring good jobs to the table and leverage other firms and other players into the process. Not only do these companies create multiple jobs, they influence the work practices of their suppliers, triggering a cascade effect on the modernization of the workplace and the workforce.
- Taking responsibility for outcomes and doing what was necessary to get the job done. They helped form new organizations, restructured relationships, and reshaped the labor market when necessary, to meet their goals.
- Diversifying their funding sources. Finding multiple funding sources has allowed WRTP to stabilize the organization, expand services, and replicate its program in other industry sectors.
- Taking a sector approach. A sector focus allowed WRTP to specialize its services, and develop a high degree of competency within that area.
- Integrating workforce and economic goals. WRTP structured its services and strategies to serve businesses, workers, and the community at large. Workforce services were tailored to meet the precise needs of individual companies.

At the systemic level, success factors include:

- Maintaining strong networks and partnerships among the relevant parties. Workforce efforts require coordinating the actions of a large network of actors to meet one's goals. To replicate WRTP, Parker notes that organized labor must have a seat at the table (at least where this makes sense).
- Keeping training providers competitive. WRTP demands that all training providers compete for business, a systemic condition that forces providers to assess regularly how most effectively and efficiently to serve businesses and workers.

Has WRTP mastered all the workforce challenges? No, like all successful organizations, it remains a work in progress. At the program level, WRTP has a number of funding sources but they are almost all grant related. It is working to further diversify funds to non–grant-related revenue, and thinking about how it might move to self-sufficiency through service provision. At the system level, managing the rift between the workforce and economic development worlds continues to challenge WRTP. According to Parker, until both sides understand that the only possible approach is an integrated one, intermediaries cannot reach optimal success.

The Gulf Coast Workforce Board

The Workforce Investment Act envisioned WIBs to play a strategic intermediary role in regional labor markets, particularly in the area of planning and labor-market facilitation. Early observers have noted that many cannot provide the relationships, supportive environment, and industry expertise of the best intermediaries at present (Kazis 2004). While many WIBs have a long way to go in this effort, some practices are emerging that are worth investigating. The next case study looks at a WIB that has started to implement programmatic features that are increasing its capacity to assume an intermediary role. This case focuses specifically on those features.

The Gulf Coast Workforce Board is the workforce development board for the thirteen-county Houston-Galveston Gulf Coast region in southeast Texas, which covers 2.6 million workers and over 100,000 businesses. It was established in 1996 prior to the establishment of the WIA. To increase its ability to serve as an intermediary, the workforce board decided to address one of the largest weaknesses of public training, its lack of connection to employers or the demand side of the labor market. The WorkSource, the Gulf Coast Workforce Board's service network, implemented two features to increase its ability to collect, interpret, and craft information that would allow it to better respond to and influence the regional labor market. Those features include a sector-based industry model and the implementation of business liaisons.

The purpose of the industry model is to bring together all relevant workforce and economic development players, especially employers, from an industrial sector to form a regional committee. That committee identifies sector workforce needs and uses that information to distinguish which needs the public training regime can fulfill. The unspoken goal is to create an effective industry network whose common understandings can reshape the labor market to provide opportunities for regional residents. The Health Services Steering Committee, for example, brought together the eighty-five area hospitals to review workforce practices and strategies and to create common sector goals. Like WRTP, this sector approach brought large local employers with significant numbers of jobs to the table.

This committee is trying to establish an industry model for the ideal health-care work environment. Some of the features they are working to implement include employee evaluations (with rewards tied to performance measures), general training sessions, and the breaking down of organizational silos within hospitals and other health-care institutions. Committee members make presentations to regional employers to illustrate the values these changes offer, which include decreased turnover, errors, vacancy rates, and increased patient and employee satisfaction. The committee also undertakes ongoing analysis of the shortage of faculty at local nursing schools and coordinates loaned faculty programs from area hospitals. The committee can point to some practical successes, including committing staff nurses to teach in area nursing schools, securing funding to supplement nurse faculty salaries, obtaining $5 million to train existing staff as nurses and other professionals, and convincing legislators to provide money to educate more registered nurses. By working together, they have enacted small shifts in the opportunity structures in the labor market, specifically in the area of nursing.

The second feature, industry liaisons, is articulated through the establishment of a team of business consultants. While the consultants' main task is to market The WorkSource's services to employers, in effect, they have the ability to create trust-based relationships with employers, which serve as important information channels to enhance the WIB's intermediary role. Notably, these business consultants are required to concentrate their efforts on priority employers. These are defined as employers with over 100 employees in growth industries, with over 500 employees and varied job categories in any sector, and, critically, any employer with well-developed relationships with existing personnel. By recognizing the importance of preexisting personal relationships, the program is creating critical mechanisms for information brokerage that can help it meet its goals. Although the consultants are marketers, their real task is to build and maintain personal relationships to better customize employee recruitment and training with employer needs and follow up in order to maintain business satisfaction. Business consultants also work with The WorkSource's resident services that support jobseekers. The business consultant is the staff person through whom information concerning supply and demand is integrated and shared. In fact, consultants also screen and approve referrals to priority jobs. They are key nodes within the information framework. All intermediaries need to know where these nodes are and whether they are working effectively if they are to be valuable intermediaries.

The business consultant strategy was implemented in September 2002, and by April 2003, The WorkSource had placed 6,227 jobseekers in priority companies, a figure that exceeded their expectations. Their goal was to have 2,320 placements by August 2003.

The WorkSource has learned a few lessons on information brokering through its efforts. First, to better serve the business community, it needs not only institutional features but also personal and professional networks, which are critical to connecting to businesses. The Workforce Division manager, Marilyn Stadler, emphasized the need to build numerous ways for employers to provide feedback. While it is important to have major employers on the board, staff also must be "externally connected" to employers and their representatives if they are to recruit and retain business involvement. As well as the liaisons and the sector committees, board and staff members need to be involved in economic development groups to exchange information and to interact with elected officials in order to educate and advocate. To the degree possible, they built these features into their local program design.

Entering into information networks provided useful data on how to best position services in a competitive market. Since The WorkSource competes with private outsourcing organizations, they have learned to market their services as prepaid through taxes and have started to build business and credibility vis-à-vis the competition. They are learning to speak business-ese. As noted above, intermediaries need to be bilingual, and talk comfortably to supply- and demand-side players.

However, the Gulf Coast Workforce Board and The WorkSource did meet some challenges to their ability to fully develop that information brokerage role. First, the performance measures the government requires them to collect are not meaningful to employers and discourage employer involvement. How an intermediary measures its effectiveness is an important signal to the marketplace about whether it can broker information among players as a central node in the networks, or it is representative of a more limited viewpoint. Second, The WorkSource did not have sufficient extrabudgetary funds to join economic development groups, such as Chambers, which limited the organization's ability to network with businesses at sufficient levels. This is partially a function of the nature of government funding, which does not allow a WIB full discretion in the use of finances.

Finally, the fragmentation of the workforce system was an obstacle to effective information management. The WorkSource staff found it particularly challenging to manage the range of contractors because the latter are paid through different sources, serve different customers, and have different missions. This makes it particularly hard to sustain a common message in the region and identify collective long-term needs.

Conclusions

In comparing these two cases, certain common lessons emerge about information management. First, workforce organizations interact in a wide range of networks in which they gather the information they need to meet their missions. However, the degree to which the workforce organization can then shape that information, allowing it to function as an entrepreneurial intermediary, depends on the degree to which players on the supply and demand sides view the organization's ability to meet their needs. In other words, serving dual customers is not sufficient. Intermediaries need to deliver quality services to their dual customer bases and these customers must perceive the services as excellent, reliable, and responsive.

Customers determine quality and reliability from varying sources of information. Even if certain features, such as The WorkSource's business liaisons, signal an openness to meet business needs, the performance measures, which are understood as incentives to action, can contradict that message. Thus, intermediaries as information brokers must ensure that their design and their actions complement the messages they are trying to deliver.

Second, a sector focus provides a useful background for framing the issues and managing information. This helps to cut down on the number of players and activities that must be coordinated. It also allowed WRTP to develop an expertise and deliver quality services, which ultimately allowed it to leverage changes in employer culture for the betterment of the community.

Third, workforce development functions in a competitive marketplace. Good intentions are insufficient to be a good intermediary: a good intermediary must channel information in a way that lets it compete. The WIBs and one-stops face an uphill battle in fully developing this role, given the constraints they face. Even though The WorkSource has implemented many design features that have increased its competitive capability, it still runs into bureaucratic barriers. Thus, while WIBs and one-stops are important players in the system, they will require complementary intermediaries, especially in large and diverse labor markets, to develop a fully functional and comprehensive workforce system.

Finally, cities and regions must consider the impacts of the design of both the workforce system and of specific local programs and intermediaries. Even the best-designed programs face systemic challenges, the most compelling being the fragmentation of the system. Even the best-designed systems can host poor programs. Intermediaries must be viewed from the point of view of both program design and their systemic impact. At the systems level, intermediaries should be able to create new meaning and new understandings that start to shift the design of the workforce system to one that prioritizes human capital development and looks to expand the overall pool of talented and skilled individuals in a region.

Having intermediaries is not the only part of the infrastructure a community needs in order to manage workforce challenges in the information age. Cities and regions also need another important element, credentialing strategies, which provide jobseekers and employers with formalized information on skill attainment. The next chapter examines these issues in detail.

Note

1. The application of Imai's work to our understanding of the role of intermediaries was first used by Berry (2004).

— 4 —

Enhancing Mobility: Skill Standards, Certification, and Credentials

As this book has argued, the emergence of the information age coupled with changing demographics signals the need for a coordinated approach to building a workforce system to enhance our human capital base. That system must respond to two fundamental needs: ensuring that businesses find the skills they require in the short and long term and supporting more mobile individuals to accumulate skills for career advancement and to navigate a more volatile labor market. Improving the transfer of information about the capabilities of workers and better engaging employers in the process are essential objectives for achieving these goals. Enhancing and expanding the use of credentialed skill standards is a practical, albeit challenging, strategy for meeting these objectives.

What are credentialed skill standards? To sufficiently define this, we must break it down into its component parts. First, skill standards are skills that have been recognized as being necessary for success in a particular industry or occupation. They are work-related competencies that define levels of achievement based on what a person needs to know and what a person needs to do. For example, in the manufacturing industry, workers require skills in statistical tools and systems, manufacturing processes, tools and equipment, and inventory and materials handling. Alternatively, obtaining a clerical position requires computing skills and knowledge of certain software programs.

Standards can be subdivided into five categories that build upon each other. These include: core academic skills (see below); general workplace readiness skills (see below); industry core skills, which are standard skills and knowledge for a particular industry, and are usually imparted through career majors (e.g., hospitality, health care, and manufacturing); occupational family standards, which are standards shared by occupation sets within or across

66

industries (e.g., medical diagnostics, which includes imaging, radiography, laboratory work); and occupational or job-specific standards, which focus on specific occupational skills. Certification is usually based on occupational specific standards (Ledebur et al. 2002).

Standards form an essential bridge that connects the needs of businesses, individuals, the community, and the nation because they facilitate the flow of information in a labor market that is more volatile, more mobile, and more skills dependent. Standards help the workforce system by better furnishing a common language that workforce, economic, and community development practitioners can use to communicate, while giving educators the tools to assess student performance. By providing common documentation of industry skills, businesses, individuals, and education and training providers can train to standards, certify and demonstrate competencies, and facilitate communication around a common framework (Ledebur et al. 2002). Put in another way, because skill standards provide a way to coordinate across training and education programs, they increase the power, value, and transportability of certifications obtained through training. Skill standards, therefore, are the basis of certification.

Second, certification is an award provided to a student or trainee by an entity that recognizes an individual's competencies through predetermined qualifications. Those qualifications usually comprise education, some type of experience, and test scores; and in some fields such as health care, licensing is an essential component of certification (Mahlman and Austin, undated). Certifications are awarded by both credentialed and noncredentialed entities. Credentialing refers to the provision of certification to both the individual meeting the skill qualifications and the institution providing the training for those qualifications. Entities that are credentialed have had an external body certify that they are teaching the appropriate skill sets. The credential means that the certification is portable across national, and even international, labor markets. Certification from credentialed entities, therefore, is integral to the effective implementation of skill standards. Noncredentialed entities, such as local training programs, may impart approved skill standards, but the certification often is only recognized in the local labor market, providing no real portability for the jobseeker over time. This issue will be discussed more in depth below.

In sum, credentialed skill standards refer to the awarding of a certification to a jobseeker that signals the employers that he or she has achieved a predetermined qualification recognized by a credentialing body. Inadequate standards and limited certification create information bottlenecks in the labor market. Thus, to meet the needs of the new economy, we need to see an enhancement and expansion of credentialed skill standards.

Skill certification is important for all skill levels. Trends occurring in the low- and high-skill labor markets make this clear. During the tight labor market of the late 1990s, business demand for disadvantaged workers escalated. Businesses displayed an increased willingness to hire from labor pools they had previously ignored and to pay higher wages to these new hires. Research by Holzer, Raphael, and Stoll (2003) on business hiring practices during this period reveals that, at the same time that employers increased their demand for skill certifications (as opposed to general credentials such as high school diplomas), they also increased their use of screening methods (e.g., tests, background checks). The availability of new technologies (e.g., the Internet) has reduced the cost of testing and background checks, which helps to reinforce the overall trend toward increased skill demand driven by the knowledge economy. Employers, therefore, are looking for more reliable information to document the attainment of certain capabilities.

For individuals, evidence suggests that certification opens labor market access and increases earning potential. A study of California-based former welfare recipients who received community college credentials shows that the participants were more likely to work year-round than before and substantially increased their earnings, especially if they pursued a vocational certificate or degree rather than an academic track (Mathur et al. 2004). Moreover, the study found that longer vocational certificate programs had a more substantial impact on earnings. However, those who did not complete either a certificate or a degree remained disadvantaged in the labor market. Even though attaining some schooling did leave former welfare recipients better off than before, without that transportable validation of their skills, the study found that leaving poverty behind and advancing were still very difficult. Notably, for those who did succeed academically, most of the students reported that receiving social and employment services from the community colleges, such as child care, work-study, financial aid (especially fee waivers), and targeted academic and employment advising, made the difference in their ability to do so. In sum, for those with low levels of skill attainment, certification is becoming an increasingly important component for creating opportunity.

At the upper end of the skill spectrum, emerging trends also suggest a need for increased skill certification. These trends are most apparent in the information technology (IT) and communications industries. The rapid development of IT industries over the past two decades and competitive demand for skilled workers led to the emergence of what Adelman (2000) terms a "parallel postsecondary universe" of skill credentialing in IT. This certification system, which surfaced outside traditional education networks, was established to expand the labor pool and facilitate its flow on a global scale. The system's initiators, the primary IT equipment vendors, including Microsoft, Oracle, Novell, Sun Microsystems, and Cisco, used these certifications as a way to demonstrate knowledge of their product and to support their sales and marketing strategies (Jacobs 2004).

According to Adelman's research, the drivers behind this new system wanted a labor force that would be loyal to an occupation and to equipment standards rather than to an organization or employer. In addition, these skills should be applicable in many countries in many languages. Certification, therefore, recognizes skills attached to an occupation that can be transferred among organizations. While this new universe does not provide licenses per se, it is akin to the licensure of allied health workers, which is competency based and allows for the relatively free flow of health-care workers nationally and internationally. The goals behind this system are instructive. Rather than fostering firm-based training, which might limit skills to the need of a particular firm and tie the trainee's future to that firm, it looks to support the sector as a whole, which means broad, transferable skills. From an economic development point of view, therefore, training should be tied to industrial or occupational sectors rather than to firms.

The development of this parallel universe has been rapid and widespread. According to Adelman's research, since the first credential, the Certified Novell Engineer, was issued in 1989, over 300 certifications have been established. By 2000, about 1.6 million individuals have obtained about 2.4 million IT certifications, for the most part between 1997 and 2000. Over half of those individuals did so outside the United States. Certification is awarded upon passing an exam, which has launched an entire industry that prepares students for examinations. These exams are continuously updated in response to new knowledge and practice. As of 1999, Adelman had identified examination centers located at 5,000 sites in 140 countries and 25 languages. Maintaining active certification often requires individuals to continue their education and periodically retake the examinations. In many cases, obtaining advanced levels of certification, such as moving from Associate to Professional to Expert in the Cisco certification system, requires professional experience in addition to passing examinations.

Although private companies manage the testing centers, Adelman notes that the vendors (e.g., Microsoft) and industry associations (e.g., the Computing Technology Industry Association) actually develop the form and content of the test and award the certification. Increasingly, cross-recognition of certification is also developing. For example, Microsoft will waive its networking examination for individuals certified by Novell or Sun.

In terms of organization, the certification sponsors authorize various agents to provide course work in order to ensure that the content and instruction quality meet their standards. For example, Sun MicroSystems has partnered with New Horizons Computer Learning Centers to offer its Java courseware. New Horizon instructors then have and maintain certification from Sun. Thus, instructors are certified in both the content areas and in teaching and assessment. Finally, the industry established a Council on Computing Certification to establish industry standards and accreditation standards for the certification programs. These certifications are highly portable because the standards that underpin them are recognized across national borders (Adelman 2000).

As this universe has evolved, higher education agents have entered the picture. Adelman highlights several examples. Pima Community College District in Arizona allows students to turn their certification preparation into credit by taking an examination. Regents College in New York has teamed up with private vendors, including Microsoft, to provide a Computer Information Science B.S., which offers credit-by-certification exams. In other cases, an education institution can buy the online curricula from the vendor to provide it to students or to become partners with the private vendor and offer certification options on campus. The University of Akron, for example, is a Novell Partner. Finally, many vendors are working with high schools and colleges to build solid pipelines to the labor force. Cisco Network Academy, for example, has numerous sites around the country and abroad in which students can obtain credits toward a Cisco Certified Network Associate credential.

Data available on community colleges gathered by Jacobs (2004) at the Community College Research Center suggest that this trend toward certification is becoming increasingly widespread. Generally speaking, by 1999, noncredit offerings (certification as opposed to degrees) exceeded credit offerings in community colleges by 9 percent. Looking at IT specifically, in the 2000–2001 academic year, 25 percent of community colleges offered IT certification programs. In addition, community colleges conferred 20,450 IT degrees. In a targeted study on this activity, Jacobs found that community colleges often run their noncredit certification and credit programs alongside each other. He also found that individuals used certification within the industry to increase their mobility in the job market. However, Jacobs found little evidence that certification alone at this level of technical knowledge opened up access to the job market. Employers preferred degrees to just certification. He also found that certificate programs were more expensive than more standard programs and were not tied to public support such as the WIA. He concluded that colleges actually were responding more to private markets than a more generalized need for skill standards. Even so, Jacobs still determined that the impact of certification and skill standards on community colleges overall has been positive. While it has not created a new delivery system, it has opened up community colleges' understanding of learning and the effectiveness of its workforce programs. The challenge is to better integrate certification into more standard credit programs.

The IT experience with the rapid development of standards and certification offers us some general lessons as to its importance and its limitations. Adelman concludes the following. First, the student rather than the institution is the heart of the system. The student enters the system at any time (it is open access), determines his or her best way of learning, and is not bound to a school or a company or a place. Second, the system is grounded in competency-based education and performance assessment, which has no equivalent in the traditional echelons of higher education. Third, although it is influencing higher education, it is not higher education because it is strictly about skills development based on standards. Higher education serves a wider mission of developing the whole person. Fourth, industry certifications do not replace experience or degrees, and in fact, employers do not require it per se. However, they do reward it financially. Typically, individuals receive a 4–14 percent increase in salary after receipt of the certification. Finally, students obtain certification to support increased mobility as well as wage enhancements because the certifications are both transparent and portable, unlike more generic workforce training received on-site, which has no recognition off-site, and thus provides no portability or proof. In conclusion, certification based on recognized skill standards trends are indeed emerging at higher skill levels, but they are not replacing degrees; rather, they are enhancing them. They signal businesses that individuals have solid skills as well as a more rounded education provided through a degree, and for individuals, they provide more strength in the labor market. Degrees at this level are still the key to the labor market door, but certification then impacts how well they navigate the maze once inside it. At this higher level, certifications add to mobility and lifelong learning.

It is important to note that the inability of the education and training system to meet demand partially explains the emergence of this parallel universe. A study done by Davis and colleagues (2001) on the supply of IT workers in Northeast Ohio's higher education system illustrates the challenges on the ground. One of the main insights emerging from the study was the incompatibility between the classification of IT work and what education programs taught. In different institutions, IT programs were housed within different academic disciplines, which influenced instructional content. Alignment was better in schools with independent IT departments or divisions. This disconnect had a substantial impact on the labor market, whereby demand for IT workers outstripped supply by large margins. What this example suggests is that skill standards still matter at higher skill levels, and that institutions of higher education do not always impart them in an effective way when viewed through the lens of potential employers. While many high-skilled professionals have licensing procedures to validate skills obtained, in IT, one of the newest skill sets to emerge, the system is in the process of being built.

Understanding emergent certification trends is an important step in responding to the needs of a twenty-first-century workforce system. We can come to several conclusions. First, credentialed skill standards support individuals navigating the labor market, but certificates do not replace degrees. While certification based on skill standards opens access to the labor market for low-skilled individuals, at higher levels of skill, they serve as resume enhancements. Businesses' willingness to reward certification indicates that standards and certification improve information to the benefit of the labor market. Thus, certifications, as we shall see later in this book, are an important component of lifelong learning.

Second, communities must address equity concerns. Specifically, certification is expensive and relies increasingly on individuals who choose to enhance their skill base; thus, it may be difficult for disadvantaged and transitional populations to access. Moreover, real advancement is eventually attached to degrees, so certification needs to be integrated into a higher education pathway for individuals to fully thrive. For those struggling to overcome the barriers created through disadvantaged starting points (documented in chapter 3), a lot of up-front support is required.

Third, if education and training institutions cannot respond sufficiently in meeting emerging skill needs, then the private sector will. This has some thought-provoking implications. The IT system is global in reach and has supported the dominance of certain firms in the market by tying skills and certification to specific vendors and their products. The creation of an international labor market based on common skill sets benefits individuals by increasing their opportunities, but also makes it easier to transport jobs abroad. Skills need to be tied to industries and occupations not vendors, or else we run the risk of creating betamax skills. In tight labor markets, skills attached to declining vendors may become obsolete. Thus, the need for communities to invest in responsive human capital systems that are grounded in industrial and occupational skill standards is even more apparent. The private sector is faster and often better resourced. It seems education and training entities may be responding to immediate market cues, rather than long-term systemic demand. Although that parallel system could easily be defined as continuing adult education, its creation has had a cascade effect on public training and education venues. While short-term advantages can be gained by letting the private sector lead, long-term sustainable development requires the strategic leadership of education and civic institutions as well.

Finally, insufficient standards may deny communities access to talented, skilled immigrants and other newcomers. Skilled workers may be unable to obtain work for which they are trained due to the lack of professional certification or restrictive certification demands. Inadequate standards as well as inadequate certification denoting the achievement of standards create information transmission problems in the labor market and act as a detriment to communities wishing to develop, attract, and retain a strong human capital base. IT standards have emerged in order to create common technical skill standards that support a global labor force. Thus, developing common standards and recognized methods to certify them is of paramount importance to meet the labor market needs of the twenty-first century.

In sum, certification based on recognized standards facilitates labor market flows for both disadvantaged workers and high-end workers. Systems that validate skill sets, and ensure employers a recognized set of skills, make it easier for individuals to navigate the labor market. Credentialed skill standards, therefore, are an important component of a twenty-first century workforce system.

Skill Standards: Where Do We Begin?

The discussion of credentialed skill standards in fact starts with schools. Although skill standards refer to work-related competencies, they assume individuals have core academic skills that provide the foundation for attaining a more demanding career-related skill base and prepare them to function in society. In today's world, the lack of these skills hampers the capacities of individuals and, by extension, communities.

Variation in educational quality not only affects individual opportunities but also shapes opportunity sets for metropolitan regions. Metropolitan regions marked by a well-educated population have a higher per capita income level. Over the past twenty years, there has been a divergence of incomes among regions driven by educational attainment (Gottlieb and Fogarty 2003). This divergence, according to Gottlieb and Fogarty, is "the geographical equivalent of growing income inequality among individuals in our society. The so-called new meritocracy [knowledge economy driven by human capital] is as unforgiving to poorly educated regions as it is to poorly educated individuals" (2003: 330). While the quality of the educational system may relate only indirectly to the quality of the local labor force—because migration can change the proportion quite rapidly (positively and negatively)—investing in human capital development still starts with schools insofar as schools teach core academic skills. Also known as basic skills, core academic skills are the foundational skills that prepare individuals for the world of work and participation in society.

Any review of current politics, media, or just talk on the street will show that the U.S. population is greatly concerned about the quality of its education, especially the apparent inability of our system to impart these basic skills. The statistics are telling. Approximately 40–44 million adults in the United States, about 21–23 percent of the population, fall into the lowest literacy ranking, according to the results of the national adult literacy survey. Another 50 million or so, according to the survey, fall into level 2, which denotes better but still limited basic skill attainment (Kirsch at al. 2002).

This concern is not new. In 1983, the U.S. Department of Education's National Commission on Excellence in Education report, *A Nation at Risk*, sounded the first alarm bells. Warning that schools were not preparing students sufficiently for employment, the report informed the country that it was necessary to upgrade the academic achievement of all students in order to meet the needs of the technological age. Given their lack of basic skills, their insufficient knowledge of the world of work, and their difficulty adjusting to the changing environment, students were deemed ill-prepared to achieve success in a high-performance, increasingly complex workplace.

A decade later, the U.S. Department of Labor issued the report "What Work Requires of Schools," produced by the Secretary's Commission on Achieving Necessary Skills (SCANS), which continued the cry for improved academics and went one step further: SCANS identified and defined the foundation skills required of all U.S. youth, whether they went directly from high school to work or went on for further education. According to SCANS, the minimum basic skills required to move from school to work are:

- reading;
- writing;
- mathematics (arithmetical computation and mathematical reasoning); and
- listening and speaking.

According to the report, less than half of all young adults have achieved the minimum skill levels for reading and writing. The figures are even lower in mathematics (SCANS 1991). In the twenty-first century, experts now recognize a fifth basic skill: science and technology literacy, which includes "knowledge of science, scientific thinking, mathematics and technology and the relationship among them and technology literacy, including competence in the use of computers, networks and digital content" (Nelson 1999, cited in

CEO Forum on Education and Technology 2001: 9). As noted earlier, all individuals in this century will need to be technology and science savvy, even if they are not all scientists or technicians.

While the discussion of foundation skills starts with schools, it does not end there. SCANS also identifies personal qualities, including responsibility, self-esteem, sociability, self-management, and integrity/honesty as core attributes for moving from school to work.

These personal or soft skills, also called life or workplace readiness skills, refer to the range of attitudes and behaviors that individuals need to be successful in the workplace and are generally assumed to be imparted through family and the community. In practical terms, these skills provide individuals with courtesy, self-discipline, timeliness, conflict management, a positive attitude, the desire for work, a willingness to learn, an ability to take supervision, an ability to work with colleagues, and the capacity to adapt to workplace norms. For many entry-level jobs, especially jobs in key service sectors such as hospitality and retail, employers look predominantly for soft skills, believing the job-specific or technical skills required can be taught on the job.

The lack of soft skills tends to be associated with low-income individuals such as welfare recipients, school leavers, or ex-felons who grew up in a social milieu in which neither family nor peers nor schools imparted such habits. Disinvestment in urban communities compelled jobs and people with jobs to leave the inner city, creating jobless communities that are unable to socialize their residents into the culture of work. The situation also produced social isolation, separating inner city residents from the social networks that help them to find good jobs and resulting in the exclusion of whole communities from the labor market with no personal knowledge of the world of work (Wilson 1996).

While the situation is particularly pronounced in urban areas, it is not solely an urban problem. Rural-based businesses also find that younger members of the labor force similarly lack these skills. Some communities have tried to address this through their schools. For example, several school districts located in rural West Texas have implemented what they term a leadership course to provide instruction in character education and business ethics.

Soft-skill attainment is a real as well as a complex problem. When talking about soft skills, it is important to be aware that, at times, we are also talking about the cultural differences of a multicultural society, which has racial undertones. Soft skills can serve as an informal gatekeeper in hiring decisions, which then underplays the importance of more technical skills, and may be used to discriminate against specific groups, especially black men (Harrison and Weiss 1998). It can also create uncomfortable workplace scenarios in which middle-aged white people tell Hispanic or African-American youth how to talk and dress (Houghton and Proscio 2001).

Given the lack of basic and soft skills, it is not surprising that many approaches to serving disadvantaged populations have focused on improving those skills. Taking an in-depth look at Support and Training Result in Valuable Employees (STRIVE), a nationally reputed program known for its effective methods for enhancing soft skills, will illustrate why the standards issue may start with basic and soft skills, but cannot end there.

Support and Training Result in Valuable Employees

Support and Training Result in Valuable Employees (STRIVE) was established in East Harlem, New York, in 1985 to assist individuals facing significant social and economic barriers in finding economic independence through work. Using a boot camp approach, STRIVE developed a three- to four-week job-preparedness program focused on soft or life skills development and job search techniques, followed by job placement. Today, STRIVE has twenty-one affiliates in the United States and abroad: it is one of the few community-based programs to be successfully replicated on a wide scale. The STRIVE network has a common benchmark of placing 75 percent of its graduates, of which 70 percent remain employed after two years. In 2001, for example, 4,000 were trained and 3,000 were placed (STRIVE New York 2005).

Although each affiliate organization shares the same philosophy and approach, local programs are customized to respond to local needs. Each program reflects the particular needs of local clients, the makeup of the local business community, and the expectations of local funders.

To ensure a connection with its participants, STRIVE hires trainers and support staff who are either program graduates or individuals with backgrounds similar to the trainees. These individuals know the environment their clients come from and serve as living examples that barriers, no matter how high, can be surmounted. STRIVE's commitment to its mission guides its development, and consequently has required the program to expand and adapt in response to advanced learning about the workforce development needs of some of the hardest-to-serve populations. Thus, STRIVE is a particularly important case because its evolution reflects state-of-the-art learning of what works and what does not in workforce development.

One of the most important lessons that has emerged from STRIVE's experience is that just providing soft skills does not alleviate poverty or create real opportunity for advancement. Many of STRIVE's graduates were placed in low-skill, low-wage jobs and were unable to escape the poverty trap based merely on the acquisition of soft skills. To increase the wage potential of their trainees, STRIVE affiliates then added occupational training modules, appropriate to meeting local demand, or partnered with other training agencies that could provide hard occupational skills for STRIVE graduates. For example, STRIVE New York established a Career Plan program, which offers training in several fields, such as Brownfields Environmental Technology, Artisan Baking, and Cisco Academy network certification, that are linked to career planning, attitudinal development, and certification (STRIVE New York 2005).

The second lesson follows from the first. STRIVE affiliates have found it necessary to create links that allow students to acquire additional skills for true advancement. While basic and soft skills are an essential start in the skills acquisition path, they are only the start. Basic and soft skills impart a level of readiness for more comprehensive human capital development.

The third lesson—placement is easy, retention is hard—led STRIVE to assume a more intermediary-type role in relation to its clients. The individuals in STRIVE programs face enormous barriers to job retention, including the need for child care, mental health problems, transportation issues, substance abuse, and legal issues, which leads to high turnover after placement. In response, STRIVE has developed a career advancement program that connects its graduates to whatever services they need to stay in a job and, ultimately, develop a career path. A STRIVE graduate can call STRIVE for assistance at any time, for any reason. The service is available for the individual's entire lifetime. For the first two years, the service is proactive, with STRIVE staff regularly following up with its trainees. After two years, the service is passive; the trainee must contact STRIVE to receive assistance.

The last core lesson STRIVE learned is that in order to be effective workforce agents, they must have strong relationships with the business community. STRIVE DC, for example, emphasizes the importance of building solid employer relationships. The STRIVE model drives home the basic argument of this book: for a workforce system to function effectively and efficiently, both employers and workforce programs need to be engaged in an interactive manner that creates a shared language, shared assumptions, and shared information.

The story of STRIVE puts a very human face on what the research results have clearly revealed. More than forty years of research on training programs confirm that basic and soft-skills training are critical but insufficient (Grubb 1996). Studies on stand-alone basic education and GED preparation have demonstrated questionable results for placement and retention (Harrison and Weiss 1998). Training is most effective when it integrates basic and soft-skills training into occupational or work-based training. For individuals, this approach has been shown to increase earnings and access to benefits and improve an individual's ability to find steady work even if it is not in a single job (Smith et al. 2002; Zandniapour and Conway 2001).

For businesses, an integrated training approach provides more productive workers. A study of state-financed incumbent training programs reveals that these programs, which were established to improve the competitiveness of businesses, incorporate basic skills training in their training modules (Creticos and Sheets 1990). The study also finds that the training modules used in these programs closely resemble the materials employed by community colleges and other institutions training individuals for vocational careers. Good business-focused vocational programs, therefore, incorporate basic skills into occupational training.

In sum, in the knowledge economy, basic and soft skills have become pretraining issues. In today's world, basic and soft skills are sufficient only to enter the world of work; they are not enough to guarantee either a high-paying career or the successful completion of postsecondary education. The knowledge economy demands a higher level of human interaction to innovate and create new knowledge. That higher level of interaction demands that individuals develop interpersonal and cognitive skills. The SCANS report also identified these workplace readiness skills:

- creative thinking;
- decision making;
- problem solving;
- seeing things in the mind's eye;
- knowing how to learn; and
- reasoning.

These skills are best taught in an applied setting. Learning based on real world problems imparts problem-solving and decision-making skills. Vocational and career education traditionally have been best at providing this style of education and supporting this type of learning (Carnevale 2004). This helps to explain why training and experiential learning approaches that integrate basic skills into work-based training may be so successful.

Academic and workplace readiness standards have been developed and are generally well accepted. The challenge remains to increase the number of individuals with these skills. At the policy or systems level, the demand for skill standards targets the industrial and occupational levels.

Creating and Implementing Industrial and Occupational Skill Standards

One of the biggest challenges in delivering occupational skills is the scattered and uncoordinated nature of the standardization of these skills. While certain professions require degrees and have established exams denoting certification (e.g., accounting, health care) and are thus only deliverable through educational institutions, many technical skills and occupational categories are not so well organized and are offered in many arenas. As the IT example underscores, courses have mushroomed across the country and they are only now establishing an institution to accredit the certificate-awarding venues. The end result is that for many industries and occupations, diverse schools and training agents offer something they call certification, but businesses may not recognize the training or it may be useful only for the individual in the regional labor-market area of the school or training program. In other words, the standards may be highly local and hold no currency in another region or state. Let us take a more detailed look at the case of the William F. Goodling Regional Advanced Skills Center in York, Pennsylvania, where local businesses did come together to define skill standards. The case reveals the strengths and limits of a local approach, while also providing some important lessons on what it takes to develop skill standards.

William F. Goodling Regional Advanced Skills Center

In York, Pennsylvania, manufacturing firms faced shortages of skilled technicians and the institutions able to provide them. In this region, the educational institutions did not provide a sufficient pipeline to skilled workers. At the postsecondary level, the region had no community college. Local universities, which do not fill vocational needs as their primary mission, had politically blocked the establishment of a community college in order to reduce competition for local students. At the secondary school level, students in York County must choose a vocational track in ninth grade, which can be early to choose a career track. Those who might have later pursued a vocational route in eleventh or twelfth grade no longer have the opportunity open to them, either in high school or beyond. This has contributed to a very limited pipeline of individuals prepared for technical careers. Additionally, there is still the major limitation of lack of parental support for blue-collar career choices.

To increase the pool of skilled workers, the York County Economic Development Corporation worked with area businesses to develop the William F. Goodling Regional Advanced Skills Center (ASC). The center provides customized training to meet the training needs of local industry clusters. ASC started with four cluster areas: machining, plastics injection molding, printing, and welding. New training tracks such as IT and electrical maintenance technology have been added as ASC has evolved. Businesses have been major partners in the design of the center, its curricula,

79

and the development of equipment lists, assuring that training meets local business skill requirements.

Trainees at ASC receive certificates or diplomas based on skill standards developed by local businesses. However, ASC is not an accredited body, so the certification provides no college credit. In addition, lack of accreditation also denies the institution access to Federal Pell grants that can support individuals who might choose to pursue these technical fields but do not have the financial ability to do so. Thus, ASC had no natural pipelines to potential workers; the supply side activities were missing. While ASC was developed to fill a real gap in workforce development, their experience reminds us that the labor market is comprised of both individuals seeking jobs and businesses providing them. While we know from studies on training that investment in supply-side programs does not work in isolation from the wider market, the York case shows that a demand-side-only focus to increase the pool of skilled workers can also face significant constraints.

In response to these insights, ASC widened its mission and became certified to train dislocated workers as part of the WIA public training regime. ASC also constructed a partnership with the Crispus Attucks YouthBuild Charter School to offer an internship program to Charter School students. Once a week, students can attend ASC for vocational training in manufacturing machining and computer-aided design. This expansion into a wider realm of workforce development activities was a necessary evolution to help expand the supply side of the market.

According to Chuck Thomas, executive director, this was still not enough. He recognized that, to meet the needs of jobseekers and to really expand the labor pool, the region needed a community college that could provide the necessary accreditation and access to financial resources to support individual career development on a different scale. He noted, "We thought we could do it without having a community college involved but they are the ideal workforce partner from the individual side." In 2002, the local school district invited Harrisburg Area Community College (HACC) to start providing classes locally. The community college president was invited to, and now serves on, the ASC board. In fall of 2005, HACC opens its York location.

The ASC story shows why credentialed skill standards matter. Focusing only within the demand framework has a limited impact on regional economic opportunity. Thus, standards are a necessary but insufficient factor in enhancing the capabilities of the workforce system. Their real value is in their ability to provide the foundation for certification and credentialing, which requires accredited educational and training venues.

We now turn to the case of the Bread and Butter Café in Savannah, Georgia, to better understand the value of these insights.

80

Bread and Butter Café, Savannah, Georgia

In Savannah, Georgia, three organizations, America's Second Harvest, Union Mission, and Savannah Technical College,[1] came together to create the Bread and Butter Café. The café is a community project designed to offer meaningful employment opportunities to the city's homeless population in area restaurants, a strong local industry marked by high staff turnover. The café trains individuals in an actual restaurant setting that is open to the public. Given the highly stigmatized nature of the homeless population and employers' doubts about their employability and skills, the program has implemented the following features to address these concerns.

- Prescreening of applicants, including English and math tests and drug testing at entry and randomly throughout the training process. As we discussed in earlier chapters, the problem of insufficiently screened job applicants is most often cited by employers who hire from public and community training problems (Kazis, Prince, and Rubin 2003; Mills and Kazis 1999). Equally important, these tests demonstrate that individuals graduating from the program have already attained core academic skills that will allow them to complete the course and later pursue additional education and training required for career advancement.
- Holistic training including life skills, jobs skills, job readiness, job placement, and retention services, in addition to direct work experience as the trainees prepare food in the restaurant. As noted above, both research and practice indicate that the combination of pre-employment skills, industry-based training, support services, and on-the-job skill upgrading has the most significant impact on wages and job retention (Giloth 2000). The restaurant setting provides the added value of generating revenue that supports the program and exposing the public to the homeless, which helps to reduce the stigmas attached to this population.
- Case managers who oversee job retention issues, which includes maintaining good relationships with employers. Retention rates of graduates are 80 percent. The Bread and Butter Café' acts as a new-economy intermediary and mediates between workers and employers to ensure that the needs of both sides are met.
- Students' skills are certified by the Savannah Technical School, which standardizes the skill base for employers and provides the trainees with college credit should they continue their education. Some program graduates have gone on to pursue their Associate's Degree in Culinary Arts. The program did not seek to create new standards but

built on existing standards embedded in existing relevant curricula. This benefits participants because the program embeds its trainees into the existing network of higher education, which puts them on a potential career track if they so choose, exposes them to opportunities they may not have considered, and familiarizes them with the system as a whole.

The Bread and Butter Café has designed its programs to meet the needs of some of the hardest-to-serve individuals. By providing college-based certification attached to career advancement paths to workers in an industry marked by chronic workforce concerns, the program contributes to the overall stability of the industry as a whole, creates economic opportunities for individuals, and meets business demand. By adding certification to the mix, Bread and Butter becomes an economic development engine, because it strengthens the overall quality of the labor pool and the industry, not just the individual, even though the individual is the program's central target.

The ASC and Bread and Butter Café examples demonstrate that standards and certification are important workforce issues, especially for those individuals not possessing a bachelor's degree, which still represents the majority of the population. In fact, skill standards have grabbed the attention of federal and state policy makers.

Over the past decade, the federal government and a number of states have introduced the idea of voluntary, industry-recognized skill standards.

Existing Skill Standards

In 1994, Congress mandated the National Skill Standards Board (NSSB) to develop a voluntary, industry-driven, national skill standards system that could serve as a basis for certification. The NSSB brought together business, labor, employee, education, and community and civil rights organizations to build a voluntary national system of skill standards, assessment, and certification systems. NSSB identified fifteen industry clusters for which to develop skill standards. Industry's role is to identify the priority occupations and the necessary skills, but the framework has them work in full partnership with labor, civil rights organizations, and community-based organizations. By the early twenty-first century, NSSB industry coalitions had established skill standards in manufacturing and sales and service. Skill standards were being developed for education and training, hospitality and tourism, information and communication technologies, and the public administration, legal, and protective services industry sectors. In 2003, NSSB sunset and two successor structures were established to continue its mission: the National Skill Standards Board Institute, which will continue the work of convening interested parties in skill standards development; and the National Skill Standards Board Education and Research Institute, which will oversee information storage on issues of quality assurance and system integrity (National Skill Standards Board Institute 2005).

The NSSB standards highlight an important skills strategy: occupational clusters, which are job skills that cross industry sectors. The NSSB's standards in sales and service represent this approach. There are examples of the use of the strategy on the ground. For instance, the National Retail Federation and the Jewish Employment and Vocational Services have partnered to create the Customer Service Training Collaborative (CSTC) in Philadelphia. The CSTC provides participants with skills relevant to positions in retail, banking, hospitality, insurance, call centers, public service, and other related areas. Once an individual obtains the initial set of skills, they can then build career ladders based on common skill sets across industries. For individuals, the CSTC opens up advancement prospects that are tied to occupational skills but not limited to a single industry. The curricula have been reviewed by businesses across a wide range of related industries, thus enhancing an individual's mobility within the Philadelphia region (Prince 2003).

States have also been working on setting skill standards. At the state level, this activity has been around for a long time in vocational education or what is now termed career technical education. Texas and Illinois, for example, have separate agencies whose responsibility is to endorse skill standards at the state level. States have used standards to develop curriculum, provide program approval for training providers, and assess students (Ledebur et al. 2002).

Once standards are in place, they need to be aligned across the labor market, and that takes partnerships. Take, for example, the Northwest Center for Emerging Technologies (NWCET) in Bellevue, Washington, located at Bellevue Community College. This nonprofit Advanced Technology Education Center, funded by the National Science Foundation, has built partnerships among businesses, education, and government to promote IT education and has created skill standards for eight IT career paths (Lerman, Riegg, and Salzman 2000). Such activities start to overcome the supply-demand disconnections identified in the Northeast Ohio study, and to disseminate standards at a higher level than the existing, vendor-based certifications can offer.

Recognizing that skill standards already exist in many sector and occupational categories makes the difficult job of moving standards forward a little bit easier. Rather than reinventing the wheel, states and regions can simply borrow existing systems, which has the added advantage of enhancing labor-market mobility across wider labor markets.

Conclusions

This chapter clearly demonstrates that the standards and certification world is as complex and fragmented as the more general workforce system. How can a community cut through the confusion and identify core strategies for implementing credentialed skill standards?

Two of the most critical forces within the region for creating and implementing credentialed skill standards are an engaged business community and strong community college(s). In Europe, which has a higher level of business involvement in skill development specifically and the training regime more generally, credentialed certification has greater validity in the labor market (Rosenfeld 1998). Without business engagement, standards and certification do not hold the same degree of power for the individual. Standards must be business-approved if they are to create effective labor market links.

However, as the York example has shown, it is not enough simply for businesses to designate desired skills. Those skills must be delivered through channels that support individuals. Again, taking the European experience, which has a longer history of using skill standards, we learn that Europe's success in the use of standards is a function of its investment in curriculum development, teacher training, and the establishment of institutions that can accredit both the qualifications and the institutions that provide them (Vickers 1995). According to Vickers (1995), standards do not drive reform. Rather, reform results from building the capacity needed to deliver standards in schools and training institutions. Thus, standards are only the palette on which certification and credentialing are drawn. The ASC and Bread and Butter Café cases suggest that the participation of a two-year college was integral to their ability to be effective in training individuals to meet high-demand jobs. Standards and certification, therefore, require capable institutions that can deliver them. Within the U.S. system, one of the central institutions for meeting this goal is the community college.

Community colleges have the potential to effectively cater to business skill demands and the wide-ranging needs of individual students. As accredited entities, they are able to provide credentialed occupational and sector-based skill standards that support labor-market mobility, fully making skilled labor a public good within the region. Since they also are linked to a range of educational, social, and other services, they offer an effective bridge to transition disadvantaged individuals into more secure, better-paying career paths. Community colleges adapt relatively quickly to labor-market demands. In the case of IT certification, community colleges rallied quickly to provide multiple IT training options. Even though this may have been a response to short-term market demand, it demonstrates the potential of community colleges if given a more strategic leadership position within a workforce system.

The centrality of the community college also hinges on its ability to provide remediation services, among other support for individuals with weak academic skills. As we have seen, for disadvantaged workers and for employers who rely on the low-skilled, low-wage workforce, just providing soft and basic skill training is essential but insufficient. These skills are best provided if they are effectively integrated into a more holistic integrated approach to training. Partnerships such as we have seen in the Bread and Butter Café that link two-year schools, community organizations, and employers may provide more substantial ways to move these efforts to scale.

The good news is that much of this work has been done. Regions do not necessarily have to go out and create skill standards, but rather to identify those existing in wider markets and apply them locally. The community college is a central institution for coordinating these types of activities.

Skill standards start with the attainment of basic and soft skills but they do not end there. Basic and soft skills are part of a continuum of learning opportunities that each workforce system must provide. We must fully accept the fact that basic and soft skills can no longer be considered sufficient training exercises. Rather, they are essential pretraining activities that allow individuals access to more demanding occupational training and education.

Ultimately, providing standardized technical skills for existing jobs is necessary but insufficient to the task of creating a skilled and motivated workforce for the community and the nation more broadly. People-centered places are more than factories for producing certificates and standards; they are environments that support human capital development. Consequently, training efforts and skill standards need to be integrated into a web of opportunities and services for additional training that ultimately ends in the provision by educational institutions of recognized credentials on which individuals can further develop. Accredited certification through educational institutions that individuals can use as the basis for later degree attainment is the greatest guarantor of advancement to an individual and of a talented workforce for businesses and the community. By increasing the number of individuals with credentialed skill standards, we increase the size, capability, and scope of mobility of regional talent, which benefits the region and all who live and work in it.

Note

1. Since the initial research on this case, America's Second Harvest has pulled out of the partnership, taking the trademark with them. But there is some hope they may eventually return. If they do not, there is a serious risk that the program will decline. The problems with the program are fiscal in nature and do not undermine the analysis of its programmatic strengths.

— 5 —

Increasing the Pool: Talent Expansion Strategies

Building intermediaries and expanding the type and content of credentials are important systemic methods for better aligning supply and demand in the labor market and increasing the overall pool of skilled workers in the region. The third leg of the infrastructure of a good workforce system includes having a portfolio of strategies aimed at attracting, retaining, and developing talent. While creating intermediaries and credentials target improvements in the workforce system, talent expansion strategies focus on the individual level. The purpose of talent expansion strategies is to encourage certain types of individual behavior: to persuade people to live, study, work, advance, and play in the region.

Talent is mobile. Specifically, college graduates are the most mobile sector of the population (Krieg 1991). Consequently, the problems of brain drain, which refers to the loss of talent from a region, and brain gain, strategies to attract talent, have taken center stage in workforce-oriented economic development activities. Whichever way you choose to phrase it, the lack of skilled labor poses significant economic challenge to communities. First, it puts pressure on wages as a means to attract skilled workers to a region, which if not successful, will price local goods out of global markets and pressure businesses to relocate to places where workers can be found. Second, it means businesses and employers will be unable to obtain specialized human capital across a range of ages and skill levels, especially for driver and cluster industries (Gottlieb 2004).

Finding ways to increase the pool of skilled labor also presents considerable policy challenges to communities. If individuals with higher skills are increasingly mobile, then the incentives to invest in talent are small because improving the skills of workers increases the difficulty of keeping them at home. Consequently, the knee-jerk reaction of many communities to skill shortages has been marketing efforts to recruit skilled workers, supported by efforts to invest in and revitalize cities to offer amenities and quality of life

87

options that are believed to be attractive to highly skilled, young workers. However, this chapter will argue that while marketing and revitalization efforts may be useful, they are a wholly insufficient approach to talent development and cannot substitute for a more comprehensive human capital development strategy. In fact, many of these efforts may be based on erroneous assumptions about why talent relocates.

Moreover, focusing on either attracting or retaining talent is only a partial approach to building a human capital base, and ultimately, will result in a race to the bottom. The talent wars, the current competition among firms and communities to recruit skilled workers, overlook a critical fact: the pipeline for this talent is decreasing, especially for workers schooled in science, math, and engineering. Accelerated global competition for talent and more stringent U.S. immigration rules are starting to undermine the ability of the United States to access talent from global labor markets, while demographic data suggest that the number of native-born science and engineering students is declining while retirements among the science and engineering workforce are projected to increase. According to 1999 data, one-third of all science and technology Ph.D.s, half of all computer scientists, and over half of all engineers were born abroad (National Science Board 2003). John Yochelson, president of Building Engineering and Science Talent, a workforce initiative of the Council on Competitiveness, expresses the problem well:

> Higher Education is being asked to meet three converging requirements: the replacement need to fill the shoes of the current science and engineering workforce (half of which is at least 40 years old); the structural need for scientists and engineers in promising technology sectors; and the competitive need to keep pace with an international surge in production of science and engineering talent. . . . Despite efforts to diversify the scientific talent pool, the profession remains 3/4 male and 4/5 white. (cited in Building Engineering and Science Talent 2004: 1)

Clearly, a short-term focus marked by competitive poaching of skilled workers is not in anyone's best interest. The real challenge to communities is not just to attract and retain skilled workers but to find ways of increasing the number of students graduating from college generally (two- and four-year colleges), and those specializing in science, technology, math, and engineering fields specifically. This is not to say arts, humanities, and social sciences are not vital, creative forces. They are. The need is for a broad range of talents, including the science and technology pool, which faces increased demand but dwindling supply, hence, the need for some strategic attention. Additionally, building up the skilled-labor pool also requires that regions better access the voice of talent and potential talent as well as understand how to create an environment that fosters talent expansion.

To broach these issues, the chapter is divided into two sections. The first part of the chapter reviews what the research tells us about talent location patterns, in order to help formulate talent expansion strategies. The second half of the chapter then looks at talent expansion from a broader perspective, using Cleveland as a laboratory for exploring the range of issues that are involved in workforce retention.

Talent Development: Jobs Versus Place

One of the core divisions in the economic development debate over talent involves the issue of what really entices talent to a particular region: jobs or the quality of a place, especially its cultural, recreational, environmental, and social opportunities. The debate has been fueled by recent work by Richard Florida (2002), who argues that the creative class (e.g., scientists, artists, engineers, designers), which now comprises about one-third of all jobs, is the core economic force of the twenty-first century. To thrive in the knowledge age, cities need to provide places that attract and stimulate creative people because high-skilled people generate more new ideas. The heart of Florida's argument is that creativity, which comes from skilled people, drives growth. So for a community to stimulate economic growth, it needs more talented people. Although Florida's book has excited as much criticism as support, there is very little disagreement about the concept that skilled people matter for economic dynamism. The controversy centers on the methods to increase the regional talent pool.

How can a region increase its share of talented people? Do talented people follow jobs or do jobs follow talented people? Talented people, according to Florida, are drawn to dynamic downtowns, diverse recreational and cultural amenities, and high levels of tolerance for alternative lifestyle choices. Yet, Florida's finding could be considered correlational rather than causal. It is unclear whether talent flocks to these areas because of the amenities, or jobs bring talent that then shape the lifestyle options. Because of the increasing importance of this question, a number of studies have been initiated to understand the location decisions of skilled people.

Even before Florida's book, the Southern Technology Council (STC) undertook two comprehensive analyses of state-based migration patterns of skilled workers, especially scientists and engineering graduates (Tournatzky et al. 1998, 2001). The 1998 study found that the students who were most likely to stay in a state went to high school and college locally in states with large populations with relatively high wages. In other words, stayers stay, although large labor markets and sufficient remuneration also matter. The study also found that states with the highest net migration were marked by lower in-state public tuition. The authors concluded that providing a good education for locals and nonlocals was a reasonable strategy for retaining human capital.

Finally, and perhaps most important, the 1998 analysis concluded that retention of talented students and the migration of skilled workers were not the same phenomenon. Those states that retained their high school graduates after they graduated from a local college were not particularly good at attracting migrants to their states. In fact, the 1998 study found that states good at retaining students postgraduation were less likely to have positive net migration. The authors deduced from this that building a high-wage technology-oriented economy is still one of the best ways to attract skilled workers. This conclusion suggests that for talent attraction (as opposed to retention), jobs matter significantly.

This finding is confirmed by Paul Gottlieb's 2001 study of migration patterns of science and engineering graduates. Gottlieb argues that these patterns can be understood only within the context of regional labor markets. For example, sizable out-migration from a region may be caused by an excess supply of graduates, and thus not represent a lack of skilled labor for local jobs at all. Massachusetts exemplifies this pattern. Ohio, on the other hand, had a high supply of science and engineering graduates but lost many of them and were unable to attract new talent, predominantly due to a lack of demand for technology workers.

In the follow-up 2001 STC report, Tournatzky and colleagues found that graduates were more likely to stay if they were foreign, did not major in engineering or the physical sciences, were nontraditional students (older), attended a large college in a metropolitan area, and were in a large state. Graduates were less likely to stay if they had a degree in engineering or physical sciences, made a high grade-point average, attended a research-intensive or historically black institution, or received an above-average starting salary.

When comparing all graduate students, the study found that there was a 76 percent chance of retaining students receiving both high school and college degrees in-state, a 43 percent chance of retaining those who came from outside the state and received their degree in-state, and a 23 percent chance of retaining students who went to high school locally but college elsewhere.

Besides these larger studies of national migration patterns, a number of states and regions have surveyed their students and young professionals to determine how they make their location decisions. The State of Michigan polled more than 4,000 young people between the ages of eighteen and thirty-five to determine their lifestyle preferences. The survey revealed that young people believe that quality of life is more important than job opportunities and they prefer to live in or near a downtown area. While this survey seems to provide support for Florida's argument, the fact that 62 percent of respondents were undergraduates and 76.4 percent were undergraduate and graduate students generates an important question: Have the individuals surveyed actually faced the decision of job versus place or is this how they think they will decide? In fact, more than 70 percent of survey respondents believe they can get a job almost any place they choose to live (MEDC 2004). However, the truth behind this belief needs to be tested. We still need to know whether perceptions change once young talent is out in the field.

Regions have also undertaken similar studies, often as means to inform policy development and increase their understanding of how these issues play out in their neck of the woods. The Akron-Canton region in Ohio surveyed regional college alumni who had left Ohio and found that the majority (57.9 percent) had left for a better quality of life (Kent State University 2003). However, 47.9 percent of respondents left for jobs and 43.4 percent relocated because they were specifically recruited to a job. While quality-of-life concerns did rise to the top of the Akron-Canton survey, job and economic conditions also ranked highly. In another survey question, when the alumni were asked to cite three factors that most influenced their location decisions, work ranked number one by a substantial margin (75 percent). Community and entertainment/recreation came in second and third, being selected by 43 percent and 39 percent of respondents, respectively. In fact, the study directors concluded that: "the characteristics that respondents more frequently note that should be better enhanced to better retain Ohio graduates relate to job availability and career opportunities" (Kent State University 2003: 21).

A similar study conducted in the region of Pittsburgh, Pennsylvania, found that low salaries and lack of advancement opportunities were the main reasons graduates left the region. The salary differentials were deemed excessive for women and minorities, who were more likely to leave the region (Hansen, Ban, and Huggins 2003). Similar to the STC findings, the study also found that the best predictor of whether or not an individual would stay in the region was having attended a Pittsburgh-area high school.

In Pittsburgh, however, they were particularly interested in learning how to retain an increasing share of the science, technology, and engineering students who are attracted to the top-tier research universities in the Pittsburgh region. The study notes that only 20 percent of out-of-state science and engineering students remain in Pennsylvania after graduation. The average national retention rate is 43 percent. Although the study does not show us how to better retain this cohort, the researchers conclude that just increasing the attraction of out-of-state students to area colleges as an isolated strategy is not a way to harness new talent (Hansen, Ban, and Huggins 2003).

Comparing across studies, some interesting insights emerge. First, stayers stay, which suggests a need for programs that increase the number of local people who complete college, and make connections for students into the local economy; develop the research and commercialization capacities of the university to attract top-notch faculty and students; make college affordable for in-state and out-of-state students; and increase the local students' interest in science and technology. College access, therefore, is a critical part of talent expansion strategies, even though alone it is not sufficient.

Second, the results of the studies show that, while highly educated individuals are the most mobile, mobility changes in different stages of life. The Pittsburgh study revealed some interesting results when comparing students graduating with B.A. degrees and those with advanced degrees. Common wisdom and theory suggest that the more degrees a person has, the more likely he or she is to relocate away from the degree-awarding institution. However, the Pittsburgh study found, similar to the implications of the Gottlieb (2004) study, that on the ground, supply-and-demand conditions influence mobility. In Pittsburgh, where Ph.D. and B.S. awardees were indeed more likely to leave, their survey revealed that those with M.A., LL.D., Ed.D, and M.B.A. degrees were more likely to stay than was expected. Local demand for these professions is high, and in fact many survey respondents noted that they received tuition support for their schooling. Similarly, the Michigan study indicated that people's desire to locate closer to family increased as they got older. This suggests that an attractive place should cater to a range of lifestyle options, which supports the argument that the region is the central focus for talent expansion strategies.

Third, all of these studies taken together suggest that there is a strong relationship between generating human capital and dynamic industries: it is not a chicken-or-egg relationship but rather a function of both. Economic development in the twenty-first century means creating places that develop human capital and economic opportunities that can harness that talent. It seems that jobs, wages, and place matter.

If place alone is not sufficient, neither are jobs alone. As the experience of states in trying to recruit health-care professionals into underserved areas reveals, good jobs may be insufficient lures even when attached to some fairly lucrative incentives. In its survey of ten state practices, the National Center for Health Workforce Information and Analysis (2001) found that all of the surveyed states offered financial support, such as bonuses, grants, tax credits, and higher reimbursement levels for education and training, tied to the requirement that grant recipients practice within a specific location for a defined number of years. Overall, these programs have not had much impact on reducing the shortage of health-care professionals practicing in underserved areas. Part of the ineffectiveness can be attributed to the overall market (these areas just cannot compete with more attractive communities or the ability of private health networks to attract health-care professionals into their system). Part, however, has been due to poor management and organization of the programs, such as inadequate monitoring of service-contingent scholarships, inappropriate selection criteria for scholarships and loans, and lack of attention to retention rates of those who are required to practice in those locations. While the study found that many states have worked to improve these programs, with some success, the problem remains that most programs are small (they support only a few participants) and thus cannot have a significant impact over the longer term.

Fourth, affinity or strong social networks among families, friends, professionals, or communities can be a powerful force for recruiting and retaining talent. The Pittsburgh study finds that closeness to family and friends is an important reason for those who stayed. Similarly, the Michigan survey suggests that being close to family is an influential factor in location decisions, and that importance seems to increase with age. The Canton-Akron study finds that most alumni (72.7 percent) believe it unlikely that they will return to Ohio. Of those who are willing to relocate, the highest ranked reason is to be closer to family (38.7 percent). The studies suggest that building networks locally and farther afield might be part of a good human capital development strategy.

Philadelphia, for example, has launched the Knowledge Industry Partnership (KIP), a partnership among business, education, and government, to expand the pool of local talent and create more and better jobs (Goldberg 2004). KIP's One Big Campus initiative is aimed at making Philadelphia a premier college destination, to "create positive firsthand experiences throughout the student life cycle (prospect>student>graduate), which in turn lead to a stronger emotional attachment with the area and ultimately a personal desire to remain after graduation" (Knowledge Industry Partnership 2005). KIP's focus on embedding students emotionally into the region reflects this fourth insight revealed by our review of the research, the role of social networks in the attraction, retention, and development of talent.

It will be useful at this point to take a closer look at the relationship between social networks and job relocation patterns of skilled workers. Granovetter's (1995) well-known study on how professional, technical, and managerial workers secure information on job availability provides some insights on labor mobility. He notes that "[t]he actual transmission of information about job opportunities becomes a more immediate condition of mobility than any characteristic of jobs themselves" (Granovetter 1995: 6). Although Granovetter is referring simply to a job shift, irrespective of locational change, he brings to light an important consideration for local recruiting: social contacts that can be accessed through intermediaries and networks. Overall, Granovetter found that professional jobseekers or job changers (people may often be tagged for a job even though they were not actively seeking one) prefer to use personal contacts rather than any other means for mobility because they feel it offers higher-quality information, such as the character of the office culture, the boss, and officemates. Granovetter found that better jobs tend to be found through contacts, and probably due to this, those who find jobs in this manner are more likely to stay.

Granovetter's work notes differences in mobility opportunities according to age bracket. Younger professional workers, who have fewer developed contacts, are more likely to search through formalized means. Professional entry-level jobs, therefore, are more often filled formally, rather than informally through social contacts. When they do use contacts, they are more apt to use friends and family, while older workers have a wider range of professional contacts. Granovetter concludes:

> mobility appears to be self-generating; the more different social and work settings one moves through, the larger the reservoir of personal contacts he has who may mediate further mobility. It is because ties from past jobs and from before work are about as likely to be used as more recent ones that we have a cumulative effect, as if individuals "stockpile" their contacts. (1995: 85)

This capacity to stockpile jobs over a long time period across geography and a range of industries provides insights into the problems experienced by regions that rely on traditional industries when these industries start to decline. Individuals with stable jobs in the same firm will have fewer contacts, smaller networks, and a harder time finding work when they lose their jobs. Thus, areas with higher mobility, networks, and networking venues create the infrastructure for labor-market mobility. Granovetter has suggested that mobility of workers among organizations is often a product of routinized relationships that they maintain for a host of business purposes (e.g., sales, subcontracts, industry-wide committees and activities). Talented people belong to strong networks that foster new ideas and support mobility. Silicon Valley, for example, is comprised of dense professional networks that are believed to be a critical part of its economic success (Saxenian 1996).

In sum, the mobility of talented workers is not just about place and jobs, but about the social and economic networks they create, which structure opportunities available to them. My discussions with experts and community members nationwide suggest that individuals choose locations where they are comfortable losing a job; where job networks for their particular field are thick and interconnected, so in the event that a job is lost, they are in an area where it is easier to sell their particular collection of skills and experience. In other words, individuals are attracted to places where there are thick social networks that support their occupational and lifestyle needs.

Just as networks support entrepreneurship and business development, they support labor market opportunities, and help attract, retain, and grow a high-skilled workforce. As the above discussion indicates, talent expansion strategies are in fact a detailed and complex phenomenon. The next section looks at how we need to think about talent expansion, and what that means for policy and practice.

The Many Dimensions of Talent Expansion Strategies

Talent expansion is, in effect, a wide-ranging effort to increase the pool of educated individuals within a region. Similar to comprehensive economic development strategies that create, retain, and attract businesses, talent expansion strategies need to focus on creating, retaining, and attracting skilled workers. There are nine components to a comprehensive strategy:

1. retention of local college students, which, according to the research we reviewed, is the low-hanging fruit;
2. retention of high-achieving college students, which are the most mobile in the population;
3. the attraction of college graduates from outside the state;
4. increase in the number of local people who become college students, which includes opening college access for low-income and minority students, increasing affordability for low- and moderate-income students, and dealing with local capacity (colleges and universities' ability to handle increasing enrollments). This issue starts earlier than college, and relates to the preparedness of postsecondary students;
5. efforts that encourage and assist residents who have some college to complete their college degrees. These individuals usually have a high stake in remaining local;
6. implementation of "Bridge Programs" for low-income students and workers to obtain college credit and ultimately degrees (Stark Education Partnership, undated, citation refers to the first six factors);
7. attraction of out-of-state students to local colleges and universities;

95

8. increase in the number of students interested in and obtaining science, engineering, and math degrees; and

9. embedding of young professionals in the community to increase their commitment to the region, generate leadership, and provide a voice to the region to help it remain responsive to emerging new needs, lifestyles, and worldviews.

The challenge for most communities is to address all these issues in a coordinated fashion. Risks involve the presence of small, multiple efforts spawned by various nonprofit organizations, governmental entities, and private businesses that work in isolation from each other and from common goals. Because many facets of talent expansion efforts are relatively new, we do not have much best practice to learn from. This chapter will focus on a single region, Greater Metropolitan Cleveland, to investigate the range of activities going on across the nine dimensions. In fact, many regions could draw a map of retention efforts with similar results. Once we look at the range of activities, we can draw some initial conclusions about the challenges and potential benefits of better understanding and then better coordinating talent expansion strategies. In what follows, we examine a select range of programs in motion. The list does not at all represent a full listing of the activities occurring in the region.

Welcome to the Greater Cleveland Region

Greater Cleveland, like many other regions across the country, has been increasingly concerned about its inability to attract or retain talented young professionals. A 2001 study concluded that, when compared to other cities, the Cleveland-Akron region ranked fairly low in terms of both its demand for and supply of scientists and engineers (Gottlieb 2001). More generally, the state of Ohio is marked by an overall low rate of adults with college degrees. It ranks thirty-ninth in the nation.

Even though the statistics suggest a grave problem, the Cleveland region, which has substantial university assets, retains about 70 percent of its students. However, it loses its science and engineering students from the most prestigious universities. Irrespective of the numbers, the regional population believes that the area is not attractive to young people and must do more to retain them (Livingston 2003a, 2003b).

Notably, the Cleveland institutional landscape is marked by a plethora of activities organized by establishments of different sizes, scopes, and budgets aimed at growing the pool of educated residents. Like the general workforce environment, these activities and organizations tend to be disconnected, highly decentralized, and minimally funded, and many are not heavily publicized. Some programs have emerged as projects of affinity networks, small groups that, on their own, have taken on the mission of opening up opportunities for young people by making local business, nonprofits, and government agencies more accessible and responsive to young people. Together, they are opening up access to internships and mentoring relationships, developing networking opportunities for young professionals, marketing the amenities of the region, and getting involved in addressing quality-of-life issues that many feel handicap Cleveland's attractiveness to young professionals.

Cleveland has long been known for its engaged civic institutions and a strong history of partnerships. One of the features in Cleveland that supports this civic infrastructure is the strong network of professional staff within the civic institutional intermediaries, many of which are foundations. Cleveland institutions have devoted time and resources to build up a staff network that acts as an institutionalized network of informal power. That staff has the unique capability of translating among the government, community, and business sectors and provides the foundation of trust that enables information flows and bolsters partnerships (Adams 1998). While this structure has furnished Cleveland with a strong civic infrastructure, it may also create subtle methods of exclusion for certain grassroots organizations as well as create obstacles for more collective approaches to policy making. Not all organizations can afford professional staff. David Bergholz, former executive director of the Cleveland-based Gund Foundation, notes, " . . . yes, this town is a very top-down place. We set priorities. We make agendas. We line up the troops" (cited in Adams 1998: 12). While partnerships are abundant, they are not necessarily inclusive.

The Cleveland region, while not without its challenges, reminds us all that economic development is, at heart, an endogenous undertaking. Even with its strong top-down orientation, a number of grassroots approaches have bubbled up. And for this reason, the Cleveland region presents us with a rich laboratory for viewing what is happening below the public radar screen, which often tends to focus on large, well-funded flagship projects. The activities occurring on the ground can have a measurable impact on the type of community and quality of life available to residents through building social networks, peer exchanges, and recruiting new leaders. Furthermore, they offer a foundation on which to build a creative friendly community by leveraging and enhancing new leaders, new energy, and new ideas around a common goal: to enhance the local environment to create, attract, and retain a skilled, engaged, and innovative workforce. Even if many of these programs do not classify themselves as brain-gain activities, they are critical infrastructure for creating an environment that can attract and retain potential leaders, young and old. Moreover, they represent access to, and the voice of, young professionals.

In what follows, we look at the nine dimensions of talent expansion, to see what is happening in the Cleveland region component by component. As the reader will note, many of the programs have multiple goals and can be categorized in several ways. They have been placed according to their core activities. Additionally, many programs are young so there is a lack of data available on their effectiveness or sustainability. Communities are learning by doing, so these examples offer food for brainstorming and idea generation.

Dimension 1: Retention of Local College Students

A number of organizations are involved in local talent retention programs. Their main activities include providing internships, marketing the amenities of Cleveland, and providing networking venues to embed young people in Cleveland life. In the nonprofit world, (i)Cleveland is a network of area graduate students and professionals who want to retain students in the region. Their mission is "to ensure a talent-rich region that helps achieve economic growth by providing the best and brightest undergraduates with access and connections to area employers and an appreciation of this region as a great place to live" ((i)Cleveland 2005). Formerly known as the Graduates Council, this organization serves as a clearinghouse for local intern information. It provides online resources, career-oriented workshops, and social/networking events. Originally created by the regional Chamber of Commerce, the Greater Cleveland Growth Association, now known as the Greater Cleveland Partnership, (i)Cleveland now shares space with the Cleveland Scholarship Programs, an organization aimed at helping as many people as possible to enter and graduate from college (see below).

The (i)Cleveland network emerged as a response to local research revealing that students were not aware of available social and economic opportunities in the region. The program's goal, therefore, was to make the connections between businesses and students. One of their strategies is to embed students in professional networks. As Bridget Manke, manager of the program, notes, "In Cleveland, you can get in deeper and faster," which suggests that Cleveland in fact offers young professionals career advancement advantages, which is often unrecognized by young people who tend to rely on more formalized job-search strategies.

The program is competitive for students, and has experienced steady growth from 60 students at the program's inception four years ago to 436 participants in 2004. The challenges it faces are its small budget, which runs about $275,000, and limited internship options. The (i)Cleveland network does not place students directly into internships, but rather creates the connections between students and businesses. Of the 436 participants, only 46 had internship placements. In fact, the organization's next steps involve trying to help businesses develop internship programs. According to Manke, only about 30 percent of local employers have such programs.

Another initiative created in the nonprofit sector is the Cleveland Foundation internship program. The Cleveland Foundation, the region's largest foundation, supports internships for young professionals interested in nonprofit or government work while simultaneously providing human capital resources to support local organizations. While this is not a talent expansion program per se, and is benchmarked by intern satisfaction with the program (as opposed to their perceptions of Cleveland), it is still part of the network of activities supporting young professionals and embedding them in Cleveland networks, especially nonprofit networks. As program officer Pam George notes, "the program has never focused specifically on brain gain as a main goal, but it is a preexisting vehicle for addressing the issue." The internships are complemented by seminars highlighting host organizations, which allows interns to network among themselves and a range of nonprofit and government agencies while learning about what the city has to offer. It is one of the more highly resourced programs of this type, which allows it to recruit high-level internships because they pay the intern a stipend. Moreover, it is highly competitive, so it tends to attract high-quality students.

While both of these programs arguably could have been placed in dimension 2, I have chosen to focus the discussion of dimension 2 activities on those targeting science and engineering students because they are the most mobile as well as most difficult to develop, attract, and retain.

Dimension 2: Retention of High-Achieving College Students

Regional universities and private sector entities have become involved in efforts to retain science, engineering, and math students. Clevelandintern.net is a program developed by the Northcoast Consortium for Career Advancement (NCCA), an organization of college-based career services offices working together to retain graduates in Northeastern Ohio. It is now managed by the Northeast Ohio Council on Higher Education (NOCHE), which represents and serves twenty-four colleges and universities in thirteen counties of northeast Ohio and is dedicated to building up the region's higher education resources. Predominantly a Web-based tool for matching students with employers, the program also administers a state program, known as the Ohio third frontier internships, which focuses specifically on providing internships to science, math, and engineering students, to increase

99

the state's retention rate of this particular cohort. According to Paul Klein, director of Career Services at Cleveland State University, the third frontier internship program emerged from a partnership of NCCA, (i)Cleveland, and the Greater Cleveland Growth Association, now the Greater Cleveland Partnership. The program targets several industry sectors, including advanced manufacturing, advanced materials, power and propulsion, instruments, controls and electronics, bioscience, and information technology as well as businesses in other industries but these require an intern to operate in one of these targeted sectors.

There is also private sector activity in this area. Techstudents.net is a Web-based initiative that connects technology students and local businesses on a project-by-project basis. The initiative's goal is to retain technology students by creating student-business linkages and to encourage entrepreneurship locally. The project-by-project structure allows the student to gain work experience through entrepreneurial experience, which includes building up a network of contacts by working for multiple employers, negotiating contracts with employers for specific projects, and setting fees for service (work is set on an hourly basis). Employers gain affordable technology resources. It is of particular benefit to small employers who cannot afford employees, interns, or co-op students, but require technology skills on a short-term basis. The Website charges students a minimal fee to post their qualifications on the Internet and to search for pay-by-the hour projects. The fee was adopted as a filter to block the participation of students who are not professional and serious about the work.

Dimension 3: Attraction of College Graduates from Outside the State

As well as looking to retain the best and brightest at local schools, regional groups have also initiated activities to recruit young professionals who have studied outside the state to consider the Cleveland region as a potential place to relocate. Bulldogs on the Cuyahoga is an organization comprised of young Yale University alumni that aims to attract the college's alumni into the region. It is an example of the contribution made by young people who act in an entrepreneurial fashion to invest in their hometown. According to organization staff, the region sends ten to twenty students to Yale annually and about 60 percent return. The organization's goal is to attract 120 percent to the area. The group recruits local businesses, nonprofits, and government agencies to provide meaningful internships for ten weeks during the summer; raises about $2,000 per student to cover housing, travel, and extracurricular activities; provides alumni mentors; and organizes more than thirty events throughout Cleveland to introduce them to the area's range of amenities. Interns earn at least $2,800 during their time in Cleveland.

This program started in 2003 but has already received media attention (Townsend 2004) and spawned increased demand from businesses for interns and from other university alumni groups wishing to participate. In 2004, the second summer, Bulldogs formally partnered with three other alumni groups from Princeton, Colgate, and Case Universities under the collective name of Summer on the Cuyahoga. Case is a local school but decided to participate in order to give students experience living as real Cleveland residents. Fifty-six students, selected from an applicant pool of over 300, were housed in Case's dormitories, where they could network with each other. In the first two years of the program, 89 internships were procured, of which 75 percent went to interns not originally from the region. Interest in the program continues to increase, as other colleges have also expressed an interest in participating. Smith College is the latest partner school.

Bulldogs on the Cuyahoga modeled itself on the Louisville-based Bulldogs in the Bluegrass. The founder of Bulldogs in the Bluegrass and the Cleveland Foundation Intern program helped jumpstart the organization. The program is too new to evaluate it fully. Current benchmarks are based on the interns' perceptions of Cleveland pre- and postinternship. In all areas (professional, volunteer, entertainment, lifestyle, and involvement opportunities), interns noted a 50 percent or greater increase in their perceptions of Cleveland opportunities.

For Bulldogs in the Bluegrass, which has been active for six years, the number of those who return has thus far been small. Of 200 students who participated in the program, only 15 moved to, and continue to live in, the Louisville region. However, both groups feel that this is a long-term endeavor, and not necessarily about short-term gains (Townsend 2004). Ilona Emmerth, vice president of Bulldogs on the Cuyahoga, feels that whether or not students decide to relocate to Cleveland, the program will make them good ambassadors for the city, who help to create a positive image of the city and its opportunities. The program is as much about changing the image of the city within the networks of the best and brightest as it is about specifically attracting them to live in the area. It is based on the assumption that affinity networks have national reach, and can be very important in recrafting the image of a city not viewed well in this particular segment of the population.

The Cleveland Chapter of the National Association of Black MBAs also works to recruit new talent to Cleveland. Being part of a large national organization of about 11,000 members, the Cleveland chapter has partnered with local businesses, including Key Bank, National City Bank, Progressive Corporation, and others, to recruit new talent to Cleveland during the national organization's annual conference. Working with their corporate partners, the local chapter undertakes other initiatives of this ilk, such as the development of a welcome to Cleveland book aimed specifically at the African-American population.

While these efforts are small, they represent an important resource on which to build. Because they focus on network building, they create affinity and professional density. They socialize information and provide ways to spread that information across new geographies. They offer an overlooked and untapped, but critical, resource. While these programs have heart, they lack scale. They alone cannot change the ecosystem for talent creation, retention, and attraction, but they are critical components of it. And they are growing, as indicated by the creation of Summer on the Cuyahoga from the initial efforts of Bulldogs on the Cuyahoga.

Dimension 4: Increase in the Number of Local People Who Become College Students

The state of Ohio has been engaged in trying to increase access to college for many Ohio residents. In 1999, KnowledgeWorks Foundation in Cincinnati, the Ohio Board of Regents, and the Ohio Department of Education, supported by the Ohio Business Roundtable, founded the Ohio College Access Network (OCAN). OCAN is the first coordinating body of its kind in the nation. As of this writing, 36 college access programs serve approximately 225 of Ohio's 612 school districts, and 17 private/parochial schools in 46 counties. As a result of the program, Ohio has almost doubled the number of college access programs since 2002 (OCAN 2005).

In northeast Ohio, Cleveland Scholarship Programs (CSP) is an OCAN member. CSP, established in 1967, is the oldest college access program in the country and has been rated as one of the best charities in the nation (Charity Navigator 2004). CSP has an operating budget of $6,815,489, of which 39 percent covers student scholarship grants, 25 percent goes toward early college awareness programs, 22 percent pays for counseling and scholarship services, and an additional 6 percent covers services to college students. In 2003, CSP allocated approximately $2.8 million in scholarship aid to 2,017 students, which is roughly $1,388 each. The scholarship funding is "last dollar scholarships" or the final funding a student needs to attend college after accounting for all other financing (CSP 2003). As a result, students are guaranteed to be able to attend college after receiving this particular award.

Furthermore, CSP uses its scholarships to leverage additional financing from governments, colleges, and other scholarship programs, resulting in another $12 for every dollar they provide (CSP 2004). For example, CSP has a Cuyahoga Community College Initiative, which provides transfer scholar-ship funding for Cleveland public school students who attend the local com-munity college with CSP assistance and who then want to transfer to a four-year institution to obtain a bachelor's degree. The scholarship is $2,000 and renewable for two years. Many local universities will award a $2,000 match for students meeting their eligibility requirements.

While scholarships are their main activity, CSP also spends a lot of time in outreach to potential college students through their High School Advisory Services and centralized Resource Center for the Community. In addition, CSP administers several federally supported programs intended to open col-lege access, including the Educational Talent Search, which aims at increas-ing the number of disadvantaged youth entering college and Gear Up (Gaining Early Awareness and Readiness for Undergraduate Programs), which targets middle school students. The Gear Up program starts with an entire sixth-grade class in one middle school and works with teachers to integrate college and career planning into the curriculum. Gear Up activities include intensive academic advising, development of a student database to track each student's progress, homework roundtables, mentoring, tutoring, enrichment programs, and resources for parents.

Cleveland Scholarship Programs attributes its success to its ability to reach young people who are missed by other brain-gain organizations. And the numbers confirm its success. On average, 74 percent of college freshmen enter their sophomore year. For CSP-supported freshmen, that number in-creases to 86 percent. For Northeast Ohio, the benefits increase. As noted above, about 72 percent of Ohio college graduates remain in Ohio. For CSP alumni, that number rises to 82 percent (CSP 2003).

The Northeast Ohio Council on Higher Education has also assumed a role in college access efforts. According to Chuck Hickman, NOCHE's executive director, two of its programs under development are aimed toward increas-ing the number of residents who go to college. The first program, Creating Bright Futures, plans to increase the number of youth, particularly from de-mographic cohorts underrepresented at colleges and universities, who aspire to, attend, and earn degrees from higher educational institutions. The pro-gram, developed in partnership with the Cleveland Browns Foundation, in-cludes a televised marketing campaign, personal appearances by Browns players, coaches, and administrative personnel at middle schools in urban areas, and opportunities for precollege students to "shadow" selected busi-ness executives in the Cleveland area. Messages imparted in the campaign center on the economic and personal benefits of obtaining a college degree, appropriate precollege academic preparation, and the admission and finan-cial aid process.

A second program, College Caravan, also aims to increase the number of students attending college, particularly in economically and educationally disadvantaged locations. The Caravan brings admissions counselors to meet with high school juniors and seniors to discuss the admissions and financial aid process, and useful evaluation criteria for individual students to use in focusing on NOCHE institutions relevant to their specific interests and needs.

Dimension 5: Efforts That Encourage and Assist Residents Who Have Some College to Complete Their College Degrees

Degree completion is a subset of college access programs. It is no surprise, then, that CSP is also involved in helping those who have some college to complete their degrees. They have two programs that contribute to this goal (CSP 2005). First, the Adult Learner Program provides counseling/advising and scholarships to adults to help them access postsecondary education. The program supports adults who are reentering college as well as those entering for the first time. The scholarships support entry into both degree and certificate programs.

Second, the Community Outreach Program provides part-time college and financial aid advisers to various community agencies and social services throughout Cleveland. These advisers are available during nontraditional hours to support the needs of potential adult students. Advisers can be found at places such as public libraries and recreation centers. They help potential students to develop an educational plan, explore college and financial options, and apply for college and financial aid.

Dimension 6: Implementation of Bridge Programs for Low-Income Individuals

There is a large overlap between bridge programs and college access programs. However, bridge programs deserve separate attention to emphasize that special notice must be paid to ensure that access for lower-income individuals is opened up.

Several bridge programs available in Northeast Ohio are part of a statewide network. KnowledgeWorks Foundation, in partnership with the Bill and Melinda Gates Foundation, supports the development of small high schools in disadvantaged areas, to provide underrepresented populations with challenging academic programs that link the secondary with postsecondary educational systems. Known as early college, this effort enables students to complete their high school educational experience with either an associate's degree or transferable credit. In Northeast Ohio, Lorain County Community

College and Youngstown State University are engaged in these efforts. The city of Cleveland also has an early college initiative. Cleveland State University (CSU) has worked with Cleveland Municipal schools to offer classes that lead to CSU credits (NOCHE 2004)

The Cleveland Chapter of National Black MBAs just relaunched the Leaders of Tomorrow program, which pairs high school minority students with a member of the chapter who serves as the students' mentor. It targets inner-city youth who have average grades to open up their social networks, to provide encouragement and a role model, to improve their grades, and to plan for careers. The program was developed nationally by the National Black MBA Association and has been in operation for thirteen years, although it was established in Cleveland in the fall of 2003.

In Cleveland's program, the youth and the mentor sign a contract that commits both to interacting on a weekly basis for a minimum of one year. In addition to this big brother/big sister interaction, the student also attends monthly workshops, allowing networking and mutual learning among the students from different schools. Efforts are now being made to better tie the students into the workings of the Black MBA Association, by charging the students with developing a community service for the organization as a whole. While there are no local benchmarks as yet, the national program has seen a 25 percent increase in the math grade point average (GPA) and a 9 percent increase in the English GPA of the mentored students. Kim Holder, the Leaders of Tomorrow Program chairperson for the association, noted that the program has already had an impact by creating long-term relationships with teachers and counselors, and building connections between the business community and local students to demonstrate to businesses the assets local students can provide. According to Holder, students are learning the value of education and developing local networks to support their career and educational aspirations. Although this program does not provide college credits, it does offer resources to lower-income individuals to help in career planning and advancement.

Dimension 7: Attraction of Out-of-State Students to Local Colleges and Universities

The Northeast Ohio Council on Higher Education is in the process of developing College 360, a four-year $5 million program that seeks to: attract prospective students to Ohio schools; engage them in civic life through service learning and community volunteer opportunities, events that showcase premier cultural and recreational venues, an online campus events calendar, and regular student meetings with regional business and civic leaders; and then link them with prospective regional employers via internships. According to Hickman, this program is based upon similar efforts that have been implemented in Philadelphia (discussed earlier) and will draw heavily on active participation from education, business, and civic interests throughout Northeast Ohio.

Dimension 8: Increase in the Number of Students Interested in and Obtaining Science, Engineering, and Math Degrees

All communities need specific programs for both high school and college students to attract them to, and retain them in, math, engineering, and science degree programs. In these fields in particular, the challenge is in the preparation needed for students to follow this path. Success in science and math is dependent on strong academic preparation in high school, especially in math, and on following a full-time, traditional college path (National Science Board 2003). Math, science, and engineering paths do not seem amenable to nontraditional students or students with heavy financial obligations. In fact, the rising cost of education may be a deterrent to increasing this cohort because increasing tuition tends to increase the number of nontraditional students. In fact, only about 27 percent of today's undergraduates fall into the category of traditional student (National Science Board 2003).

A second challenge lies not just in attracting freshmen to the field, but in keeping them there. Over half of those selecting the path as freshmen do not complete a science and engineering degree within five years, and underrepresented minorities drop out at a higher rate (National Science Board 2003).

In Cleveland, the presence of the National Aeronautics and Space Administration (NASA) Glenn Research Center provides unique resources in this area. The center provides a wealth of programs to K–12 to expose youth to science and technology and entice them into the field. An exemplary program is the Science, Engineering, Mathematics and Aerospace Academy, which is a joint venture with Cuyahoga Community College to increase the number of underrepresented and underserved students interested in science, math, engineering, and technology careers (NASA 2005).

While the example cited focuses on secondary education, regions, especially their local universities, will need to find ways to attract, support, and retain science and engineering students in postsecondary institutions as well.

Dimension 9: Embedding Young Professionals in the Community

Finally, the last set of efforts involves attempts to make the region more attractive to young professionals by embedding them in affinity networks and building a cohort of young leaders. Some examples of Cleveland programs are listed below.

- Cleveland Bridge Builders brings young people together to discuss civic issues and expose them to civic leaders to build connections to Cleveland.
- Ethnic networks, such as MotivAsians for Cleveland and the Cleveland Network of Indian Professionals, have emerged to support young professionals and to increase their leadership opportunities in the region.
- Industry networks, such as the Young Lawyers Section of the Cleveland Bar Association and The Web Association, connect young professionals in specific fields.
- Regional marketing efforts such as coolcleveland.com and the Young Professionals Section of Cleveland.com, which is offered by the *Plain Dealer*, the regional newspaper, try to position Cleveland as a cool place for young professionals. According to editor-in-chief of Cleveland.com, Denise Polverine (2004), the purpose of this section of the local news Website is "to shine the spotlight on all the young professionals in town who are involved and who care about this city and the future . . . We need to celebrate all the young, smart people in town who plan to stay and make this city their home." The Young Professionals section provides a comprehensive news source targeted at this cohort. Polverine believes that the launch of the Website has resulted in increased attention to the topic of brain drain and has encouraged organizations to act. She notes: "I think *The Plain Dealer* has really started the discussion and has gotten the community to talk about this issue. I think there are so many ways that young people can get involved in this city. The only way we can change things is to get involved and get other young professionals involved in the community."

Conclusions: Lessons from the Metropolitan Cleveland Laboratory

Cleveland might be considered typical of many U.S. cities. There is a lot going on when you look down the streets and around corners. However, since many of the programs in Cleveland are small and minimally funded, they remain disjointed and unable to achieve any type of scale. There also may be an overemphasis on some areas at the expense of others. For the organizations to reach their full potential individually and for the regions, there needs to be a better sense of what is really going on, how it fits together, and what is missing. One observer recommended the need for more multiorganization

107

events for young people, to cross-fertilize, cross-network, and expand their reach. In other words, to develop a well-networked population of young leaders that continuously expands.

Building local networks of young leaders may also have been subject to the exclusionary nature of Cleveland's existing civic infrastructure. Another observer notes that current programs tend to focus on individuals who were already insiders, those already well connected within the local community. The challenge is to find ways to reach the wider population and open up new venues to move young people into leadership roles. Part of the answer is about better jobs; part is about expanding the talent pool; and part is about the community adapting itself to the range of lifestyle choices that diverse people choose. People-centered places recognize that jobs, talent, and place all matter.

Attracting talent is not about sports stadia, jogging trails, and sufficient nightlife per se, but about engaging students and young professionals in the social, informational, and occupational networks of the region. These amenities may act simply as signals that a city has the networks, opportunities, and lifestyle choices in which individuals can embed themselves. Changing populations, and engaging new populations in meaningful ways, will influence the shape of the city in a way that reflects new lifestyle options. While the Greater Cleveland region has a lot going for it, those initiatives currently are small drops of water in a much larger ocean. They do, however, matter significantly, because they have started to change the conversation about who Cleveland is and where she is going. Talent expansion is first and foremost a social endeavor with substantial economic impacts. It requires social as well as economic approaches to reach talent expansion goals.

This whirlwind tour of Cleveland demonstrates that a kind of chaos marks all attempts to expand the talent pool. There are so many ways to approach talent expansion, at so many levels, and a significant number of small, medium, and large organizations is involved. The real jewel of information from our journey is the recognition that there are indeed grassroots efforts; in fact, talent itself is becoming involved in recruiting talent. This example should in many ways drive home the main theme of this book: people matter most. We can use our talent to help build up our talent because people have an interest in doing so. What we still need to figure out is how to align these grassroots attempts so that they can reach a scale sufficient to provide an extended infrastructure for talent development.

And finally, before concluding this chapter, a word on the role of employers is warranted. Wages, benefits, and good work environments are very much a part of the debate over talent expansion. For example, some textile companies at which I once conducted interviews in the rural South offered low-skilled, entry-level positions, and faced challenging labor shortages in the late 1990s. There just did not seem to be any people available to work (it was not just a skills issue). The problem in these cases was not lack of people per se, but often the inability of these companies to adapt to tighter labor markets and provide better working conditions or benefits. With tight labor markets, individuals have a choice of posts, and will go to the place that offers the best opportunity or can accommodate their needs. Companies in the same rural region that provided good working conditions, benefits, training, and promotion opportunities had developed worker loyalty and did not suffer this fate. Moreover, when a new business came to town, that business had over 1,000 applicants for jobs, suggesting that in demanding labor markets, businesses also need to adjust to the needs of their workforce.

As the Pittsburgh study shows, many talented people leave for better wages. In addition, anecdotal evidence from interviews in Cleveland suggests that recruiting individuals is hard because of local wages, as well as national images of a region that is racially divisive, environmentally insensitive, and overall in decline. While communities, their universities, and their citizens are working to open up college access and to provide attractive and exciting living environments, they also need to encourage businesses to enact sound practices that attract and retain a talented workforce. In the end, talent expansion, like workforce development in general, is not about doing one thing; it is about being a different kind of place in which governments, businesses, community groups, and individuals think about investing in people in new and broader ways.

— 6 —

Bringing the System to Scale: Engaging Employers

A significant weakness in the workforce systems of most regions is the lack of employer participation. Employers contribute substantial resources to an effective workforce system. They articulate skill needs, invest in incumbent training, employ new workers, provide internships and mentors, participate in workforce programs such as career fairs, and serve on boards and committees that plan, run, and advise workforce programs. Equally important, employers' hiring processes and assumptions structure labor market opportunities. Employers build relationships with individuals and institutions that create systems of preferential treatment for hiring and advancement (Rosenbaum 2001; Harrison and Weiss 1998). Employers' disengagement from the past training regime left parts of the workforce system, especially those oriented to serving disadvantaged and low-skilled populations, outside the main labor market. Finally, employers' workplace practices and investments in human capital are essential components of lifelong learning and talent expansion strategies. Employers' engagement in the system, therefore, is a necessary precondition for an effective workforce system and the emergence of a lifelong learning culture.

Successfully involving employers in the workforce system encompasses three separate but interrelated dimensions: (1) recruiting and retaining employers' involvement as partners in workforce programs; (2) convincing employers to regularly hire workforce program graduates, especially those who have traditionally been outside the labor market; and (3) increasing employer investment in training generally.

As many communities are aware, engaging employers can be challenging on all three dimensions. As program partners, businesses are not always willing or reliable participants, even though such relationships can serve their interests. When communities do succeed in recruiting employer participa-

110

tion, the employers often do not stay attached very long to many programs, especially after their immediate needs have been served (Bailey 1995). Employers' reluctance to invest in training and hire public training graduates has been well documented in earlier chapters. Irrespective of the challenges, employer engagement is an essential piece of workforce development. Without such engagement, it will be not be possible for a workforce system to reach a scale significant to impact the quality of the labor force.

To find ways to help communities master these challenges, this chapter will start with a look at both theory and practice to explain why obtaining employers' cooperation is so difficult. The second part of this chapter will examine a number of programs that have succeeded in engaging employers across these dimensions and isolate their success factors.

Challenges to Employer Engagement

Each of the three dimensions creates a different set of hurdles that communities must address. Connecting employers to workforce programs struggles with the well-known collective action problem, whereby agents will not participate if they can reap the advantages without cooperating (Olson 1965). Clearly, workforce programs conform to this logic. Although all employers benefit from a workforce program that improves their access to skilled employees, that access will be improved whether or not they participate in the program. Given these conditions, theory tells us that cooperation is more likely to occur when incentives are available to induce participation and when the targeted group is relatively small and homogeneous and has articulated common interests (Olson 1965). We also know that cooperation is more likely under conditions in which repeated instances of cooperation will be required at unknown times in the future. Under repeat conditions, cooperative, as opposed to competitive, approaches have proved to be more effective remedies to the existing challenges (Axelrod 1984).

Applying these ideas to the workforce system, employers respond to three general types of incentives (Bailey 1995a). First, some businesses participate for philanthropic reasons in order to support their local communities. While philanthropic motives can get a business to the table, practitioners and researchers generally agree that this is inadequate to sustaining long-term commitments. Second, businesses may participate because they derive some individual benefits, such as good public relations, financial incentives, and access to labor. Finally, businesses may get involved to achieve a collective industrial benefit, such as the overall strengthening of the workforce.

These incentives, however, are quite weak due in part to the competitive nature of the labor market. The literature reveals that government services offered in competitive market environments tend to perform poorly because service recipients can buy those services elsewhere and thus do not need to interact with government providers. Without knowledge of the needs of core consumers in service provision, government agencies that function in competitive environments struggle to maintain quality services (Hirschman 1970).

Workforce programs compete with private sector providers. Since employers have access to employees from other venues, they have no reason to get involved with workforce programs either as partners or as consumers. As a result, this employer-involvement gap results in poorly performing workforce programs unattached to market demand. Therefore, the problems of engaging employers in the workforce system as both program partners and consumers of training services need to be resolved simultaneously. To accomplish this, communities must increase business voice in programs and improve the quality and relevance of training to deliver the skills employers want to buy.

The Workforce Investment Act (WIA) has applied these principles as the foundation of its reform of the workforce system. To this effect, its core strategies focus on strengthening business voice and improving training services. Early evidence suggests that generally the WIA has not been effective, although there are individual Workforce Investment Boards (WIBs) and one-stops that can point to improvements. In what follows, we will examine in some detail what we know about the WIA's efforts to engage businesses, in order to understand why theory and practice seem to be at odds. We will see that the ideas still seem sound, but the details of implementation have been insufficient.

To enhance the voice of employers, the WIA's main thrust has been to require that businesses represent a majority on the local WIBs and that a business representative chair the board. A study of employer use of WIA services, by Kazis, Prince, and Rubin (2003), has shown that although businesses judge the plan to increase business voice through board involvement favorably, they also feel that the nature of such participation has been limited.

The employers surveyed note that even with a role on the WIB, their actual influence on the agencies and service providers that make daily decisions about services has not been augmented measurably. Those employers observe that business board members have less of a stake than other board members who are fighting to maintain turf in a rapidly changing system, which serves to lessen the impact of their voice on decision making.

Moreover, WIB members may be direct service users, but they do not have to be. They often include business representative organizations and business service providers, such as law and accounting firms and others who may not directly hire individuals from the public training system. This lessens the ability of businesses to provide feedback on the actual services. Boards include a handful of firms and business representatives that may represent only a fraction of local employers. When business groups such as chambers and industry associations are used as private sector board members or intermediaries, they may not be able to articulate the range of workforce needs of a region's employer base (Berry 2004). Emerging new sectors can also be overlooked if they are not yet organized or recognized.

To meet the second challenge, delivery of a variety of quality skills, the WIA has attempted to widen the applicant pool to offer businesses a range of individuals with different skill levels in the implementation of universal services. The WIA also provides training to increase the skill levels of certain individuals, and has implemented performance measures to monitor those services.

Again, the evidence to date suggests that the WIA remains far from its goals. Although a wider population of jobseekers is using the one-stops, overall that pool still remains narrowly centered on no- to low-skilled employees (Buck 2002). Placement is the one-stop service most used by businesses and serves as a bellwether for business engagement. The employers surveyed indicate that insufficient screening of job applicants has led to poor-quality referrals (Kazis, Prince, and Rubin 2003). An earlier study of business involvement in welfare-to-work echoes some of these conclusions. Researchers found that employers were similarly challenged by the inability of the workforce system to customize activities to meet employer demand, the poor quality of job referrals, insufficient screening mechanisms, and the inflexibility of public agencies (Mills and Kazis 1999).

In addition, evidence shows that employers are not supportive of the "work-first" approach underpinning both welfare reform and the WIA. The work-first orientation has made it harder to access training dollars, reducing the number of individuals demanding and receiving training (Buck 2002). The businesses surveyed about the WIA stressed their need for potential employees to be better trained to ensure a certain standard of skill. Employers noted that the one-stops provide insufficient access to training resources that would increase the value of the applicants to business clients (Kazis, Prince, and Rubin 2003). Similarly, employers interviewed about the welfare-to-work reforms revealed that the focus on work first was not always in their best interest and wanted policies that better married the need for placement with the need for skills training, including preemployment skills, and skill advancement strategies for incumbent workers (Mills and Kazis 1999).

Finally, the employers noted that the performance measures selected did not reflect their interests. Rather, they were representative of federal objectives instead of business need (Kazis, Prince, and Rubin 2003).

Our review of the WIA suggests that just putting businesses on the board is insufficient for developing business voice and improving training quality. It is also clear from the discussion above that businesses do want their voices heard. Therefore, the WIA's objectives were on target, but the strategies to achieve them were inadequate. Sufficient mechanisms for engaging employer voice at the level of service delivery are not in place. Our review of employers' input and the WIA experience suggests several strategies that would be more effective. The surveyed employers felt that the absence of a personal relationship, such as an account representative, was a significant weakness of the WIA (Kazis, Prince, and Rubin 2003). As has been noted in earlier chapters, trust is an essential foundation of a functioning system. *"Not only must they [employers] receive information, they must receive it in a context of social infrastructure that reassures them of its trustworthiness and relevance"* (Rosenbaum 2001: 150; emphasis in original). Engaging businesses means establishing trust, and that means using methods for transferring information that are based on personalized relations.

Another lesson emerges from the generalized nature of business voice on the board. Theory suggests that it is more effective to engage smaller, more homogeneous groups that have common interests. Employers are a large, disparate group with diverse, and at times, competing interests. Experience suggests that a better strategy might be to segment the market and develop business voice pertinent to each particular segment (Berry 2004).

We have established the challenges of employer engagement in workforce programs and started the discussion of strategies to overcome those challenges. We still need to elaborate the difficulties of convincing employers to increase their overall investment in training. Turning now to the story of a western region's experience with business training consortia will illustrate those challenges in detail. A local two-year technical school, which was part of a state network, had multiple campuses located throughout the region. The college's regional headquarters hired an aggressive, entrepreneurial manager to coordinate their workforce efforts across the region, using the campuses as a natural network to access local employers in the various subregions. The college put together a business consortium to bid for the customized training funds available from the state. The college took responsibility for putting the grant proposals together, and then would be responsible for managing the distribution of the training funds once awarded.

The consortium received the grant but then the member employers did not use the funds and did not train their employees. The college found itself having to go out and convince the businesses to use the free training, with little success. The consortium comprised assorted local small employers whose only common tie was their mutual participation in that consortium. The small businesses struggled at the financial margins and were unwilling or unable to find the time to take their employees out of the workplace to receive training. Moreover, because the firms came from different sectors and had no recognized or articulated set of common training needs, it was difficult to identify training courses that could strategically benefit them.

This tale reminds us that small businesses in highly competitive markets, which are most in need of subsidized training resources, have the most difficulty taking advantage of them. Those small businesses also have little understanding of how to use training as a vehicle for strategic modernization (Creticos and Sheets 1990).

We have seen that engaging businesses on all three levels is fraught with difficulties and failure. But the picture is not only gloom and doom. Let us return to our western region and see what they did next.

The college decided to try again, but the consortium they put together this time was distinctly different in important ways. The second consortium included the major employers from a single economic sector, the health-care industry, which was an important part of the regional economy. The regional health-care sector, similar to regions across the nation, regularly struggles to attract and retain professional and paraprofessional health-care workers. The repeated nature of the workforce challenges and the small number of employers with homogeneous workforce needs were already involved in multiple activities to strengthen the sector. The regional education and training organizations were also heavily engaged in addressing these issues. All the regional two-year and four-year schools offered a series of education tracks leading to varied health-care careers. Partnerships and joint efforts among the local universities in this particular area are quite strong. The preexisting partnerships, the common set of training needs among the business participants, the chronic nature of workforce challenges, and the ability of local training agents to serve those needs allowed the college to be an effective intermediary for engaging businesses and delivering services in this instance.

Strategies to Engage Employers

The experiences of the WIA and the western region have begun our discussion of what works and what does not work. This section aggregates the experiences of the following six programs to identify common effective strategies for engaging employers.

- *Wisconsin Regional Training Partnership* (WRTP) is a union-employer partnership created in 1992 to stabilize the struggling manufacturing sector. It developed a threefold, sequential strategy: modernize manufacturing practices to better compete in the global market; train workers to improve productivity, especially in light of modernization; and recruit and train entry-level workers, especially those from disadvantaged populations. Their services are intensive and demanding, starting with redesigning the labor management relationships before service delivery actually begins. It has expanded since its inception and now works with firms in the hospitality, construction, health-care, finance, and technology fields.

- *Bread and Butter Café* is a community-based training program targeted at serving the Savannah homeless population. It trains these individuals for work in area restaurants in an actual restaurant setting open to the public.

- *The Gulf Coast Workforce Development Board* and its service network, *The WorkSource* serves the thirteen-county Houston-Galveston Gulf Coast region in Southeast Texas.

- *The William F. Goodling Regional Advanced Skills Center* (ASC) in York, Pennsylvania, has emerged in direct response to business demand for an institution that provides technical skills training to area residents to meet the needs of the region's industrial clusters. As it evolved, ASC has also become WIA-recognized, increasing its access to potential students.

- *Eastern Idaho Forum for Information Technology* (EIFIT) is a business association representing technology companies in the Idaho Falls region of Idaho. The regional economic development entity launched the organization in order to develop a business voice to help guide economic development strategy. Once created, EIFIT then used its organizational power to work with the local community college to meet its training needs.

- *Empower Baltimore Management Corporation* (EBMC) manages the Baltimore Empowerment Zone. EBMC manages thirteen programs related to workforce development. This case focuses on one specific program: customized training, which provides training to Empowerment Zone residents customized to meet employers' workforce needs. EBMC assumes full responsibility, including recruitment and screening of individuals and the costs of training (training is provided by the employer and EBMC reimburses them for the expenses). In exchange, the employer must agree to hire trainees for a minimum of thirty-two hours per week over at least one year for at least $8.00 per hour and with some potential for advancement. Workers receive stipends during training, which lasts about three months.

Comparing across these programs, the following common strategies emerge: (1) targeting sectors and sector leadership; (2) creating business intermediaries when they are not available; (3) building and working through personalized relationships; (4) ensuring quality; and (5) developing and integrating multiple information-gathering methods.

Targeting Clusters and Cluster Leadership

The research for this book involved the use of several methods to identify exemplary case studies, including querying leading workforce- and economic-development-related organizations on best practices, my own years of experience in the field, and a practice-focused literature review. All the programs gathered through these methods had some type of industry-sector focus. The exception was STRIVE, but some STRIVE affiliates were evolving to incorporate sector strategies in their approach. Overall, the most visible trend for mobilizing business participation in workforce efforts is the use of formalized clusters or industry sectors (Council for Urban Economic Development 1998). The terms "cluster" and "sector" are used interchangeably, but they do differ. A cluster is a:

> Geographically bounded concentration of similar, related, or complementary businesses with active channels for business transactions, communications, and dialogue that share specialized infrastructure, labor markets, and services that are faced with common opportunities and threats. (Bosworth 1996, cited in Harrison and Weiss 1998: 6)

Industry sectors, alternatively, may not share infrastructure and specialized institutions at the regional level. The term "sector" also incorporates occupational sectors, and is thus a more convenient and encompassing term for use in this chapter. Whether it is a cluster or sector, the basic strategies remain the same.

A sector focus provides a series of strengths for workforce development. First, sectors allow a workforce program to specialize in and standardize its product for a specific industry. By developing industry-based expertise, workforce programs develop a reputation for excellence, an important component for building trust and delivering quality services.

One concern expressed by critics of sector-based approaches is that they may limit mobility to a single industry. This book argues that improved mobility must be a core objective of a workforce system. Do sector strategies subvert that goal? The answer is no, rather they support mobility within the sector. A study of the relationship between community colleges and cluster

117

strategies found that community colleges provided training for the sector as a whole, but ensured that the content of the classes concentrated on the problems and needs of local industry (Rosenfeld 1998). Specifically, the colleges examined in the study trained students broadly for advanced manufacturing, but the coursework focused on industry-specific problems in textiles, furniture, or metalworking. Thus, individuals entered the specific local industry but their advanced manufacturing process skills were relevant across the range of industries. In addition, many programs targeted sectors that have a high degree of local stability, such as hospitality and health care. Even though there may be variability in the actual employers, as in the hospitality sectors, or the occupational categories, as in health care, the demand for base skills will be regular.

Some targeted sectors, however, do remain volatile. If a region loses the ability to compete in all manufacturing processes, there will be a loss of mobility for some individuals. But it is key to remember that even sector strategies and sector approaches cannot be static. The labor market in the new economy is dynamic, requiring workforce and economic development organizations to be equally dynamic. In all our cases, we see expansion into new industry sectors; in some, we see closure of sector courses that are no longer relevant, and in others, a reorientation of the focus within the sector as opportunities and needs shifted and expanded. How to keep programs dynamic will be discussed later, as it is another feature of effective programs.

Second, sectors identify relevant voices and do not need to rely on a generalized business voice that does not sufficiently represent business needs. By targeting business voice, it resolves WIB problems that involve a disjuncture between the businesses on the board and those who might use its services. Sector approaches target a smaller, homogeneous group of firms with a shared labor pool and common training needs. These firms regularly interact, creating an environment of repeat conditions and common challenges, which increases the power of incentives to encourage cooperation. Sectors provide a natural venue for articulating training needs, and maintaining oversight for the continued relevance of training approaches and providers.

As an example, The WorkSource developed an industry model composed of sector steering committees to feed specific training needs into the public training regime. The industry approach gave them the ability to bring together the eighty-five area hospitals to review workforce practices and strategies and create common goals. They found that they needed to broaden the nature of business engagement for it to be effective.

Third, sectors are partnership based and bring a range of workforce and economic development actors, including employers, unions, local government, and community-based organizations, to a common table. These part-

---

Exhibit 6.1

Summary of High-Road Partnerships

All partnerships provided worker training, and most provided placement and referral services. Looking more specifically:

Training and education	Number of partnerships
Technical and occupational training	13
Job or skill upgrading	12
Entry-level training	11
English as a second language	8
Basic skills education	7

Groups served	
Incumbent workers	13
New workers	11
Youth	9
Displaced workers	8

Funding sources	
State and local incumbent training funds	9
Union-management negotiated funds	8
Private foundations	7
Departments of Labor and Health and Human Services Welfare to Work Funds	6
State manufacturing extension funds	6
Community colleges	6
State Education Departments	3

Source: Herman (2001), pp. 2–4.

---

nerships are well networked in the community, providing sector strategies with depth and reach (Herman 2001).

Fourth, the expertise and partnership components of sectors help employers to pursue high-road as opposed to low-road strategies of competition in globalizing markets. High-road strategies aim to increase business competitiveness by improving jobs, skills, and opportunities, usually through improved processes and products and the application of new technologies. Low-road strategies seek to improve competitiveness by decreasing production costs, predominantly through wage and benefit reductions, downsizing, and outsourcing. Exhibit 6.1 summarizes a study of fourteen high-road sector strategies implemented through business–community–union partnerships. We can see that high-road sector strategies provide scope to workforce efforts, as they are able to supply and integrate multiple services, including basic skills, entry-level training, industrial modernization, and incumbent training, to a range of workers, including new workers,

119

incumbent workers, youth, and displaced workers (Herman 2001). Sector strategies are a natural way to connect the spectrum of services needed in a functioning, dynamic, adaptive workforce system.

Fifth, because they provide scope, sector strategies in the cases examined have effectively reached out to disadvantaged workers, helping low-wage workers obtain and advance in good jobs. Recent research reinforces these conclusions (Elliott et al. 2001; Zandniapour and Conway 2001; Foster-Bey and Rawlings 2002). Because they focus on industry-specific skills, sector strategies lead to improved wages and clearer career paths. The WRTP, for example, raised wages by an average 165 percent, from an average $8,500 to $22,500. As another example, EBMC placed 956 trainees between 1998 and 2002, earning an average $8.81 per hour, which represents an increase of 68 percent or $1,700 per quarter after training.

Sixth, some programs targeted sector leaders as a critical strategy for engaging businesses, and building the reputation and expertise of the program. For example, WRTP initially concentrated on recruiting large firms in a single sector, which allowed them to develop the appropriate expertise, and open up their entry into the sector as a whole from the point of view of both marketing and reputation. The WorkSource, similarly, brought large firms to the table in their sector approach. Large firms offer a significant number of jobs and influence the work practices of their suppliers, thus providing an entry to engage new businesses. Targeting sectors and initially focusing on leading employers bring scale to workforce efforts, allowing programs to reach out to a large number of workers. When recruiting initial businesses, aim high. Focus on visible, respected leaders with deep relationships to the cluster and the community. Their involvement signals the seriousness and relevance of the effort.

Finally, sector workforce strategies can be used to support entrepreneurship efforts. The EBMC's Entrepreneurial Training Program provides one example. This initiative trains residents in entrepreneurial skills, in an effort to encourage local business ownership, and, subsequently, to generate jobs in the Enterprise Zone. To compete in today's knowledge economy means developing all knowledge-based assets. Entrepreneurship is an important part of a human capital strategy. The study of cluster/community colleges highlights a program in Ireland that trains students in the craft and design of furniture making, an advanced manufacturing process (Rosenfeld 1998). The courses include entrepreneurship training because many graduates start their own businesses or work for smaller companies that offer more opportunity for innovation and modernization than do the more traditional large firms. Integrating entrepreneurship into sector-based training and education approaches offers strategies to struggling regions.

In sum, sector strategies present regions with a powerful tool for engaging employers, structuring workforce programs, opening up opportunities for transitional workers, supporting entrepreneurs, and offering a spectrum of integrated services.

Creating Business Intermediaries When They Are Not Available

Some communities may not have organizations that represent the range of business voices and needs. In these cases, appropriate strategies would be aimed toward helping them to get off the ground. WRTP realized that for businesses to recognize the benefits of training, the training had to be integrated into comprehensive modernization efforts. But there were no local organizations available to help businesses think through and implement modernization strategies. So they created one. They became the catalyst for establishing the Wisconsin Manufacturing Extension Partnership.

In eastern Idaho, the regional economic development organization seeded the creation of the Eastern Idaho Forum for Information Technologies (EIFIT) to tap into the voice of a small but emerging industry sector. Although EIFIT was not created to serve workforce needs but to support local business development, it did become involved in these issues. By bringing the group together, some common training needs were identified. EIFIT worked with the local community college to develop courses to meet collective training needs (Pages and Garmise 2001). In the case of new and emerging industries, a catalyst may be required to get them together to develop a voice that could then contribute to training venues. The EIFIT example reminds us that the task of creating intermediaries to mobilize particular voices may fall on public agencies.

Building and Working Through Personalized Relationships

While intermediaries and organizations matter, personalized relationships are also significant components of successful workforce systems, and they are essential for recruiting and retaining business participation. Businesses believe that personalized relationships are part of a good business partnership. Effective workforce programs build personal attention into their program structures.

Building wide-reaching relationships can start with a single contact. For example, EBMC built a customized program around a relationship cultivated by the EBMC president and Johns Hopkins University Hospital. Once established, the program was then replicated in other hospitals around the region. The WorkSource, another example, identified companies with preexisting relations with their staff as one of the core categories of their priority company strategy.

Another common strategy is to create staff positions whose role is to build relationships with business. The WorkSource established a team of business consultants whose job is to market its services to employers. The consultants are tasked with building personalized relationships to better customize employee recruitment and training to employer needs and follow up to maintain business satisfaction. Bread and Butter Café relied on its case managers, whose main task is to support the trainees in retaining their jobs, and who are responsible for maintaining good relationships with employers, recognizing that to meet its core goal of retention the program must meet business goals as well.

Finally, the timing of employer engagement also influences a community's ability to recruit business participation because it has a strong influence on building trust. Businesses are more likely to participate if they are involved in designing the program, and thus trust that it has been organized with their needs in mind. Therefore, they should be recruited early in any major initiative (Poczik 1995).

Ensuring Quality

A 2003 study of business engagement in nonprofit workforce programs found that consistent quality in the preparation of jobseekers delivered through personalized, responsive services was a core strategy for ensuring continued business engagement (Clymer 2003). The cases provide further support to these conclusions.

Bread and Butter Café, for example, screened its participants before entry. The screenings included English and math tests to demonstrate at least a sixth grade competency as well as entry and random drug testing to guarantee that trustees are and remain drug free. Once in the program, trainees received expert training from the local college, soft skills to ensure workforce preparedness, and direct restaurant experience, resulting in highly qualified workers. In fact, the organization started up an entire new program in response to demand from employers for a different type of worker—those trained for institutional kitchens (e.g., schools, cafeterias)—as well as restaurant-oriented cooking. The Community Kitchen Program emerged and targeted former welfare recipients who find the daytime hours, more secure wage structure, and higher benefits more appealing than restaurant work with its fluctuating hours and minimal benefits. In this case, the program's ability to meet employer demands enabled the organization to tap into another hard-to-serve population.

In addition, WRTP learned through its experience how important it is to ensure training quality. While WRTP delivers basic training internally, specialized training is provided through commercial vendors. Problems with training quality in the beginning compelled WRTP to implement design adaptations. It does not have regularized contracts with vendors; rather, WRTP keeps the vendors competing for business to ensure that businesses receive quality services.

To cite another well-known example, Focus Hope in Detroit, which prepares low-income black youth for good jobs in the auto industry, prescreens its participants by requiring them to have a high school diploma or GED and to be drug free. Focus Hope then requires its participants to have an excellent attendance record and focuses on work habits and skill development, thereby certifying the quality of its graduates (Rosenbaum 2001).

Developing and Integrating Multiple Information-Gathering Methods

In workforce development, businesses' lack of engagement in workforce programs may not necessarily indicate poor service delivery as much as it suggests poorly targeted service delivery. The difference is fundamental. Programs maintain the relevancy of their skills through business engagement complemented by regular mining of the labor market (Clymer 2003). Workforce agencies, therefore, need to continuously assess the labor market by gathering and integrating information from multiple sources to ensure that training is relevant to the market.

The case of ASC is instructive in this regard. Even though this program was requested by businesses and developed in partnership with businesses, keeping training relevant requires diligence and hard work. Chuck Thomas, ASC executive director, notes that it can be difficult to keep up with business trends and overall economic changes in the region. Businesses open and close all the time. In response to evolving needs, they have to develop modules for new economic sectors, while old modules go unused. The lesson here is a simple but important one: to maintain the relevancy of training policy and recruitment efforts, workforce and economic development organizations must ensure that the directions and information they receive really help them to stay in tune with skill needs in the economy.

Strategies for information gathering include extensive review of labor market information and multiple methods for gathering business feedback. Besides having businesses on governing boards, workforce programs gather business feedback through committees, interlocking boards, and contractual partnerships.

Using businesses on committees, as opposed to or as well as on boards, is a common strategy for keeping training relevant. Many community colleges, technical schools, and school-to-work programs have business advisory committees to oversee their curricula and training design. The extent to which the committees are used varies as does the quality of their feedback. Committees can be effective vehicles for oversight, without the heavy demands made of board members. For Bread and Butter Café, using the technical school to deliver training suggests that these relationships were preestablished, which helped to ensure that the training provided was relevant.

An interlocking board/committee strategy refers not just to having businesses on the board or committees of workforce organizations, but also to having workforce staff hold board or committee positions in business organizations. ASC representatives, for example, are on the education and training committee of the local manufacturers association.

Mike Jefferson, director of Crispus Attucks Center for Employment and Training, a partner of ASC in workforce development, sits on the Youth Council, the chamber board, and the Susquahannah Regional Airport Authority. These activities help him to gather information about current issues and events, and to let the community know about his program. He participates in order to tie his organization into the information and opportunity networks in the region and to stay on top of demand.

Finally, it is not unusual for workforce organizations to have contractual partnerships with business organizations that provide critical information on skill needs and changing labor market demands. For example, the Manufacturing Association of South Central Pennsylvania contracts with ASC to deliver training to its members, and is an important source of information in helping them to maintain the relevancy of their training.

In sum, workforce programs must focus on continuous improvement and continuous relevance and that means developing and integrating multiple sources of labor market information. According to Diane Bell, EBMC president and chief executive officer, making real change in the community means achieving those results over and over again, based upon attention to data, trends, and learning. Business channels are critical, but insufficient. Labor market data must also be included.

Conclusions

In this final section, we will sum up the lessons about business engagement and workforce development. First, the primary goal of the workforce system is to provide quality employees, not simply to place workers. A focus on placement misaligns the performance measures and ignores the needs of both employers and employees. Engaging employers is most effective when they trust that workforce activities meet their needs.

Second, sector strategies appear to be the most effective for engaging employers, designing workforce programs, and developing training expertise. Effective sector strategies require identifying sector leadership. That may mean targeting leading firms. If firms are small, then the most effective strategy may be to encourage them to organize an association to provide that leadership. Sector strategies, especially those focused on sector leaders, can also help a region reach scale in terms of talent expansion. Scale depends not only upon employers who hire individuals and help to define skills, but also upon employers who start to invest in skills internally as a regular, commonplace practice—who make lifelong learning part of the overall regional business culture. Engaging sector leaders provides a potential way to lead that change. They not only lead by example but may then require suppliers and partners to enact similar changes.

Third, putting businesses on the board is insufficient for obtaining the depth and scope of information required to keep abreast of labor market demand. It can be an important part of an information development strategy, but on its own, it will not be enough for workforce programs aimed at reaching sufficient scale. Rather, to be effective, a workforce system needs a range of access to diverse business voices, complemented by strong labor market and economic data.

Fourth, workforce programs exist in a competitive market environment. Strong performance means adapting to this environmental reality. It does not mean that programs cannot develop and meet societal goals, but the market sets up parameters to action that cannot be ignored.

Finally, our review of employer engagement strategies reinforces the point being made throughout this book that building personalized relationships is a fundamental component of building a workforce system. Not only did employers indicate a desire for more personalized relationships, but, where those personal relationships existed, things happened. A workforce system is a structural construct that is implemented through people. To move it from the level of theory to actual practice, people are the glue that make and maintain the connections. People learn to speak the multiple languages of business, government, and the community. While we talk of formal partnerships, networks, and relationships, they are built, maintained, and adapted through the formal and informal actions of key people who hold those connective positions including liaisons, case managers, and the staff of intermediaries who are usually assigned this specific task.

Although we are talking about economic actors engaging to effect economic outcomes, the nature of such activity is in fact a social undertaking that hinges on social relationships. Only people connect to people. Systems create the framework that helps us identify who needs to work with whom and what needs to be done. But people do it. This chapter, which has focused on organizations, reminds us again that human capital always counts.

— 7 —

Instituting a Lifelong Learning Culture: Connecting Services to Support Advancement

The transformation of the economic structure together with the acceleration of technological progress has redefined the nature of career advancement. Upward mobility now requires enhanced labor market transparency through improved information flows and better engagement of businesses and individuals in continual skill acquisition. To strengthen the human capital assets of a region, a workforce system must provide institutions and strategies that foster lifelong learning, which has been defined as "certificates, licenses, diplomas and other proof being collected by learners following completion of final degrees" (Brown 2004: 2).

Lifelong learning has already become a permanent feature of the information economy, whether we as a society have fully embraced it or not, due to two reinforcing trends: shifting corporate structures and the regular injection of new technologies into most industrial sectors. Corporations are changing from large, vertically organized structures to flatter, less hierarchical companies. That shift has made promotion opportunities less likely in a single organization. As a result, career paths are moving from an internal career ladder that offers straightforward, linear trajectories within firms to a vaguer, messier career staircase or lattice format requiring horizontal moves across firms, and possibly even across economic or occupational sectors, to advance at a later date (Atkinson 2001).

Moreover, when economies restructure, significant proportions of the population may find their existing skills irrelevant. As we have seen regional economies move from traditional industries, such as textiles, steel, shipbuilding, or the military, to new industries, such as environmental science, information technologies, and health care, people have not been able to make the shift without extensive training, or in many cases, a return to full-fledged education. In the absence of extensive retraining, many individuals have moved

126

into lower paying, low-skill service jobs often with no benefits, which has significant long-term costs to the economic health of the community.

Equally, technological innovation requires regular improvement in the skill base. For example, recent research demonstrates a strong relationship between the business use of computers and the increase of skills required in the workplace (Autor, Levy, and Murnane 2003). Not only white-collar work is affected. Traditional blue-collar jobs in manufacturing, automotives, electronics, and many other fields are similarly growing more complex, requiring more sophisticated skills for more sophisticated equipment. And this is only what we know about today. Given the speed of technological change, many of the businesses and jobs that will be available years from now do not exist today. The inability to prepare individuals for the jobs of tomorrow creates additional pressure on communities to develop responsive, adaptive, lifelong learning systems that assist individuals in building upon their existing skill base and moving through a continuously changing labor market.

With employment security reduced and technology continuing to progress rapidly, people must reinvent themselves and acquire new skills throughout their lives. In the knowledge economy, this has shifted the onus of education and training from the firm to the individual (Atkinson 2001). Businesses, which depend on skilled labor, will move to a place that has the skills they need if the community cannot develop or attract them. For communities to remain competitive, therefore, they will need to be more involved in creating workforce systems oriented around lifelong learning.

While we hear much talk about the need for lifelong learning, this is also a somewhat new feature in human organization, so we have few existing models that describe it. Based on the research underpinning this book, this chapter proposes guidance to communities for developing a lifelong learning system.

At its most basic level, a lifelong learning system is composed of three core features. First, a region must provide access to the spectrum of networked educational and training opportunities, from those dealing with illiteracy to advanced degrees, covering toddlers to retirees. The key word here is "access." Not every region has research universities and not every high school can offer advanced placement courses but regions will need somehow to create access to them. This will be discussed in more detail below. Additionally, the spectrum of services needs to include issues such as financing, child care, health care, and other services that support individuals as they travel up the ladder. It is often these components that impede individuals from attaining further education and training; not a lack of will or ability.

Second, this spectrum of programs must be integrated, so that individuals can move fluidly among them. Third, economic and workforce developers need to reorient their worldviews from one based on job development to one

127

based on career-path development. This reorientation in thinking will help refocus their efforts toward programs that support upward mobility for both jobseekers and incumbent workers. In other words, the goal is not to place people in jobs, but on pathways. Special emphasis should be placed on, but not limited to, supporting disadvantaged workers entering the labor market. This chapter will first discuss why providing an integrated spectrum of education and training programs, the foundation of a lifelong learning system, is so critical to economic competitiveness, and then outline some strategies communities have undertaken to start making those connections. The chapter concludes with a look at specific programs launched to support upward mobility for low-skilled, low-income individuals, because for many communities, this is the heart of strengthening existent human capital resources and expanding the talent pool.

Lifelong Learning: The Need for an Integrated Spectrum of Opportunities

Many regions indeed possess a range of social service, economic development, training, and educational institutions relevant to workforce development. As has been seen in chapter 2, these efforts tend to be scattered and isolated from each other. While that spectrum of services first needs to be in place, if it remains fragmented and disconnected, it cannot support lifelong learning in a significant way. W. Norton Grubb explains why:

> But this piecemeal approach, valuable though it might be in specific instances, misses the point. The real problem with existing job training programs is not that a component here or there is inadequate but that their offerings consist of a welter of different services, some job-specific training, some remedial instruction, some work experience, and some supportive services, none obviously more effective than any others and all poorly coordinated. Furthermore, individual programs of limited intensity are not linked to other opportunities, even though they are intended for a population with substantial needs. (1996: 105)

Grubb concludes that the most effective method for strengthening the skills and thus the opportunities of the disadvantaged is to reintegrate training back into the education system. It is important to note that the isolation of the training realm from the education realm is not just a problem for aiding the low-skilled; it is also a serious impediment to the creation of a lifelong learning system and building of the higher skill base that businesses and communities need to compete.

The gap between education and training is significant. While both systems are designed to prepare individuals for the work world by furnishing them with a recognized set of skills appropriate to a particular career or range of career options, they traditionally provide very different levels of skill preparation. Education is considered the first chance system. K–12 provides the foundation skills upon which career, technical, or occupational skills are built. Postsecondary training then hones those skills and offers professional, occupational, or generalized credentials that prepare individuals to enter the work world. Training represents the second-chance system for those who either did not receive a good education, who left education early, or who now need to acquire new skills to stay, advance, or change jobs.

Table 7.1 outlines the major differences between the two systems. Summing it up, education is long term, available to everyone in the population, delivered by educational institutions through a classroom format, aimed at developing the overall capacities of the individual, and managed by state and local governments. Training is usually short term, open only to eligible populations (e.g., veterans, low-income individuals, the disabled), delivered through a wide range of institutions that use multiple teaching methods, aimed at getting people into jobs, and it is overseen by the federal government (Grubb 1996).

Of the two systems, education provides the greatest benefits for all involved. For individuals, as we saw in chapter 1, education provides the greatest returns in terms of both wages and quality of life. When used as a substitute rather than a complement to education, training provides minimal benefits. Grubb's (1996) evaluation of the history of U.S. training efforts shows definitively that while training has the positive initial effect of a modest increase in wages, such increases are not enough to lift individuals out of poverty and they diminish over time. Education, alternatively, increases wage potential as time passes.

For businesses, a better educated workforce is a more productive workforce. A study by the National Center on the Educational Quality of the Workforce (1995) found that a 10 percent increase in workers' education levels (a little over one more year of school per person) led to an 8.6 percent increase in productivity across industries and an 11 percent increase in nonmanufacturing firms. In fact, the study found that increases in education levels outperform increases in both capital stock and man-hours for productivity gains.

Ultimately, since lifelong learning refers to the accumulation of additional certified skills above and beyond the first degree, the system for advancement really starts with education. Much of the training we associate with the public training regime should now be considered preeducation preparation. The ultimate goal of the training can no longer be just to get individuals in a

Table 7.1

The Differences Between Education and Training Programs

Characteristic	Education	Training programs
Time span	Long, 1 to 4 years in length	Shorter, from 4 weeks to 1 year, averaging about 15 weeks
Population	Open to all members of the population	Open to eligible populations
Institutional framework	Programs occur in standardized education institutions (e.g., high schools, vocational schools, colleges)	Programs offered by the wide range of players, indicated in chapter 2
Service delivery method	Provide a standard service via classroom instruction with supplementary activities such as labs	Multiple teaching methods used including classroom instruction, on-the-job training, and counseling sessions
Goals	Broad goals covering moral, intellectual, and political as well as occupational needs	Focus solely on getting people employed
Lead players	State and local governments are the lead players	Federal government is the lead player
System hierarchy	Education is the first-chance system to enter the labor force; it is older and better organized with institutionalized political support	Training is the second-chance system for those who did not make it in the first chance or need to retool in light of economic change; it is much younger, more chaotic, and highly subject to political pressures, adding to its chaotic nature

Source: W. Norton Grubb, *Learning to Work: The Case of Reintegrating Job Training and Education,* pp. 2–5. © 1996 by the Russell Sage Foundation. Reprinted with permission.

job, but to support individuals in the development of careers. Given the impact of education on productivity, such a goal is in the best interest of business as well as individuals. A training system disconnected from the education system, therefore, provides little long-term benefit to anyone. Training and the training system alone are not the endpoint but one stop on a skills development continuum.

The first step in building a lifelong learning framework then is to reintegrate training into education, but, clearly, lifelong learning goes well beyond this. It also comprises more clearly articulated links among educational institutions and the development of connected, supportive services that allow individuals and employers to take advantage of those opportunities. Issues such as access to affordable child care, health care, high-speed Internet services, and financial aid that allow individuals to pursue these opportunities now affect a much wider spectrum of the population, not just the disadvantaged. As we will see below, successful advancement programs have had to address these particular issues.

But how can we create lifelong learning systems? Clearly, everything we have looked at thus far in this book is part of the picture. Skill standards and certification provide the foundation for lifelong learning. Intermediaries build support networks for individuals with long roads to travel. Strategies to expand the overall pool of talent and engage businesses help regions to better steer and comprehend the labor market in the new economy. The next critical piece is to build a chain of relationships among training, education, and service providers, which individuals and employers can use to build and revise skills. Those relationships ultimately will be grounded in articulation agreements that allow for credit accumulation and transfer over time. Those partnerships will span institutional sectors and place-based boundaries if they are to be successful. There are already several types of linkages in place serving as models for building lifelong learning systems, including linkages between training programs and educational entities, between high schools and postsecondary institutions, among postsecondary institutions, and between public agencies and education institutions.

The first type of relationship is between training and educational entities. The Bread and Butter Café is an example of how this works. The nonprofit partners provide the pretraining and other support services, while the local technical school offers occupational training attached to certification and college credit. Individuals can later return to the technical school to complete their associate's degree, building on their prior experience and credits.

The second type of relationship is between high schools and postsecondary institutions. One widespread model of this type of relationship is a federal program called Tech Prep. The program starts in eleventh grade and includes either two years in postsecondary school or a two-year apprenticeship and culminates in some type of certification on completion. It consists of a four-year planned sequence of courses between a high school and a community college in a technical field. Tech Prep programs often include guidance and preparatory services to help youth make career-shaping decisions at an early age. They require high schools and two-year schools to align curricula based on skill standards.

The need for high school and postsecondary linkages should not be

131

restricted to vocational career paths. High schools will also need to build relationships with universities to support career development for their students. Take the interesting example of Abilene, Texas. Within the city limits, there are three universities (and a fourth one is located in the neighboring town), but none of these institutions offers a B.A. or B.S. in engineering. To allow students to pursue an engineering career, Abilene independent school district has an articulated career pathway with Texas Tech in Lubbock, Texas (163 miles from Abilene), that feeds students interested in engineering degrees. While students leave the region to pursue a degree, the purpose of such an initiative is to build the overall base of human capital assets within the state. This effort also increases the overall number of science and technology workers that have some affinity to the region.

The third type of connection integral to building a lifelong learning strategy is among postsecondary institutions. Looking again at Texas, Texas Tech in Lubbock has created the Pathways program with twenty-five community colleges in Texas and New Mexico. The purpose of the program is to expand the number of students attending and completing community college and transferring to complete their bachelor's degree. Texas Tech provides guidance and financial counselors to partner campuses, assistance with the transfer process, and retroactive degrees, which allows students to send credits back to the community college to obtain their associate's degree, creating an easy, seamless system for students who want to continue their education (Texas Tech 2005). In fact, it can be quite common for community colleges to create articulation relationships with local universities, especially in particular career paths, as many community colleges play the role of feeder institutions. As another example, in the Orlando, Florida, region, two- and four-year schools have come together to form an education consortium to meet both education and economic development objectives. The consortium is currently developing an academic course exchange that will allow students in any participating university to enroll in, and transfer credits from, any course offered by any consortium school (Orlando Business Journal 2004).

Some of these postsecondary interinstitutional relationships are moving in more sophisticated directions, often with the purpose of enhancing the science, engineering, and more technically related workforce. The National Science Foundation Advanced Technological Education Program (ATE), for example, seeks to enhance the education of technicians in the science and engineering fields through partnerships between academic institutions and employers, with an emphasis on career path development between secondary schools and two-year schools, and two-year and four-year postsecondary schools. An evaluation of the program noted that it has been successful in promoting collaboration among community colleges, high schools, and four-year colleges (Bailey et al. 2003).

One exemplary project supported by the ATE program aimed to integrate the training of technicians and engineers for the semiconductor manufacturing industry. Three universities partnered with three community colleges in three contiguous states (New Mexico, Arizona, and Texas) to design computer-based training modules covering nine different skill areas. The project was a response to the concern that postsecondary institutions were not meeting the industry's workforce demand. Specifically, technicians needed a better understanding of scientific and mathematical principles, engineers needed to know the machinery better, and they both needed to understand the skills and roles of the other. In addition, the project expected that increased interaction between technicians and engineers would foster lifelong learning habits, cross-train community college and university faculty, reduce later costs of training on the part of businesses, and encourage technicians to later pursue engineering degrees. Businesses have been important partners in the effort, especially in the area of module review, equipment donation, provision of industry information, and skill set identification (Wood et al. 2000).

The semiconductor industry was selected because, structurally, it is particularly amenable to this type of project. Technicians and engineers work together more frequently than is normally found in traditional manufacturing settings, and quality standards are particularly stringent. While this model may not be useful in traditional manufacturing, evidence suggests that it is relevant to emergent industries, such as microelectromechanical systems, known as MEMS, and nanotechnology, which are closely related to semiconductor applications, techniques, and quality standards. The model also suggests a mode of thinking integral to lifelong learning frameworks: ensuring that all courses introduce students to potential next steps for advancement.

Before moving on, it is worth looking at two of the challenges this particular project faced, because they are representative of typical challenges of longer-term partnership training efforts that underpin the foundation of a workforce system. The first challenge was an unexpected downswing in the economy after the project was initiated, which led to a decline in demand for technicians and individuals choosing semiconductor training paths at the community college level. Out of the first cohort of 249 students participating in cross-training modules, only 45 were technicians (Wood et al. 2000). Many more have been trained since then, but this experience reminds us that short-term business cycles are important components of individual choices and contribute to cyclical gaps in labor market activity. Workforce systems with improved information flows can improve this situation but will never entirely eliminate it.

This first challenge was a structural one. The second difficulty was of a programmatic nature. Basically, it is hard to coordinate the schedules and manage the demands of six autonomous institutions, which makes momentum hard to maintain over time. The challenges of managing multipartner projects, however, are balanced by the benefits of having a greater wealth of perspectives and resources. Since partnerships increasingly are the heart of city and regional governance, we must remember that they are not, by nature, easy.

Finally, the last type of partnership critical to building a lifelong learning infrastructure is between regional and city agencies and education and training institutions. It may be incumbent on public agencies and intermediaries to create new relationships or to stimulate the creation of new institutions to establish better access to the full range of education and training opportunities. Returning again to the city of Abilene, we see what a region with insufficient postsecondary science and technology education did to build those assets. The city worked with Texas Tech to establish a satellite campus in downtown Abilene, which offers a master's degree in computer software engineering and will add research capacity in the application of intelligent software. The program was designed so that students at the local universities taking approved coursework could feed directly into the program (Cooke 2002). Bringing in Texas Tech also provides the city with enhanced resources to promote technology commercialization and entrepreneurship, in turn promoting all facets of knowledge development.

Looking at the range of partnership types and cases, several important lessons emerge for building lifelong learning structures and creating new economic opportunities for regions. First, public agencies may need to serve as catalysts for building new and different relationships among education and training institutions in order to help bolster local opportunities and lifelong learning structures. Second, for many communities, building human capital assets may require crossing jurisdictional boundaries and working with nonlocal education and training partners to tap into wider resources. The key to building a spectrum of services is not always to create new institutions, but to build access in new ways (e.g., distance learning and Internet systems also have a role to play here).

Third, community colleges are key nodes in lifelong learning networks and hold a special place in the design of the workforce system. They offer a natural link between the worlds of training and education, so it is no surprise that community colleges have been known to assume an intermediary role (Giloth 2004a; Fitzgerald 2004). State laws regulate what community colleges can do. To be able to effectively access the power of community colleges may require working with state governments to review and revise those regulations.

For individuals to navigate through the labor market over the course of a lifetime and for businesses to continue to compete in a globalized, hypercompetitive economy, the workforce must continuously update its skills and increase productivity—hence lifelong learning. For individuals facing economic and social disadvantage, especially those lacking basic skills, specific initiatives to support their upward mobility will be essential. As we have seen in earlier chapters, business-led programs supporting upward mobility tend to favor more professional staff, who already have a high level of credentialing in place. Given that the ultimate goal of a human capital strategy is to expand the talent pool, developing programs that support lower-skilled individuals to move up the training and education ladder works to the benefit of all.

Upward Mobility Programs: Creating Career Ladders

Upward mobility, advancement, or career-ladder programs provide basic skills, job-specific skills, or some combination of the two, with the express purpose of helping individuals, often disadvantaged, advance from their current positions to higher-paying ones. This workforce development approach often consists of building a career ladder, defined as a "series of occupations linked by common skills" (Prince 2003: 3).

Three general strategies for promoting upward mobility have been identified (Fitzgerald and Carlson 2000). The first strategy advances individuals through the provision of education and training. The second strategy focuses on increasing wages through the professionalization of existing jobs. The third strategy is the creation of new tiers within occupations that are linked to pay increases as one moves through them. The case of WRTP discussed earlier, for example, started with the restructuring of occupations and then linked advancement to the accumulation of training over time.

Advancement programs can be implemented internal to a firm or they can create linkages that help individuals to move between firms, usually within an economic sector but not always. Upward mobility programs are more easily designed within industry sectors, but they can be based on common skill sets that cross sectors. In Grand Rapids, Michigan, for example, Burger King employees can move up into higher paying manufacturing jobs, creating cross-sectoral paths for advancement (Giloth 2000). In Philadelphia, the National Union of Healthcare Employees provides up to $5,000 per year in tuition reimbursement for participants who graduate from their nurse's aide training courses to enter a licensed practical nursing program (more on this program below). Employers engage in these types of initiatives because hiring from within reduces labor turnover and retains employees already steeped in the organization's culture and social structures.

To establish advancement opportunities internal to firms, several factors must be in place. Companies must be willing and able to hire from within; they must have clear, formal promotion paths that are universally applied; and those paths must be accessible from entry level positions, including low-skilled positions (Tao et al. 1992). Internal career laddering efforts include a formal training component, but effective programs also disseminate information detailing a company's promotion opportunities and procedures (e.g., available apprenticeships, job rotations, certification opportunities) and ensure that employees understand the company's philosophy and the opportunities for, and advantages of, lateral job moves. Advancement, therefore, is a function of socialization within the work environment as well as obtaining new skills. Thus, internal advancement efforts must also include a focus on more informal practices, such as work groups to socialize individuals into work expectations and practices, the availability of mentors to guide individuals through these diverse and complex paths, and other linkages related to career movement (Tao et al. 1992). For example, Cape Cod Hospital and its union provide a book that describes all available career ladders in the hospital. It lays out the requirements for each job, as well as available educational opportunities and funding sources to help workers plan for advancement (Fitzgerald and Carlson 2000).

According to Fitzgerald and Carlson (2000), creating upward mobility strategies within economic sectors depends on several components. First, employers must provide details on job structures and advancement routes. Second, individuals must have access to specific job-training efforts connected to those paths. Finally, supportive institutions such as intermediaries and governments should be available to provide financing and management resources to connect the various pieces of the career ladder.

Finally, career ladders can be developed around occupational sectors that crosscut industry sectors (e.g., customer service skills). This model tends to focus on entry-level employment because, as individuals move up the ladder, advancement is increasingly attached to industry-specific skills. Core success factors for these approaches include a reliable referral source for the individuals participating in the program, and an organizing intermediary that can recruit, place, and monitor individuals and work with employers (Prince 2003).

Intermediaries are important players in career-ladder programs in industry and occupational sectors, but there also are examples of intermediaries working with companies to create advancement programs internal to an employer. In this case, intermediaries often serve as catalysts for the development of the program, and then can replicate and transfer that model to other employers, thus increasing the scale and impact of such an effort. The Empower Baltimore Management Corporation (EBMC), the management arm of the Baltimore Empowerment Zones, provides a good example of this method. The EBMC worked initially with two hospitals to develop a customized training program for surgical technician skills. For one hospital, Johns Hopkins Hospital (JHH), the program was for new entrants. For the second hospital, the University of Maryland Medical System (UMMS), the program targeted existing employees wishing to advance. In both cases, the course was offered by a community college, lasted for ten months, and included classroom study, laboratory work, and a clinical rotation. The programs had dramatically different completion rates. For UMMS, 96 percent completed the program. For JHH, only 44 percent did so, even though for individuals completing the training, on average, their salaries increased from $16,992 to $28,346 (Roberts 2003). Differences in program design explain these results and will be discussed in detail later in the chapter.

The program also had some important impacts on employers' human resource and public policies. JHH learned the importance of helping workers learn basic academic skills to support their advancement and implemented a Skills Enhancement Initiative to do just that. UMMS discovered the value of recruiting from within and launched initiatives similar to the Surgical Tech Training for pharmacy technicians and medical coders. As a result of this experience, UMMS now encourages hospital staff to create an environment that promotes advancement for entry-level workers. Finally, the state of Maryland then used the EMBC's program as a model for the development of its Skills-Based Training for Employment Promotion (STEP) program to train low-income workers for advancement. STEP funding was used to extend training opportunities in the health-care field (Roberts 2003).

Health care has been a common target nationally for developing sector-based upward mobility programs. The sector has many entry and paraprofessional positions and regularly faces shortages. While many programs in this area are quite young, some have been around for a considerable time. For example, the Philadelphia District 1199C Training and Upgrading Fund was established in 1974 by the District 1199C, Philadelphia's largest health-care local union, to provide training services to support their members' advancement. The program receives financial support from employers through collective bargaining agreements negotiated under the auspices of Taft-Hartley education funds. This support, which comes from fifty-four employers, represents 43 percent of its budget, and finances the programs available to union members only. The rest of the budget is made up of tuition and fee-for-service funds (10 percent) and public grants (46 percent, including funding from the U.S. Department of Labor, the Pennsylvania Department of Education, the Pennsylvania Department of Labor and Industry, the Pennsylvania Department of Public Welfare, and the Pennsylvania Workforce Development Corporation). While initially available only to union members, the Fund now provides many services to Philadelphia residents to aid their entry into the health-care sector.

The activities of the Fund are housed in the Breslin Learning Center, a 35,000–square-foot facility that employs a staff of 120, and serves about 17,000 people annually. The center is open fourteen hours a day for seven days a week. Because most participants are working full time, many programs are part time. In addition, the Learning Center has developed a range of specialized courses to meet specific employer needs.

The sheer strength of this model is its ability to tailor services to meet the needs of workers over the long term. From adult basic education, covering remedial math and English and GED preparation, to full-time scholarship programs (including a leave of absence) for members to pursue full-time education to receive A.S., B.S., master, and Ph.D degrees, many of the programs are consecutive, and provide college credit and certification, allowing individuals to pursue career advancement tied to degree attainment over time. Services also include skill, academic, and career evaluation; career counseling; and placement assistance, including interview and resume-writing skills. In addition, the program also administers a number of certification examinations on-site.

Because the Fund aids disadvantaged and incumbent workers alike, has well-developed employer engagement, and has effectively integrated a spectrum of services from remediation of basic skills to B.A., it provides a useful working model of a lifelong learning system, albeit within a single industry sector. Once new workers have entered into this world, they step onto well-established ladders to advance within the sector. The fact that the Fund has lasted thirty years, and continues to be cited as a successful model speaks to its success (Prince 2003; Fitzgerald and Carlson 2000; Pindus, Flynn, and Nightingale 1995).

One of the strengths of this particular model is the centrality of the union. In a review of health-care-based career ladder programs, Fitzgerald and Carlson (2000) found that the strongest program they studied, the Cape Cod Hospital career-ladder program, was effective due in large part to unionization. Unions serve as a critical intermediary that have the capacity to focus on improving wages, working conditions, and advancement ladders internal to an employer or an industrial sector. For example, the average hourly wage of a nonunion nursing assistant is $8.55, while a union assistant receives about $10.17. The programs support health-care professionals but they also provide entry to nonprofessionals (e.g., housekeepers) to move up within the hospital. Basic education classes, for example, are taught by the community college on-site. Courses last two hours and are offered between shifts. Both the hospital and the employee donate one hour of the time. The employee quits work an hour early or starts one hour later for the duration of the course. For individuals already at higher levels within the hospital, traineeships are available to support their career development. Traineeships allow workers to learn additional procedures on the job. Once completed, the worker can apply for a higher position when a job opens up. Fitzgerald and Carlson note that although the program has been good, the most frequent advancement is within the lowest skill and wage levels, moving housekeeping to clerical or secretarial staff.

Fitzgerald and Carlson also point out that even when career ladders are available, they can be difficult to pursue. They discuss the case of Bethel New Life, a Chicago-based community development corporation that started a Health Care Career Ladder project to move low-income women from home health aid to CNA to LPN, RN, or another allied health profession such as lab technician. Between the years 1997 and 2000, the program served 150 participants who began as home health aides. Of those participants, 95 (63 percent) completed CNA training, increasing their hourly wages from $5.40 to $7.20, and 5 enrolled in RN programs at the community college. Fitzgerald and Carlson found that the CNA appeared to be a stopping rather than a starting point, which may be partially explained by the fact that studies for advancement past this point take a long time to finish while working full time. They conclude that, for some, career ladders can be "too much too soon." For some individuals, it might be more effective to improve the working conditions and overall pay of CNAs, particularly as there are opportunities for professional growth within this job field, such as doing more specialized work in intensive-care areas involving restorative care or oncology. Overall, they remind us that, again, we need a spectrum of approaches that allows individuals to advance in different ways at different times.

In the next section, we will review the factors that comprise successful programs and the most common obstacles that impede success.

Making Advancement Programs Work

Fitzgerald and Carlson (2000), who reviewed a number of sector-based career-ladder strategies, found a mixed bag of results. They identified obstacles that held programs back as well as success factors. Obstacles include:

- Employer's resistance. Employers must be willing to create jobs with career advancement potential (with downsizing, there are now fewer rungs connecting higher and lower positions) and support their workers to obtain the training, with benefits such as time off for training and some subsidy for the training.

- Costs of individual trade-offs. Workers face many obstacles to obtaining the increased education required for advancement, including familial responsibilities, physical and financial access to training, time management, lack of role models, and others. It is hard to find the time to acquire additional training under these circumstances. For people entering the job market from a transitional place, it may take awhile for them to adjust to their new roles and responsibilities before they can even consider advancement strategies. In sum, success is less likely when workers are required to commit to training on their own time (e.g., many have another job); training expenses are added to budgets that often are already overstretched (e.g., tuition, child care); training has stigma attached to it, such as basic or remedial training; and there is a lack of any type of clear benefit associated with the training.
- Lack of amenability to laddering. Not all industries are amenable to laddering, especially if they are made up of many small firms (e.g., printing). In these cases, advancement strategies require intermediaries that make connections across firms and industries.
- Unmapped career paths. Careers need to be mapped if ladders are to be developed. This is not always the case.
- Weak intermediaries. Some intermediaries are stronger than others. In particular, unions and community colleges often provide the widest range of resources and support that can make these programs work.

Fitzgerald and Carlson also note that success factors include having sufficient training resources, involving the workforce in the design and implementation of training, and having sufficient collaboration between labor and management in overseeing the program. These factors are easier to organize in unionized employers or sectors.

The evaluation of the EBMC customized training program came to similar conclusions. The UMMS program, which had clear positive outcomes for employer and employee alike, allowed participants to work half-time during the course but receive their full salary. In addition, the community college provided the classes inside the UMMS facilities. Those courses were tailored to meet the specific need of Empowerment Zone residents. The JHH program, alternatively, was for new entrants, who received only a $100 stipend per week during their participation in the program, and thus had to earn an additional salary. Furthermore, the classroom and laboratory components were provided on the community college campus, which was quite a distance from the Empowerment Zone. Finally, the courses were not at all customized to meet the special needs of Empowerment Zone residents (Roberts 2003). Consequently, UMMS, which provided a higher level of support attached to clear advancement prospects was more effective in graduating individuals, suggesting that wages are only a part of the incentive for individuals to invest resources in their own advancement.

Thus far, we have looked at upward mobility models focused on creating opportunities predominantly for disadvantaged and low-skilled individuals. However, upward mobility strategies are not limited to this realm. Incumbent training programs, which have traditionally focused on improving business competitiveness by augmenting workforce skills, are an integral part of this environment. In fact, WRTP and the Philadelphia District 1199C Training and Upgrading Fund started by focusing on incumbent workers and then expanded to creating opportunities for disadvantaged community members. Starting with incumbent training demonstrates to employers the value of training and builds trust between employers and intermediaries. That trust opened the door for harder-to-serve individuals, because the intermediary is accountable for outcomes, thus sharing the risk with the employers. A deeper look at incumbent training programs is merited.

Incumbent Training: A Linchpin of Lifelong Learning

As we have seen earlier in the book, employer-based training is generally considered the most effective vehicle for training delivery, but employers typically spend more of their training dollars on the better-educated workers at the top of the workforce pyramid. Getting businesses to extend those resources down the pyramid has been difficult, and the workers, the communities, and the businesses themselves lose as a result. Ultimately, firms cannot improve competitiveness and productivity if they invest public and private training dollars only in college graduates who hold managerial and professional positions (Thurow 1985 cited in Creticos and Sheets 1989: 24). Incumbent training, in the knowledge economy, has become a linchpin of a lifelong learning system because it can enhance the skill base in a way that makes individuals, businesses, and communities more competitive.

To encourage businesses to invest in their workforces, forty-five states have established some type of program to finance incumbent training. In 1998–99, state spending for these programs totaled $593 million (Department of Labor 1999). State-financed incumbent training programs generally are organized in two ways; either the state provides grants or tax credits to businesses to pay for training or the state directly delivers these services. Grant programs may provide the grant directly to the training provider, and in some cases may require that businesses use community colleges, or they may provide the grant or credit directly to the business, which then chooses a provider (Council for Urban Economic Development 1999).

State-financed incumbent training programs have a long history. When they were first implemented in the 1960s, states used them primarily as incentives to attract new businesses or help businesses expand, which restricted their use to the training of the unemployed or new hires for new positions created by the locating or expanding company. In the 1980s, as the numbers of dislocated workers increased, existing businesses expressed their resentment regarding their inability to access training dollars, new technologies were implemented, and U.S. companies appeared to be losing competitiveness globally, states modified their incumbent programs. They started to provide financing to existing businesses to retrain, and thus retain, workers whose skills had been made obsolete as a result of new technologies and new methods of work organization.

Early program innovators, such as the Employment Training Panel in California and Prairie State 2000 in Illinois, required businesses to prove that they were making technological and organizational changes in their production process and that workers would need new skills to adapt. By creating a direct link between retraining and business strategy, this use of incumbent training instituted the first attempt to integrate training initiatives into economic development objectives (Creticos and Sheets 1989).

A large-scale, national evaluation of twenty-four state-financed incumbent training programs undertaken by Creticos and Sheets (1989, 1990) identified four variables that should be used to assess incumbent programs specifically, and these remain the standards by which all workforce programs should be judged. These variables are:

- employees' achievement of certified competencies in transferable skills;
- the performance of the work units affected by the training;
- the company's overall competitive standing; and
- the earnings of the trainees.

These evaluation criteria emphasize that the goal, therefore, of all training programs must be to improve both the position of the worker, through increased competencies and improved wages, and the position of the firm. Competitiveness and worker training are intimately linked. Workforce development efforts need to recognize and enhance that relationship.

The results of that evaluation revealed important lessons about the value of public investment in work-based training and how it is best delivered. The lessons identified by Creticos and Sheets (1989), which are reviewed below, are applicable across workforce programs and represent good general lessons for communities building workforce systems.

First, state grants expand the scope, reduce the timeframe, and increase the number of individuals involved in training. Public programs, therefore, have a clear and positive impact on extending training opportunities in the workplace.

Second, training projects are most effective when linked to well-defined business goals and performance objectives. Incumbent training that is not complementary to business strategic goals will not help the business or have a significant impact on the trainee's position.

Third, state training funds are least likely to replace private investment in training when grants are used for direct instructional costs of classroom and laboratory training rather than for paying the wages and salaries of trainees. One of the most controversial aspects of incumbent training is that instead of creating new opportunities that would not have existed without it, public financing merely replaces what the private sector would have invested on its own.

Fourth, while small businesses are the most in need of subsidized incumbent training, small business management often does not know how to use training as a vehicle for strategic change, and needs additional assistance in this area. State involvement helps businesses, especially small businesses, overcome a range of barriers that limit their retraining efforts, such as poor management-labor relationships, negative prior training experiences, fear of poaching or loss of employees before their return on investment is met, and a feeling that retraining is a luxury.

Fifth, incumbent training programs are important vehicles that can help businesses overcome the uncertainty they have toward training and can persuade them to use training to improve their performance and build learning into their company culture. In other words, effective public training programs serve as catalysts to increasing overall business understanding of, and investment in, the value of training.

In addition to outlining the value of public training to the community, Creticos and Sheets also identified six lessons for delivering effective incumbent training programs, which are detailed in Exhibit 7.1. Key success factors include the commitment of management, the organization of training around business principles, and employee comprehension of the purpose of the training, among other factors.

Many challenges surround the expansion of incumbent training. Even the most effective state programs are available only to a small set of firms. There is little federal funding available for incumbent training. While some WIA funding may be used for incumbent training, in practice that use remains limited. Finally, incumbent training needs to be better integrated into workforce training systems so that it can be used as a tool to open up

Exhibit 7.1

Six Lessons for Delivering Effective Incumbent Training

1. Upper management needs to be committed to training.
2. Training must be organized around clearly identified, measurable business objectives.
3. Employees need to understand the objectives for the training. In successful programs, employees are somehow involved in detailed discussions about the business's competitive situation.
4. Behavioral objectives for the training must be clearly established and imparted using a competency-based curriculum.
5. Class-based learning must be combined with on-the-job or appropriate laboratory training that shows the practical relevance of the course work.
6. Pre- and postassessment of individual skills should be conducted to demonstrate learning and to determine which basic skills need to be integrated into the curriculum. This may be more useful for training of technical skills and may not be appropriate in all cases.

Source: Creticos and Sheets (1990: 49–51).

opportunities for advancement. Even with these limitations, it is not uncommon for states to have trouble recruiting companies to use their programs. As noted in earlier chapters, mobilizing business involvement, even in situations where business interests are clearly met, is not always easy or straightforward.

Even with the challenges, incumbent training can no longer exist in isolation from the wider workforce training system. It is a central foundation of a lifelong learning framework that leverages business investment in the overall development and maintenance of the skill base. Incumbent training is also a core component of upward mobility strategies that help individuals access good jobs with family-sustaining wages.

Conclusion

A people-centered place will provide an exhaustive array of linked services that allow anyone, at any age or skill level, to develop and advance within a career. Those services will be linked in formal and informal ways, and the career pathways they connect will be tied into the public, private, and community sectors. The networks will tie local and regional populations into wider education and training opportunities.

Lifelong learning is first an institutional infrastructure of educational, social, and economic services, and, second, a culture, a way of thinking about life, neighborhoods, and economic growth that is accepted by individuals, businesses, and governments. Lifelong learning will not work if all three are not engaged. Every individual is a unique combination of public, employer, and personal investment in skills and development. Every business has a labor force with these characteristics.

If we accept that the central goal of a human capital development strategy is to expand the overall pool of talent, then to design and support methods that increase the skill base of individuals at various points in their lives is an essential feature of meeting that goal. Talent is not just a function of skills but is the continuous development of skills and competencies to meet new challenges and harness new opportunities.

Creating a lifelong learning culture grounded in career-path development will not be easy. It means breaking down cultural and structural barriers that impede collaborative work across the education, public, private, and community sectors. It means thinking through new ways to deliver financing, child care, health care, and other services that allow individuals to pursue new paths based on skill attainment. It means engaging businesses not only in rewarding individuals for their efforts, but also in becoming key partners in encouraging those efforts through their own internal workplace practices and investment decisions. And it means accepting and allowing governments and intermediaries as the movers and shakers of the system—catalyzing new types of partnerships and providing incentives and services that make the connective links between career pathways and services.

All of this activity starts first by eliminating the historic divisions between the education and training systems. Their separation has created two worlds. The need for talent and skills now demands that they be reconnected. Only by reconnecting them can communities dig deeper and wider to build talent.

Communities wishing to enhance their lifelong learning systems will need to map their service offerings, ensuring that they provide or can access training on any part of the continuum of learning requirements. They may also have to help catalyze the relationships between training and education providers to fill service gaps and help individuals to move fluidly among options and build their careers. Finally, communities need to find ways to leverage business investment in incumbent training in a more expansive way that taps into and complements the lifelong learning system and spectrum of services.

Ultimately, a workforce system aligns the connections among these various component parts to foster talent expansion and better facilitate labor market transitions. The final chapter sums up the lessons for system building that emerge from this book.

— 8 —

Conclusions: People-Centered Economic Development

When listening to the discussion of workforce issues, the talk revolves around problems to be solved, chaos to be tamed, and predictions of doom and gloom if we do not act soon. In this final chapter, I would like to propose another way to frame this discussion. Workforce development is not a problem—it is an opportunity—the chance to unleash the creative, productive, and innovative forces, found only in people, for the economic and social betterment of our cities, states, and nations. People-centered development has the unique advantage of promising increased equity, efficiency, and economic vitality.

The Secretary's Commission on Achieving Necessary Skills (SCANS) report, which identified the skill needs of the information age, summarizes the challenge:

> For the last 40 years, we have worked to further the ideal of equity—for minority students, for the disabled, and for immigrants. With that work still incomplete, we are called to still another revolution—to create an entire people trained to think and equipped with the know-how to make their knowledge productive. (SCANS 1991: xiii)

I would argue that these are not two revolutions but one and the same revolution. Herein lies the real opportunity. Equity is first and foremost a function of skills, of preparing all people for whatever career options they choose to pursue. Extending equity, intrinsically, expands the talent pool. By creating equity, we create the foundation for our businesses to compete and our communities to thrive. Equity is not just the right thing to do—it has become the essential component of a successful economic development strategy because without talented, creative people, we will not have the assets to compete globally. People and their ability to innovate are the economic drivers of the twenty-first century, if we recognize and invest in their development. It will not be enough to focus on talent attraction. That is a race to the

146

bottom because it is neither sustainable nor practical. All the trends in place are clear: we have to expand the pool of talent. Competitive places will have the infrastructure in place that support people's development. By nurturing human talent, we invigorate our economy, because knowledge and the ability to apply and innovate that knowledge, is an asset unique to people. It is people—not technology, not buildings, not finance, not roads (although these remain important)—who create, innovate, invent, repair, maintain, nurture, apply, and transfer knowledge and then find economic and social uses for it (entrepreneurship). Competitiveness is about finding ways to maximize that capacity.

This book provides the initial outline of what a people-centered place looks like. People-centered places focus on knowledge creation, and are working to build workforce systems that invest and nurture the creation, retention, and attraction of their talent. The conclusions will summarize the lessons learned and key recommendations for putting a people-centered workforce system together.

Lessons Learned: Building a Workforce System That Creates, Retains, and Expands Talent

A system is defined as "a group or combination of things or parts forming a complex or unified whole" (*Random House Dictionary* 1980: 883). While no region has a strategically developed workforce system, all regions have complex, fragmented institutions involved in recognizing, developing, and transferring skills that de facto comprise a system. Training and educational institutions are central to the system, although the system is not reducible solely to these actors. Within the existing system, regions have institutions that have been around for generations with cultures and objectives that may no longer align with current needs, and new institutions that view the world through a different lens, all of which, together, influence the shape and function of the labor market.

The main objective of this book is to start the conversation around what a people-centered approach to economic and workforce development would look like. It starts with a cultural shift in our understanding of economic development—one that recognizes human capital development and the local environment that promotes it, as the foundations of a dynamic economy.

In practical terms, that cultural shift would be grounded in a shared language among public, private, and community sectors that facilitates information flows within the labor market, better aligns goals across the system, and provides the basis for the emergence of networks that link the various institutions within the system. For that type of system to emerge several features are required: entrepreneurs who give the system shape by leveraging and merging resources and implementing and advocating new approaches; tools that enhance labor force mobility and transparency to tighten the supply and demand sides of the market; and strategies focused specifically on expanding and widening the overall pool of talent. Even with these features in place, and many communities are involved in these activities, the overall culture has to change and be brought to significant scale within the region. Bringing about that sort of cultural shift requires that employers and people recognize its value and are able to engage in it. People-centered places have found methods to engage employers and embed individuals in a way that allows them to develop and enhance their talents from any potential entry point (low or high skilled, young or old).

This book has identified multiple means to build and strengthen these five components, which are summarized below.

- Develop and strengthen intermediaries as system entrepreneurs. Intermediaries serve this role by brokering information to craft new understandings across the labor market, leveraging and linking resources, experimenting with new approaches, advocating for change, and bridging across sectors to create new opportunities. Intermediaries find ways to more tightly align supply and demand in a more volatile, skill-centered labor market.
- Enhance labor market mobility by augmenting the use of credentialed skill standards to support increased workforce mobility; to provide a common language in the labor market to align training options, worker expectations, and business needs; and to provide a fundamental underpinning to a lifelong learning system.
- Implement workforce talent expansion strategies to strengthen and expand the existing human capital base, including methods to increase college access, to attract and retain skilled workers, and to embed young professionals in the civic, economic, and social life of a region. These strategies also include rewriting and promoting new stories and understandings of place and opportunity. People-centered places recognize that jobs, place, and regular access to skills all matter for a healthy economy.
- Better engage the business community in system design and as training consumers. Not only does the increase of business voice across the system help align supply and demand, business activities influence the shape, size, and culture of the talent pool. Without employer acceptance of the importance of continuous skill development, the system cannot reach scale. In effect, it will not be a comprehensive system but remain

a series of component parts that may change individual lives, but fail to revitalize regions.

- Create a continuum of linked workforce, economic, and social services to support labor market mobility, advancement, and lifelong learning. These services should be available at all skill levels and all ages, and be adaptive to existing and emergent opportunities. Services not only help increase the size of the talent pool but also help the latter to maintain its competitive edge. To develop and expand talent in a way that makes a place competitive requires us to recognize that talent development is multifaceted and continually in motion, which means communities need a range of adaptable services to build and maintain it.

Combined, these five features will better enable a region to build skills, facilitate labor market mobility, and create new understandings of place grounded in the importance of human capital development. Different strategies will need to be implemented at different levels within the workforce system: system level, sector level, firm level, and individual level. Figure 8.1 diagrams what this system might look like. It outlines how information travels within the labor market, particularly the institutions through which that information flows. Those institutions mediate the power and transparency of that information in ways that either tighten or fragment the labor market.

Credentials, intermediaries, and talent pool expansions link the supply and demand sides of the system. These systemic components are more than just bridges—they transform the nature of information to create a common language and align expectations between workers and employers. The primary goal of a community is not only to increase the number of talented people but also to reframe the culture to support business and individual pursuit of knowledge accumulation.

Credentials enhance the transparency of the system by ensuring that what you see is what you get. They signal employers that potential employees have the right skills, provide individuals with evidence that they have attained the appropriate skill levels, and provide educational and training institutions the material they need to ensure individuals leave with job-appropriate skills. They work to align and tighten the labor market in ways that empower individuals, minimize risk to employers, and ensure that supply-side institutions meet labor market needs. However, given what we know about the impact of institutions and perceptions on the fluidity of the labor market, credentials are essential but insufficient.

Intermediaries complement credentials because they can shape expectations between the supply and demand sides through their activities. As we saw earlier, intermediaries signaled employers as to the type and skills of

Figure 8.1 **Foundations of a Regional Workforce System**

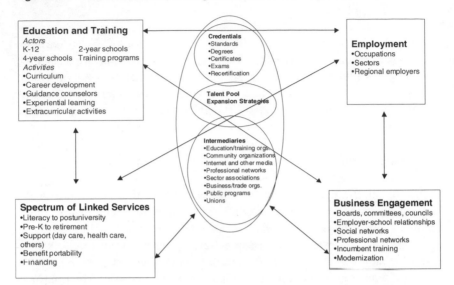

potential employees in ways that either opened doors or kept them shut. The Laufer and Winship study (2004) we reviewed previously showed that some intermediaries carry negative stereotypes, which impedes their ability to place workers, irrespective of the individual's skills. On the other side, intermediaries such as Bread and Butter Café and WRTP opened doors and created opportunities by changing perceptions.

Negative stereotypes do not hinder the labor market mobility of only the unskilled. Thomas and Ong (2002) discovered that California-based aerospace engineers, downsized as a result of economic restructuring, were not being hired by the growing electronics industry in need of engineers due in large part to stereotypes. They found that electronics employers believed that aerospace engineers, acculturated to bureaucratic organizations in which they did specialized work at inflated salaries, would not adapt well to the organizational culture of small firms in which individuals had to work in teams, communicate directly to production workers, wear multiple hats, respond to faster turnaround times and higher production levels, and receive lower wages. According to Thomas and Ong, employers used these stereotypes to screen workers. Intermediaries create a mechanism to remove these very real and very intangible barriers to work by better preparing the expectations of each side and facilitating the movement of individuals across sectors and jobs.

Finally, regions will need to think strategically about expanding the pool of talent. Expansion strategies enable a region to grow its current workforce in alignment with longer-term community and business goals. Expansion strategies go hand in hand with job and place development. Not only do expansion strategies build the workforce, they start to target the overall livability of place and its capacity to nurture people in a multitude of ways.

Credentials, intermediaries, and talent pool strategies tighten the alignment between supply and demand in the labor market at the system level. These features rest on the ability of a region to engage businesses and embed individuals in a web of opportunities for skill enhancement. Business engagement and a network of services provide the practical alignment between supply and demand that works at the individual and firm levels. It is these efforts that ultimately bring the system to scale and instill the cultural changes needed to develop a lifelong learning culture, the cognitive infrastructure for continuous skill building and adaptation.

In addition to the five components summarized earlier in this section, a sixth, the nature and composition of leadership within a region, also shapes the effectiveness of a human capital system. In what follows, we will look at each of these six areas, and summarize what we have learned about system building to date.

Laying the Infrastructure

A competitive human capital system is based on information flows that support labor force mobility and skill enhancement. Therefore, the infrastructure of a good workforce system targets those areas that improve and enhance the flow of information. That infrastructure is comprised of intermediaries, access to credentials, and talent expansion strategies because they provide the conduit that channels labor market information flows between the supply and demand sides of the market.

Intermediaries link the currently highly fragmented components of the system. They gather, interpret, and broker information to transform regional understandings of economic opportunities and workforce quality and to better align supply with demand. Intermediaries succeed not by providing information per se, but by offering better information through trust-based channels. It is their ability to insert information within a social context that allows them to succeed.

Specifically, the information brokerage role allows them to socially mediate information in a way that aligns expectations among the various players in the system to facilitate labor market exchange and to experiment with new approaches. When structured appropriately, they can change the terms of the labor market to open up new opportunities in the system. By serving as a bridge, they help mitigate risk for businesses to allow them to hire from previously untapped labor pools, diffuse training innovations throughout the system, and move comfortably across political jurisdictions.

In a strong workforce system, there will be different types of intermediaries holding different positions in a regional workforce system to meet the full range of business and individual labor market needs. Some will create entry points for the disadvantaged into mainstream labor markets, others will bring businesses firmly into the system, others will build career ladders for area residents, and yet others will be Web-based entities that connect knowledge workers to national and global markets. Education and training institutions, especially, but not limited to, community colleges, increasingly may take on this role. Some intermediaries may have to fill in spaces where neither the public nor the private sectors work effectively, such as in the provision of soft skills or the enhancement of remedial skills. Different intermediaries will work at different levels of the workforce system. WRTP, for example, enacted systemic, sectoral, and firm level changes. Bread and Butter Café targeted change at the individual level while its sector focus helped strengthen the local industry

However, having multiple intermediaries is insufficient to the task at hand. Many communities will be able to identify the presence of varied intermediaries within their borders. Intermediaries must work effectively as well. As chapter 3 has outlined, successful intermediaries have several common attributes, which are recapped below.

- They serve dual customers. For an intermediary to be effective, it first has to convince all parties involved that it meets and respects their needs. As we have seen, neither demand-side nor supply-side intermediaries function efficiently in isolation. Only by catering to the needs of both sides of the market can effective labor market marriages be made.
- They diversify and integrate funding sources to ensure their own survival and expand, innovate, and take on risk. Workforce funding is highly volatile and increasingly unreliable. Effective programs look for creative ways to finance their mission, and do not let financing dictate activities.
- They focus on outcomes rather than rules, making them adaptive and flexible.
- They provide access to the range of services that support workforce attachment.
- They focus on industrial sectors to gain a recognized expertise, which allows them to advocate for change.

- They recruit leaders to increase their access to firms with quality jobs. Involving leaders enables efforts to reach scope and scale, which contributes to cultural change and skill building, and lays the foundation for a lifelong learning culture to emerge.
- They ensure quality training and quality jobs, which builds trust on the demand side, allowing for the implementation of new opportunities and new approaches. Trust is a precondition for innovation and taking new risks.
- They collect and interpret labor market data from a variety of sources so they stay on top of trends and opportunities. Labor market skill needs are not fixed, even if economic sectors are relatively stable.
- They understand the market and know when it is necessary to use it to their advantage and when they should try to alter the terms of trade.
- They build formal and informal relationships throughout the community. Intermediary staff and leadership network extensively throughout the community, and it is through those relationships that they create paths to jobs, learn about new innovations, and advocate for new approaches.
- They develop and nurture their staffs who build relationships, work with clients, and deliver services. Human capital always matters.

Intermediaries broker information and craft it to meet societal objectives. They work on systemic, sector, individual, and firm levels. Intermediaries, however, work predominantly on a local or regional scale. Regions are part of a global system. To compete on this level, the regional labor pool must be recognized as globally competitive. Expanding credentialed skill standards is a necessary part of a competitive infrastructure because of the ability of credentials to signal, globally, the achievement of recognized standards.

The globalization of the labor market—especially the technical and scientific labor market—issues challenges to regions that do not provide large talent pools. Businesses troll for skills on a global level. The example of information technology (IT) certification suggests a scenario that opened up large opportunities for individuals, businesses, and entrepreneurs not only in the United States but also abroad. The bottlenecks emerging in the U.S. technical labor market have been addressed through increased training, international recruitment of labor, and outsourcing abroad, which has been facilitated by the global nature of IT certification. Although certification does enlarge the pool of applicants on a global scale, the increase in certified and recognized standards also ensures that the skills are here and businesses know how to find them. Ironically, improved standard-based certification and credentialing strategies support globalizing markets while also providing a response to globalization.

Credentials and certification facilitate individuals in moving more freely through the labor market, which helps individuals and businesses manage the volatility and uncertainty of twenty-first-century labor markets caused in part by a globalizing economy. Increasing the labor market mobility of individuals may seem like a counterintuitive strategy for a region, at first glance, given the overall competition for talent. Highly mobile labor markets are part of what makes the knowledge economy dynamic. Research has shown that the regular flow of knowledge workers among firms helps to explain the vitality of technology regions (Saxenian 1996). In fact, one of the results of the creation of the Eastern Idaho Forum for Information Technology was that it led to a more fluid labor market among participating firms, which businesses cited as a positive outcome (Pages and Garmise 2001). Businesses can benefit by strengthening individual labor market mobility because the end result is to increase the overall size and quality of skilled workers, providing steady access to top skills in both tight and loose labor markets.

Finally, credentialed skill standards provide the direct linkage between educational outcomes and private sector needs, which strengthens the alignment between supply and demand and supports individuals to be better entrepreneurs of their own career. For individuals to navigate an increasingly volatile labor market, they need the tools for career growth. Credentials are one of the main tools in a career development toolbox.

The movement toward an increased reliance on certification and credentials, spurred by globalizing markets, may also further increase the inequities growing within the population. Certification requires longer training time frames. Many low-skilled, low-income individuals may not be able to manage the financial cost of long training programs if not assisted throughout the process. Within the public training regime, such opportunities are increasingly unavailable. Increased focus on credentials requires complementary strategies and services to assist those for whom obtaining them will initially be a challenge.

While the need for credentialed skill standards is clear, implementing them is a substantial challenge. Currently, occupational skill standards are scattered and uncoordinated. Some standards have been developed on national and economic sector levels, while others exist only in local markets. Some are attached to certification; others are not. The lack of consistent standards creates bottlenecks in the labor market on local, national, and global levels. Overall, much work and many players have been engaged in developing and disseminating skill standards and certification with varied degrees of success. Ultimately, as we saw earlier, standards must have a national, and even global, base. At the community or regional level, there are several strategies and insights that can help communities propel this essential system infrastructure forward. These are listed below.

- Community colleges and other two-year vocational institutions represent core nodes for the development, dissemination, and accreditation of skill standards and certifications. They link the training and education systems, the training system to business concerns, and training to supportive services. They are central institutions for nurturing individual career path development, delivering technical skills, and integrating basic skills training into more developed occupational training. They often react more rapidly than universities in developing new certification needs and can borrow curriculum developed elsewhere, which allows for rapid implementation. Other intermediaries can play this role, but community colleges are especially well suited. The implication of this insight is that one of the best ways to strengthen and expand certification is through strengthening the capacities of regional community colleges and ensuring they are linked, through articulation agreements, to other education and training institutions to allow individuals to build on certification.
- There is often no need to reinvent the wheel. Communities can work with educational institutions, employer associations, unions, and other relevant parties to identify and implement preexisting standards developed at national, state, and industry levels (Ledebur et al. 2002).
- Business engagement is essential if standards are to gain broad acceptance and retain their relevance over time.
- Most training programs should be evaluated on their ability to provide certified competencies in transferable skills or their ability to place individuals on pathways toward this goal. Some individuals may need to enhance their basic skills and soft or workplace readiness skills before they can effectively obtain occupational standards. In fact, these issues need to be removed from the discussion of training and considered pretraining issues. These programs prepare individuals for entry into more rigorous, more skilled-based training and educational opportunities. They are no longer adequate and should not be seen as replacements for occupational and professional skills development. These basic skills are starting points, not endpoints.
- Partnerships are the infrastructure essential to moving this agenda forward. Certification based on standards is the outcome of partnerships between businesses and training/education entities and among training/ education entities.

Credentials and intermediaries increase the ability of regions to enhance the competitiveness of their labor pool but given the speed of change, the insufficient supply of talent, and the globalization of the economy, these alone will be insufficient. Regions must enact specific strategies to expand the talent pool. Talent expansion strategies are multifaceted and require a community to invest in the education of its workforce, the quality of place, and the development of talent-based jobs. Talent expansion is neither a jobs approach nor an amenities approach nor a training approach, but a full reconceptualization of the portfolio of strategies and tools needed to make a community economically dynamic. A brain gain/brain drain approach is too narrow to ensure the range of activities that comprise comprehensive human capital development. The end goal is to expand the overall pool of talented workers that live in a particular place. To achieve that goal, communities need an extensive range of talent expansion strategies, including:

- retention of local college students;
- retention of high-achieving college students;
- attraction of college graduates from outside the region;
- increase in the number of students entering college;
- assistance to those with some college in completing their degrees;
- bridge programs that support low-income and other disadvantaged students in obtaining college credit, with the goal of ultimately obtaining a degree;
- attraction of out-of-state students to local colleges and universities;
- increase in the numbers of students graduating with math, science, and engineering degrees;
- engagement of young professionals in social, economic, and civic networks; and
- creation of new understandings of the importance of place that nurtures the talents of workers; influences career choices; provides home, work, and play options that support varied lifestyle choices; and has in-built methods to adapt to new trends, needs, and insights about how the world works.

While this portfolio may seem overwhelming, this book has also shown that many civic, economic, social, and political groups may already be involved in these efforts. Talent expansion requires both grassroots efforts and community-wide systemic efforts. It is one of the fundamental insights of this book: talent attracts talent not only by chance but also by design. Talent is a community resource, which is why it makes sense to widen and deepen our access to it.

Therefore, if our goal is to increase the overall pool of talented workers, we must reach deeply into the population, expand college access, create job opportunities, support entrepreneurial efforts, and create effective mechanisms to access the voice of talent, and we must recognize that place is what nurtures, energizes, and influences talent development. As with most of the other elements of human capital strategies, this represents a fundamental cultural shift in our understanding of what makes economies dynamic and how our institutions need to work.

Bringing the System to Scale

Laying the infrastructure is the first step in system development. But we need to go further—we need to bring the system to scale and instill a lifelong learning mindset if a region is to build and retain a strong, competitive, and sustainable talent pool. To accomplish these objectives means changing the way individuals manage their careers and the way employers think about their workforce. Lifelong learning allows communities and regions to adapt over time as skill needs change, employers and jobs rise and fall, and technology continuously asks new things of us in economic, social, and political contexts. To reach scale and move a lifelong learning culture forward, we need to expand business engagement and ensure the existence of a spectrum of linked services that supports individual career development at any and all stages of the process.

To build this foundation, communities need to engage employers in three essential areas: as workforce program partners; as consumers of public training graduates; and as continuous investors in their own workforce. Achieving a lifelong learning system and creating and maintaining a competitive workforce will not happen if businesses themselves are not key investors in training on a regular basis. While many communities have found this element particularly challenging, there are a number of systemic elements that can be implemented to help communities move toward this goal.

First, a system needs access to a range of business voices. Simply having a majority on the Work Investment Board (WIB) is insufficient for the range of business needs within the system. Expanding voice means that organizations will need to reach out to sectors, implement interlocking board strategies, have multiple board and advisory board opportunities, have staff network at business-based functions, and develop personal relationships with business clients. For some communities, creating access to the business community may mean jumpstarting new organizations, institutions, or intermediaries such as business associations or modernization partnerships that can mobilize, articulate, and oversee common interests.

Second, training must be relevant, high quality, and where appropriate, linked to a range of services that support workforce attachment, including day care, health care, social services, and others. Building relationships with businesses will come to naught if a service cannot deliver the skills and talents businesses need from the workforce. In addition, only by providing quality skills can businesses be convinced of the value of training.

Third, sector-based strategies seem to be most effective for both organizing and delivering training. Sectors create a natural environment in which to identify and define skill standards, target appropriate business engagement, and develop industry and training expertise that the industry recognizes and validates. It is also a natural venue for developing and maintaining new cultures because they are disseminated through supply chains, professional networks, and labor market fluidity. Cultural change is brought to scale more easily through sectoral transformation rather than firm by firm.

Sector-based approaches also allow communities to reorient the nature of public training from individual to common initiatives that bring employers together to identify and develop skills as a competitive advantage (Atkinson 2001). While this may be uncomfortable, given the historic focus of workforce training on individual opportunity, it may be the only way to reach significant scale within the system. By reaching scale, we can really build skills and opportunities for all people. The key is to focus on scale and sustainability, not small innovations that may help individuals but do not affect the system or community as a whole (Giloth 2000).

Fourth, business engagement on all three dimensions is also contingent upon engaging business leadership. Starting with large firms not only brings a high level of jobs to the table, but their reputation can leverage other players and resources into the system. Their involvement signals to other firms, especially their contractors and suppliers, that training matters. Working with leaders not only brings significant voice into the system, but also leverages power and role models, which are crucial to instigating cultural changes and making any system work.

Even with the participation of business leadership, there may not be sufficient access to small businesses, which face the greatest impediments to implementing a training culture. Finding ways to access the voice of small businesses, and new and emerging sectors, may have to be a key focus in some communities. As we have seen, free or subsidized training is not always in itself an incentive, although it is an important tool in the toolbox. Ultimately, the goal of a human capital investment system is to encourage a cultural change so that more businesses more regularly invest in workforce training or provide incentives to their workforce to do so. It is not just the extent of employer engagement in the workforce system that matters, but an overall shift in how employers view, pursue, and embrace the values inherent in a lifelong learning framework.

Finally, businesses are made up of people. Businesses and people work best when relationships include a personalized element. With all this talk of systems and cultures and organizations, in most cases it is clear: working with businesses means establishing personal liaisons, which develops close working relationships, not just institutional linkages. To engage businesses, changes are required at the level of the system (e.g., WIBs), the sector (e.g., sector associations), and the firm (e.g., incentives and personal relationships).

Individuals also need to embrace a lifelong learning culture if regions are to build and retain their competitiveness in a global economy. Lifelong learning is a set of assumptions about the importance of continuously developing skills and talents and an extensive set of services that allows people of all ages and all walks of life to do so. As we have seen, creating a system that supports lifelong learning hinges on three factors: access to a spectrum of services providing the range of workforce needs to people at different stages of life; linkages among those programs so individuals and businesses can move fluidly between them; and a cultural reorientation from a focus on jobs to a focus on career path development. That continuum of services includes many services that already exist such as literacy, soft skills, child care, or access to mental health services, as well as new, innovative approaches to career financing and benefit portability (e.g., health care and pensions).

Having a range of services is a necessary but insufficient condition of lifelong learning. Those services must be connected in a way that fosters career growth. The most fundamental connection that needs to be made is a better integration of the training and education systems. The isolation of the two systems denies disadvantaged and transitional workers access to career paths and limits the overall pool of trained workers available to businesses. Lifelong learning and job development is tied to the attainment of the first degree and the accumulation of additional certification as individuals evolve. Those without degrees or on a pathway to their attainment are effectively left out of the system. If our goal is to expand the talent pool, then making sure that all people have access to career paths, rather than jobs, must be a central priority of the system. Upward mobility strategies for entry-level and disadvantaged individuals, therefore, are an important ingredient in a lifelong learning culture. Enhancing mobility rests on several efforts:

- engaging businesses to invest in entry level workers and articulate career pathways internal to the firm;
- removing barriers to workforce attachment that challenge many disadvantaged workers;

- creating pathways through the labor market that did not exist previously. For example, in Grand Rapids, Michigan, Burger King employees can move up into higher-paying manufacturing jobs, creating cross-sectoral paths for advancement (Giloth 2000);
- developing innovative financing schemes to support different types of skill acquisition. Each person is a unique package of public, business, and individual investment in his/her skill base;
- increasing resources to build up incumbent training, which is the linchpin of a lifelong learning system because it clearly marries the competitive needs of business with advancing opportunities for workers; and
- breaking down cultural barriers that make working together difficult in education, public, private, and community sectors.

The backbone of a lifelong learning system, career paths connected through certification options and cumulative college credit, will be built on four types of partnerships: between training programs and educational entities; between high schools and postsecondary schools; among postsecondary schools; and between public agents and educational institutions. Public agencies may need to serve as catalysts for increasing access to programs or making the linkages among educational institutions. Public agencies may need to think outside the box to achieve these goals, including working outside their jurisdictions to gain access to the educational resources available in other communities. Governments will be key players in stimulating new approaches to service provision.

Many communities nationwide can cite the existence of these different types of partnerships, but, in many cases, they provide only partial paths, such as an academic track between a community college and the local university, or a tech prep program, or a common nursing school. These are, however, the beginnings of more sophisticated relationships. The more these paths reflect the needs of the regional labor market, the stronger the system will be.

Creating people-centered places, ultimately, depends on the will and commitment of a region's leadership. Our review of communities and programs throughout the country suggests that leadership is required in four specific sectors: government, business, education, and the workforce itself. Each will be discussed below.

Leading the Change

As we have seen throughout this book, the government remains a critical player in any workforce system. Although it faces great pressure to limit its role, including strong budgetary pressures, the evidence shows that government involvement increases the scope and reach of training programs. Moreover, it strengthens overall business understanding of the value of training, which has helped stimulate increased private human capital investment, and assists small businesses in overcoming a range of barriers that limit their retraining efforts, such as poor management, negative prior training experiences, or fear of poaching (Creticos and Sheets 1989).

In addition, public agencies have been instrumental in creating partnerships with educational institutions and business associations in an attempt to find ways to increase educational and training options and to extend those options to a wider range of people. When necessary, public agencies have helped create new institutions and organizations in order to meet workforce and economic goals.

Finally, the growing gap between rich and poor, based on educational attainment, indicates that a public role overseeing issues of equity and accountability remains an important one. As the individual becomes increasingly responsible for attaining the increased education and training necessary to stay attached to the labor market, public activity may be an important component in finding ways to finance and stimulate those activities. In addition to financing, major questions of benefit provision and portability, child care affordability, and new methods and types of core service provision, are emerging as important pieces in the discussion of building a strong workforce. How and how much remains unclear, but these are questions that will have to be tackled in public life.

It is also clear that government action can establish disincentives to training, such as current rules and regulations present in the Workforce Investment Act. Ironically, this issue only emphasizes the importance of government activity. What government does or does not do, and the way in which it does it, influences the end result. Therefore, our goal is to involve government in a way that strengthens and prioritizes rather than deters human capital investment. If the government does not stand behind it, why would society take it on?

Equally, employers' activities are integral parts of the system because whatever they do also influences the quality of the local labor pool. Not only do we need employers and employers' intermediaries as program partners to articulate and regulate skill needs—employers are core investors in training, and their workforce policies, especially wages, benefits, and accessibility to upward mobility pathways, impact the quality of the labor force. Recruiting business leaders into system governance broadly across the region is a critical component of cultural change. For a new culture of lifelong learning to fully take root and reach scale, businesses must be

161

active participants. Recruiting business leadership into workforce issues should be a regional priority.

Education institutions are undoubtedly central players in the delivery of training and education. From the point of view of building a workforce system, communities are looking for institutions that are willing to take a leadership role, collaborate within the education and wider community, and readily adapt to and interact with the regional labor market. Simply having access to good colleges and universities, however, is insufficient for a good human capital investment system. As we discussed above, the institutions must be willing to work together to create fluid career paths among and between themselves. Within the education community, leadership from community colleges and universities is of particular importance.

Community colleges are the crucial link connecting the training and education systems. Most are engaged to varying degrees with the business community, have a range of scholarship programs available to support individuals, and are central to the provision of interim or additional certification and skill enhancement options that comprise the heart of lifelong learning. Many also have experience providing necessary support services that enable low-income and disadvantaged students to remain in school to obtain credentials.

Universities offer a different but equally critical leadership role. They create knowledge through their research activities, but, perhaps, more important, they disseminate knowledge and innovation through their teaching mission. One of their most important products is a well-trained graduate. The degree to which universities choose to engage with the regional community influences the quality of the regional labor force and the quality of life of a region. A university is also a large real estate owner, a provider of many cultural amenities, a substantial employer and user of local services, and a magnet for talent and new ideas. The engagement of university leadership is often considered a critical factor in determining the dynamism of the regional economy.

Finally, a good workforce system also needs access to the voice and participation of the workforce itself. This element is frequently neglected, but we must move it back to the center of our understanding of people-centered places. People invest in their own skills development and choose where to live, work, and play. They determine the quality of the local labor force. Part of the general neglect of trying to access the voice of the workforce comes from a broad trend away from unions. Where they are available or can be nurtured, unions are important partners in workforce activities. As we have seen in the health-care industry, they have a profound impact on the quality of jobs and the range of opportunities for advancement.

But unions represent only a small piece of the workforce voice in the twenty-first century. In particular, we need to ensure that the voices of talented young, highly mobile people, of young families, and of disadvantaged workers are also firmly engaged within the community. To expand the pool of talent, which all communities ultimately should do, we need to better understand how to develop talent, and how talented professionals make their career and location choices. From an economic development perspective, our knowledge in this area is very sketchy.

Accessing these voices is hard and often indirect. Community development organizations and intermediaries tend to provide voice to the needs of lower-income and disadvantaged individuals. Young professionals are organizing themselves using affinity and other social, economic, political, and civic networks. Although we are still learning about these efforts, our case study suggests that at the moment, they tap into a small segment of the target populations, often those that are already somewhat engaged. People-centered places listen to their people, while simultaneously trying to influence the choices of individuals to stay in school; to keep enhancing their skills; to become technically savvy; to create new businesses; to increase the number pursuing science and technology careers; and to play and live locally. Reaching out to and listening to the workforce are important parts of enhancing the capacity of the regional labor pool.

This chapter has reviewed what we have learned about creating a workforce system. The main function of a system, however, is to facilitate and enable things to happen. If the actual programs and projects are not designed well, the system alone will be inadequate to the task. Human capital development, therefore, is about good systems that support good programs. The end of the chapter will briefly summarize lessons based on a more grassroots-type scale: what we have learned about delivering good economic development and workforce programs.

In a comprehensive study, Lisbeth Schorr (1997) has identified seven attributes of highly successful social programs. These attributes, listed below, also mark good workforce programs.

- They are comprehensive, flexible, responsive, and persevering. Staff members take a flexible approach and do what needs to be done, not what rules say they can do.
- They deal with people as parts of neighborhoods and communities. They respond directly to local need.
- They have a long-term focus on prevention, a clear mission, and evolve over time as situations and clients change.
- They are well managed by an able, committed staff with identifiable skills.

- They are composed of well-trained staff members that receive adequate support to deliver high-quality services.
- They encourage their staff to build relationships and networks based on mutual trust and respect.
- They see children in the context of their families. While not generally applicable to adult workforce programs, this insight holds important lessons for at-risk youth programs and school reform agendas, in which parents are directly or indirectly stakeholders.

Schorr's attributes refer to general programmatic features of good social programs. Workforce development can no longer be considered just a social program, although many social elements need to be contained within the system. Workforce development is economic development, and there are also specific lessons that the case studies collectively illustrate about good workforce programs that contribute to economic revitalization. While many of these characteristics mirror our conclusions about good intermediaries, who usually deliver workforce programs, some go beyond that discussion. These characteristics are listed below.

- Effective workforce programs do not start with either a work-first or an education/training-first approach (Grubb 1996; Smith et al. 2002). Rather they offer a mix of services including placement, training, and post-training assistance, depending on the needs of the client and the demands of the local labor market.
- They implement dual customer strategies that recognize that both workers and employers must benefit measurably from training and education interventions.
- They use a case or account management framework for dealing with individuals and employers, to build personal relationships based on trust, rather than just institutional interactions.
- They are outcome oriented, using performance measures and evaluation strategies that are meaningful to individuals, employers, and the program itself. They deliver quality and expect quality.
- They are flexible, learning-based organizations committed to their mission, which includes social and economic returns.
- They have the right staff that understands the needs of their multiple client base and adapts gracefully to changing circumstances. Human capital always counts.
- They diversify their funding base to meet their goals, rather than adapt goals to meet funding requirements. Diversified funding allows them to expand programs and adapt to changing needs.

- They are well networked to the range of services needed to deliver and ensure quality. Good programs absorb the risk and are accountable for workforce outcomes.

Conclusions

We now are in the midst of creating fundamental new understandings of place that are centered on livability and the creativity of the human environment, rather than on the industrial or commercial environment. The knowledge economy reorients our understanding of place from a set of physical attributes to a more complex set of physical, human, social, and economic attributes that should to be evaluated in terms of their impact on human creativity, health, and productivity.

We know that knowledge transfers best through human interaction, making the region the natural environment for human capital development. We have an opportunity that is in some ways unprecedented in our understanding of economic development. There has been a natural fissure in our desire for economic development to be distributive, targeting benefits to those most in need, and our need for it to be generative, creating new opportunities and sources of prosperity where none existed before. A focus on people allows us to seal that rift. Expanding the talents, energies, and innovative capacities of individuals does both. We can meet goals of equity and overall prosperity, if we focus on the assets and potential of our people.

We have a lot of work to do. Systemic change is not easy. But most communities have started down this path and have plans to continue the journey. Human capital development is multifaceted and will take time and a great deal of learning. It requires us to be a different kind of place: one that puts the pursuit of equity alongside the pursuit of wealth; one that makes enhancing the talents of all people, not just a select few, as the overarching priority; and one that adapts the character, culture, and amenities of place to serve the lifestyles of a diverse range of people, all of whom contribute to the health and well-being of their shared community. Ultimately, human capital development is really about looking around the community and saying, "Here we do have all we need to be an exciting, dynamic, sustainable, and just place. It is all here—in our people."

References

Acredolo, Linda, and Susan Goodwyn. 2000. *Baby Minds.* New York: Bantam Books.

Adams, Bruce. 1998. "Cleveland: The Partnership City." In *Boundary Crossers: Case Studies of How Ten of America's Metropolitan Regions Work.* College Park: University of Maryland, Academy of Leadership. www.Academy.umd.edu/Publications/Boundary/CaseStudies/bcscleveland.htm (accessed March 2005).

Adelman, Clifford. 2000. *A Parallel Postsecondary Universe: The Certification System in Information Technology.* Washington, DC: Office of Educational Research and Improvement, U.S. Department of Education.

Atkinson, Robert. 2001. *Building Skills for the New Economy: A Policymaker's Handbook—A Progressive Policy Institute Report.* Washington, DC: Progressive Policy Institute.

Atkinson, Robert, and Paul Gottlieb. 2001. *The Metropolitan New Economy Index.* Washington, DC: Progressive Policy Institute.

Autor, David. 2000. "Why Do Temporary Help Firms Provide Free General Skills Training?" Working Paper 7637. Cambridge, MA: National Bureau of Economic Research.

Autor, David; Frank Levy; and Richard Murnane. 2003. "The Skill Content of Recent Technological Change: An Empirical Exploration." *Quarterly Journal of Economics* 118, no. 4: 1279–334.

Axelrod, Robert. 1984. *The Evolution of Cooperation.* New York: Penguin Books.

Bailey, Thomas, ed. 1995. *Learning to Work: Employer Involvement in School to Work Transition Programs.* Washington, DC: Brookings Institution.

———. 1995a. "Incentives for Employer Participation in School-to-Work Programs." In *Learning to Work: Employer Involvement in School to Work Transition Programs,* ed. Bailey, 14–26. Washington, DC: Brookings Institution.

Bailey, Thomas; Yukari Matsuzuka; James Jacobs; Vanessa Smith Morest; and Katherine Hughes. 2003. *Institutionalization and Sustainability of the National Science Foundation's Advanced Technological Education Program.* New York: Community College Research Center.

Bennici, Frank; Stephen Mangum; and Andrew Sum. 2000. "The Economic, Demographic, and Social Context of Future Employment and Training Programs." In *Improving the Odds: Increasing the Effectiveness of Publicly Funded Training,* ed. Burt Barnow and Christopher King, 19–48. Washington, DC: Urban Institute Press.

Berman, Jay. 2001. "Industry Output and Employment Projections to 2010." *Monthly Labor Review* (November): 39–56.

REFERENCES

Berry, Dan. 2004. "Creating and Sustaining a Coherent Voice for Employers in Workforce Development: The Cleveland Experience." In *Workforce Intermediaries for the Twenty-First Century*, ed. Robert Giloth, 193–215. Philadelphia, PA: Temple University Press.

Bosworth, Brian. 1996. *Using Regional Economic Analysis in Urban Jobs Strategies*. Cambridge, MA: Regional Technology Strategies.

Brown, Carol. 2004. "All Learning Is Learning: The Role of Credentials and Non-Credit Education in Community Colleges." Presented at the Community College Research Center Seminar All Learning Is Learning: The Role of Credentials and Non-credit Education in Community Colleges, New York, April 22. www.tc.Columbia.edu/ccrc/SeminarSeries.htm (accessed March 2005).

Buck, Maria. 2002. *Charting New Territory: Early Implementation of the Workforce Investment Act*. New York: Public/Private Ventures.

Building Engineering and Science Talent. 2004. "Report Identifies Design Principles for Success in Educating Scientists and Engineers." San Diego, CA. Press Release, February 14.

Business-Higher Education Forum. 2001. *Investing in People: Developing All of America's Talent on Campus and in the Workplace*. Washington, DC.

Carnevale, Anthony. 2004. "What Will Work Be Like in the Next Decade?" Webcast text. www.nccte.org/webcasts/description.aspx?wc=103 (accessed March 2005).

Carnevale, Anthony, and Richard Fry. 2000. *Crossing the Great Divide: Can We Achieve Equity When Generation Y Goes to College*. Princeton, NJ: Educational Testing Service.

Casson, Mark. 1995. *Entrepreneurship and Business Culture: Studies in the Economics of Trust*. Vol. 1. Brookfield, VT: Edward Elgar.

Castells, Manuel. 1996. *The Information Age: Economy, Society and Culture. Volume 1: The Rise of the Network Society*. Malden, MA: Blackwell.

CEO Forum on Education and Technology. 2001. *Key Building Blocks for Student Achievement in the 21st Century: Assessment, Alignment, Accountability, Access and Analysis*. Washington, DC.

Charity Navigator. 2004. "Charity Navigator Rating—Cleveland Scholarship Program." www.charitynavigator.org/index.cfm/bay/search.summary/orgid/3526.htm (accessed March 2005).

Clarke, Susan, and Gary Gaile. 1998. *The Work of Cities*. Minneapolis: University of Minnesota Press.

Cleveland Scholarship Programs. 2003. *Annual Report*. Cleveland, OH.

———. 2004. *Fact Sheet*. Cleveland, OH.

———. 2005. "Cleveland Scholarship Programs, Inc." www.cspohio.org/programs/index.html (accessed March 2005).

Clymer, Carol. 2003. *By Design: Engaging Employers in Workforce Development Organizations: A Publication of Public/Private Ventures Prepared for the Rockefeller Foundation's Initiative on Organizational Capacity Building*. New York: Public/Private Ventures.

Committee for Economic Development. 1999. *New Opportunities for Older Workers*. New York: Committee for Economic Development, Research and Policy Committee.

Conway, Carol. 2002. *Leave No Stone Unturned: A Human Capital Approach to Workforce Development*. Research Triangle Park, NC: Southern Growth Policies Board. www.southern.org/pubs/pubs.shtml#work (accessed March 2005).

Cooke, Daniel. 2002. "Abilene's Tech to Play Big Role in National Software Research." *Abilene Reporter-News*. www.reporternews.com (accessed August 2002).

Cortright, Joseph. 2001. *New Growth Theory, Technology and Learning: A Practitioner's Guide*. Washington, DC: U.S. Economic Development Administration.

Council for Urban Economic Development. 1999. *Performance Monitoring: Achieving Excellence in Economic Development*. Washington, DC: Council for Urban Economic Development.

Council for Urban Economic Development and the Indianapolis Private Industry Council. 1998. *Help Wanted: Building a Competitive Workforce—Conference*. Washington, DC.

Council on Competitiveness. Data Central. 2001a. "Skill Requirements Are Increasing." www.compete.org (accessed May 2002).

———. 2001b. "Without a High School Education, Workers Are Far More Likely to Be Unemployed and in Poverty." www.compete.org (accessed May 2002).

———. 2005. "Many Companies are Providing Remedial Education." www.compete.org (accessed March 2005).

Crawford, Carol, and Carol Romero, with Burt Barnow. 1991. *A Changing Nation—Its Changing Labor Force: National Commission for Employment Policy Research Report 91–04*. Washington, DC: National Commission for Employment Policy.

Creticos, Peter, and Robert Sheets. 1989. *State Financed Workplace-Based Retraining Programs: A Joint Study of the National Commission for Employment Policy and the National Governors' Association, Research Report #89–01*. Washington, DC: National Commission for Employment Policy.

———. 1990. *Evaluating State-Financed Workplace-Based Retraining Study: A Report on the Feasibility of a Business Screening and Performance Outcome Evaluation System. A Joint Study of the National Commission for Employment Policy and the National Governors' Association, Research Report #89–08*. Washington, DC: National Commission for Employment Policy.

Davis, Shara; Larry Ledebur; Rob Stuart; and Jim Roby. 2001. *Supply of Information Technology Specialists Among Northeast Ohio's System of Higher Education*. Cleveland: Northeast Ohio Research Consortium of the Ohio Urban University Program.

Department of Labor Employment and Training Administration. 1999. *State Financed and Customized Training Programs*. Washington, DC. http://wdr.doleta.gov/opr.fulltext/stat-es.pdf (accessed March 2005).

Elliott, Mark; Anne Roder; Elisabeth King; and Joseph Stillman. 2001. *Gearing Up: An Interim Report of the Sectoral Employment Initiative*. New York: Public/Private Ventures.

Employment Policy Foundation. 2001. "Economic Slowdown Highlights Critical Importance of Skills." www.epf.org/pubs/newsletters/2001/et20011127.pdf (accessed March 2005).

Fernandez, Roberto M.; Emilio J. Castilla; and Paul Moore. 2000. "Social Capital at Work: Networks and Employment at a Phone Center." *American Journal of Sociology* 105 (March): 1288–356.

Fitzgerald, Joan. 2004. "Moving the Workforce Intermediary Agenda Forward." *Economic Development Quarterly* 18, no. 1: 3–9.

Fitzgerald, Joan, and Virginia Carlson. 2000. "Ladders to a Better Life." *American Prospect Online*. www.prospect.org/web/page.ww?section=root&name=ViewPrint&articleId=4334 (accessed March 2005).

169

Fitzgerald, Joan, and Wendy Patton. 1997. "Race, Job Training and Economic Development: Barriers to Racial Equity in Program Planning." In *African Americans and Post-Industrial Labor Markets*, ed. James B. Stewart, 371–90. New Brunswick, NJ: Transaction.

Florida, Richard. 2002. *The Rise of the Creative Class and How It's Transforming Work, Leisure, Community and Everyday Life.* New York: Basic Books.

Foster-Bey, John, and Lynette Rawlings. 2002. *Can Targeting Industries Improve Earnings for Welfare Recipients Moving from Welfare to Work?: Preliminary Findings.* Washington, DC: Urban Institute.

Francese, Peter. 2002. "The American Workforce." *American Demographics* (February): 40–41.

Frazis, Harley; Mary Gittleman; Michael Horrigan; and Mary Joyce. 1998. "Results from the 1995 Survey of Employer-Provided Training." *Monthly Labor Review* (June): 3–13.

General Accounting Office. 2001a. *Workforce Investment Act: New Requirements Create Need for More Guidance: Statement of Sigurd Nilsen, Director.* Washington, DC.

———. 2001b. *Workforce Investment Act: Better Guidance to Address Concerns Over New Requirements.* Washington, DC.

Giloth, Robert. 1998. *Jobs and Economic Development: Strategies and Practice.* Thousand Oaks, CA: Sage.

———. 2000. "Learning from the Field: Economic Growth and Workforce Development in the 1990s." *Economic Development Quarterly* 14, no. 4: 340–59.

———, ed. 2004a. *Workforce Intermediaries for the Twenty-First Century.* Philadelphia, PA: Temple University Press.

———. 2004b. "Introduction: A Case for Workforce Intermediaries." In *Workforce Intermediaries for the Twenty-First Century*, ed. Giloth, 3–30. Philadelphia, PA: Temple University Press.

Glaeser, Edward, and Jesse Shapiro. 2001. "Is There A New Urbanism? The Growth of U.S. Cities in the 1990s." Working Paper 8357. Cambridge, MA: National Bureau of Economic Research. www.nber.org/papers/w8357 (accessed March 2005).

Goldberg, Debbie. 2004. "Philadelphia Aims to Reverse Brain Drain." *Washington Post*, April 2: A3.

Gopnick, Alison; Andrew Meltzoff; and Patricia Kuhl. 1999. *The Scientist in the Crib: What Early Learning Tells Us About the Mind.* New York: Perennial.

Gottlieb, Paul. 2001. *The Problem of Brain Drain in Ohio and Northeastern Ohio: What Is It? How Severe Is It? What Should We Do About It?* Cleveland, OH: Center for Regional Economic Issues.

———. 2004. *Labor Supply Pressures and the "Brain Drain": Signs from Census 2000.* Washington, DC: Brookings Institution, Living City Census Series. www.brookings.edu/metro/publications/20040116_gottlieb.htm (March 2005).

Gottlieb, Paul, and Michael Fogarty. 2003. "Educational Attainment and Metropolitan Growth." *Economic Development Quarterly*, no. 4 (November): 325–36.

Granovetter, Mark. 1995. *Getting a Job: A Study of Contacts and Careers.* 2d ed. Chicago: University of Chicago Press.

Grubb, W. Norton. 1996. *Learning to Work: The Case for Reintegrating Job Training and Education.* New York: Russell Sage.

Hansen, Susan; Carolyn Ban; and Leonard Huggins. 2003. "Explaining the 'Brain Drain' From Older Industrial Cities: The Pittsburgh Region." *Economic Development Quarterly* 17: 132–47.

170

Harrison, Bennett, and Marcus Weiss. 1998. *Workforce Development Networks: Community-Based Organizations and Regional Alliance.* Thousand Oaks, CA: Sage.

Herman, Bruce. 2001. "How High-Road Partnerships Work." *Social Policy* 31, no. 3. www.socialpolicy.org/recent_issues/SP01/sp-spring-01–herman2.html (accessed September 2003).

Hirschman, Albert. 1970. *Exit, Voice, and Loyalty: Responses to Decline in Firms, Organizations and States.* Cambridge, MA: Harvard University Press.

Holzer, Harry; Steven Raphael; and Michael Stoll. 2003. *Employers in the Boom: How Did the Hiring of Unskilled Workers Change During the 1990s?* Urban Institute White Paper. Washington, DC. www.urban.org/uploadedpdf/410780_boompaper.pdf (accessed March 2005).

Houghton, Ted, and Tony Proscio. 2001. *Hard Work on Soft Skills: Creating a Culture of Work in Workforce Development.* Philadelphia, PA: Public/Private Ventures.

(i)Cleveland. 2005. "iCleveland About Us." www.gradscouncil.com/about_us/about_us.cfm (accessed March 2005).

Imai, Ken-ichi. 1989. "Evolution of Japan's Corporate and Industrial Networks." In *Industrial Dynamics: Technological, Organizational and Structural Changes in Industries and Firms,* ed. Bo Carlsson, 123–56. Boston: Kluwer Academic.

Jacobs, Jim. 2004. "Learning in the Knowledge Economy: Credit and Non-credit Courses." Presentation at the Community College Research Center Seminar All Learning Is Learning: The Role of Credentials and Non-credit Education in Community Colleges. New York, April 22. www.tc.Columbia.edu/ccrc/SeminarSeries.htm (accessed March 2005).

Kasinitz, P., and Rosenberg, J. 1993. "Why Enterprise Zones Will Not Work." *City Journal* 3: 63–71.

Kazis, Richard. 2004. "What Do Workforce Intermediaries Do?" In *Workforce Intermediaries for the Twenty-First Century,* ed. Robert Giloth, 73–92. Philadelphia, PA: Temple University Press.

Kazis, Richard; Heath Prince; and Jerry Rubin. 2003. *Employer Use of the Publicly Funded Workforce Development System: Perceptions of What's Working and What's Not and Recommendations for Improvement.* Boston, MA: Jobs for the Future.

Kelly, Kevin. 1998. *New Rules for the New Economy: 10 Radical Strategies for a Connected World.* New York: Penguin Books.

Kent State University. 2003. *College Graduate Retention Initiative Research Report.* Canton, OH: Kent State University.

Kirsch, Irwin; Ann Jungeblut; Lynn Jenkins; and Andrew Kolstad. 2002. *Adult Literacy in America: A First Look at the Results of the National Adult Literacy Survey.* Washington, DC: National Center for Education Statistics.

Knowledge Industry Partnership. 2005. "KIP Online." www.kiponline.org/homef.htm (accessed March 2005).

Krieg, Randall. 1991. "Human Capital Selectivity in Interstate Migration." *Growth and Change* 22, no. 1: 68–76.

Laufer, Jessica, and Sian Winship. 2004. "Perception vs. Reality: Employer Attitudes and the Rebranding of Workforce Intermediaries." In *Workforce Intermediaries for the Twenty-First Century,* ed. Robert Giloth, 216–40. Philadelphia, PA: Temple University Press.

Ledebur, Larry; Jon Shelton; Greg Browning; Patricia Smith; Joan Wills; Barbara Kaufman; Shara Davis; and Peter Creticos. 2002. "State Strategies for

Workforce Development Through Skills Standards and Worker Credentialing." Prepared for the Governor's Workforce Policy Board, State of Ohio. Cleveland, OH: Urban Center, Levin College of Urban Affairs, Cleveland State University (May 31).

Leete, Laura; Chris Benner; Manuel Pastor Jr. ; and Sarah Zimmerman. 2004. "Labor Market Intermediaries [LMI] in the Old and New Economies: A Survey of Worker Experiences in Milwaukee and Silicon Valley." In *Workforce Intermediaries for the Twenty-First Century*, ed. Robert Giloth, 263–90. Philadelphia, PA: Temple University Press.

Lerman, Robert; Stephanie Riegg; and Harold Salzman. 2000. "The Role of Community Colleges in Expanding the Supply of Information Technology Workers." Paper prepared for the U.S. Department of Labor, Washington, DC: Urban Institute. www.urban.org/uploadedpdf/comm_colleges.pdf (accessed March 2005).

Livingston, Sandra. 2003a. "Brain Drain: Grads with Advanced Degrees Are Flowing Out of Ohio." *Plain Dealer*, February 23. www.cleveland.com (accessed February 2003).

———. 2003b. "Magnet for minds." *Plain Dealer*, February 24. www.cleveland.com (accessed February 2003).

Mahlman, Robert, and James Austin. Undated. "Evaluating Credentialing Systems: Implications for Career-Technical Educators: Commissioned Paper for the National Skill Standards Board." Columbus, OH: Center on Education and Training for Employment. www.cetc.org/wpapers/pdfdocs/Evaluating_credentialing_systems_for_CTE.pdf (accessed March 2005).

Mathur, Anita, with Judy Reichle, Julie Strawn, and Chuck Wisely. 2004. *From Jobs to Careers: How California Community College Credentials Pay Off for Welfare Participants.* Washington, DC: Center for Law and Social Policy.

Mathur, Vijay. 1999. "Human Capital-Based Strategy for Regional Economic Development." *Economic Development Quarterly* 13, no. 3: 203–16.

Michigan Economic Development Corporation. 2004. *Michigan Cool Cities Survey: Summary of Findings.* Lansing.

Mills, Jack, and Richard Kazis. 1999. "Business Participation in Welfare-to-Work: Lessons from the United States." Paper prepared for the Business Forum on Welfare-to-Work: Lessons from America, London, January 20–21. Boston, MA: Jobs For the Future.

National Aeronautics and Space Administration. 2005. "NASA—Science, Engineering, Mathematics and Aerospace Academy." www.nasa.gov/centers/glenn/education/SEMMA_GRC.html (accessed March 2005).

National Alliance of Business. 2001. "Skilled Workforce Shortage Could Cripple U.S. Economy: Business and Education Must Address Worker Quality and Quantity." *WorkAmerica* 18, no. 6: 1–5.

National Center for Health Workforce Information and Analysis. 2001. *The Health Care Workforce in Ten States: Education, Practice and Policy.* Washington, DC: U.S. Department of Health and Human Services, Health Resources and Services Administration.

National Center on the Educational Quality of the Workforce. 1995. *The Other Shoe: Education's Contribution to the Productivity of Establishments.* Philadelphia.

National Commission on Excellence in Education. 1983. *A Nation at Risk: The Imperative for Educational Reform.* Washington, DC: U.S. Government Printing Office.

National Science and Technology Council. 2000. *Ensuring A Strong U.S. Scientific,*

REFERENCES

Technical, and Engineering Workforce in the 21st Century: A Report of the Committee on Science of the National Science and Technology Council's Interagency Working Group on the U.S. Scientific, Technical, and Engineering Workforce of the Future. Washington, DC.

National Science Board. 2003. *The Science and Engineering Workforce: Realizing America's Potential, NSV 03–69.* Arlington, VA: National Science Foundation.

———. 2004. *Science and Engineering Indicators.* Vol. 1. Arlington, VA: National Science Foundation.

National Skill Standards Board Institute. 2005. "National Skill Standards Board Institute." www.nssb.org/history.cfm (accessed March 2005).

Nelson, G. 1999. "Science Literacy for All in the 21st Century." *Education Leadership* 57, no. 2: 14–16.

Northeast Ohio Council on Higher Education. 2004. *Fact Book.* Fairlawn.

Ohio College Access Network. 2005. "Background." www.ohiocan.org/OCAN/ItemPage.aspx?groupid=1&id=76 (accessed March 2005).

Olson, Mancur. 1965. *The Logic of Collective Action.* Cambridge, MA: Harvard University Press.

Orlando Business Journal. 2004. "Volusia Higher Education Consortium Launches Course-Exchange Program." December 10. http://orlando.bizjournals.com/orlando/stories/2004/12/06/daily40.html (accessed December 2004).

Osborne, David, and Ted Gaebler. 1992. *Reinventing Government: How the Entrepreneurial Spirit Is Transforming the Public Sector.* New York: Plume.

Osterman, Paul. 1995. "Involving Employers in School-to-Work Programs" In Bailey 1995, 75–87.

———. 1999. *Securing Prosperity—The American Labor Market: How It Has Changed and What to Do About It.* Princeton, NJ: Princeton University Press.

Pages, Erik, and Shari Garmise. 2001. *Building Entrepreneurial Networks.* Washington, DC: National Commission on Entrepreneurship.

Patel, Nisha; LeaAnne DeRigne; Mark Greenberg; and Andy Van Kleunen. 2004. *Side-by-Side Comparison of Title I Provisions in House and Senate WIA Reauthorization Bills.* Washington, DC: Center for Law and Social Policy and the Workforce Alliance.

Pindus, Nancy; Patrice Flynn; and Demetra Smith Nightingale. 1995. *Improving the Upward Mobility of Low-Skill Workers: The Case of the Health Industry.* Washington, DC: Urban Institute.

Poczik, Robert. 1995. "Work-based Education and School Reform." In Bailey 1995, 56–74.

Porter, Michael. 1990. *The Competitive Advantage of Nations.* New York: Free Press.

Prince, Heath. 2003. *Retention and Advancement in the Retail Industry: A Career Ladder Approach.* Boston: Jobs for the Future.

The Random House Dictionary. Concise Edition. 1980. New York.

Roberts, Brandon. 2003. "Empower Baltimore Management Corporation's Surgical Technician Skills Training Program." Report prepared for Empower Baltimore Management Corporation. Baltimore, MD: Empower Baltimore Management Corporation.

Romer, P.M. 1992. "Two Strategies for Economic Development: Using Ideas and Producing Ideas." *Proceedings of the World Bank Annual Conference on Development Economics* 63.

Rosenbaum, J. 2001. *Beyond College for All: Career Paths for the Forgotten Half.* New York: Russell Sage Foundation.

Rosenfeld, Stuart A. 1998. *Community College/Cluster Connections: Specialization and Competitiveness in the U.S. and Europe.* New York: Community College Research Center, Columbia University.

Saxenian, AnnaLee. 1996. *Regional Advantage: Culture and Competition in Silicon Valley and Route 128.* Cambridge, MA: Harvard University Press.

Schorr, Lisbeth B. 1997. *Common Purpose: Strengthening Families and Neighborhoods to Rebuild America.* New York: Anchor Books Doubleday.

Schumpeter, Joseph. 1976. *Capitalism, Socialism and Democracy.* New York: Harper Torchbooks.

Secretary's Commission on Achieving Necessary Skills (SCANS). 1991. *What Work Requires of Schools: A SCANS Report for America 2000.* Washington, DC: Department of Labor.

Smith, Whitney; Jenny Wittner; Robin Spence; and Andy Van Kleunen. 2002. *Skills Training Works: Examining the Evidence.* Washington, DC: Workforce Alliance.

Stark Education Partnership. Undated. *College Graduate Retention: An Initiative Planning Document for Medina, Portage, Summit, Stark and Wayne Counties.* Canton, OH.

Support and Training Result in Valuable Employees (STRIVE) New York. 2005. "STRIVE New York Free Job Training and Free Job Placement." www.strivenewyork.org/strive.html (accessed March 2005).

Tao, Fumiyo; George Richard; Hope Tarr; and Jennifer Wheeler. 1992. *Upward Mobility Programs in the Service Sector for Disadvantaged and Dislocated Workers. Volume I: Final Report.* Washington, DC: National Commission for Employment Policy.

Texas Tech University. 2005. "Texas Tech University—Pathways Program." www.depts.ttu.edu/pathway/ (accessed March 2005).

Thomas, Ward, and Paul Ong. 2002. "Barriers to Rehiring of Displaced Workers: A Study of Aerospace Engineers in California." *Economic Development Quarterly* 16, no. 2: 167–78.

Thurow, Lester. 1985. *The Zero Sum Solution: Building a World-Class American Economy.* New York: Simon and Schuster.

———. 1999. *Building Wealth: The New Rules for Individuals, Companies and Nations in a Knowledge-Based Economy.* New York: HarperBusiness.

Tournatzky, Louis; Denis Gray; Stephanie Tarant; and Julie Howe. 1998. *Where Have All the Students Gone? A Benchmarking Report of the Southern Technology Council.* Research Triangle Park, NC: Southern Growth Polices Board.

Tournatzky, Louis; Denis Gray; Stephanie Tarant; and Cathy Zimmer. 2001. *Who Will Stay and Who Will Leave? A Report of the Southern Technology Council.* Research Triangle Park, NC: Southern Growth Polices Board.

Townsend, Angela. 2004. "Area Alumni Help Fight 'Brain Drain.'" *Plain Dealer*, July 24, www.cleveland.com. (accessed July 2004).

Valdez, William. 1998. *Help Wanted: Building a Competitive Workforce: Conference Proceedings.* Washington, DC: Council for Urban Economic Development and the Indianapolis Private Industry Council.

Van Opstal, Deborah. 2001. "The Skills Imperative: Talent and U.S. Competitiveness." *Issues in Science and Technology On Line* (Fall): 1–12. www.nap.edu/issues/18.1/p_van_opstal.html (accessed March 2005).

Vickers, Margeret. 1995. "Employer Participation in School-to-Work Programs: The Changing Situation in Europe." In Bailey 1995, 26–44.

174

REFERENCES

Waits, Mary Jo. 2000. "Presentation to the Council for Urban Economic Development Annual Conference." Atlanta, GA (September 11).

Wilson, William Julius. 1996. *When Work Disappears: The World of the New Urban Poor.* New York: Vintage Books.

Wood, J.E.; F. Frenzel; F. Lavender; B. Matar; and D. Hata. 2000: "Computer-based Cross-training for Technicians and Engineers for Semiconductor Manufacturing." Paper presented at the sixth Annual Conference on Advanced Technological Education in Semiconductor Manufacturing. (ATESM), Orlando, FL (July 31–August 4).

Workforce Organizations for Regional Collaboration. 2005. "Workforce Organizations for Regional Collaboration." www.worconline.org (accessed March 2005).

Zandniapour, Lily, and Maureen Conway. 2001. "Closing the Gap: How Sectoral Workforce Development Programs Benefit the Working Poor." *SEDLP Research Report*, no. 2. Washington, DC: Aspen Institute.

Program Interview List

Augustine, Kathy. Executive Director. Hard-Hatted Women. Telephone interview. Cleveland, OH. September 2003.

Becton, Marianne. Manager. External Affairs. Verizon. Personal interview. Washington, DC. January 2002.

Bell, Diane. President/CEO. Empower Baltimore Management Corporation. Telephone interview. Baltimore, MD. October 2003.

Clements, Tim. Host Committee Chair/Secretary. Bulldogs on the Cuyahoga. Telephone interview. Cleveland, OH. March 2004.

Cruver, Sue. Workforce Coordinator. The WorkSource. Telephone interview. Houston, TX. October 2003.

DiGeronimo, J.J. Founder. Techstudents.net. Telephone interview. Cleveland, OH, September 2004.

Emmerth, Ilona. Vice President/Treasurer. Bulldogs on the Cuyahoga. Telephone interview. Cleveland, OH. March 2004.

Feldman, Cheryl. Director. District 1199C Training and Upgrading Fund. Telephone interview. Philadelphia, PA. January 2004.

George, Pam. Program Officer. Cleveland Foundation Summer Internship Program. Personal interview. Cleveland, OH. March 2004.

Guthrie, Mark. Winstead Sechrest & Minick P.C. Board Representative, Chair of Procurement Committee. The WorkSource. Telephone interview. Houston, TX. March 2004.

Hanné, Bob. Chef and Trainer. Bread & Butter Café, America's Second Harvest of Coastal Georgia. Telephone interview. Savannah, GA. November 2003.

Happach, Donna. Program Director. America's Second Harvest of Coastal Georgia. Telephone interview. Savannah, GA. October 2003.

Hart-Wright, Christine. Executive Director. STRIVE DC, Inc. Personal interview. Washington, DC. March 2002.

Hickman, Chuck. Executive Director. Northeast Council on Higher Education. Personal communication. Fairlawn, OH. March 2005.

Holder, Kim. Program Chairperson. Leaders of Tomorrow Program. Telephone interview. Cleveland, OH. May 2004.

Kilbury, Courtney. Internal Communications and Marketing Coordinator. Cleveland Scholarships Program. Personal interview. Cleveland, OH. April 2004.

Jefferson, Mike. Director. Center for Employment and Training, The Crispus Attucks Association. Telephone interview. York, PA. September 2003.

Klein, Paul. Director. Career Services, Cleveland State University. Personal communication. Cleveland, OH. December 2003.

Latiak, Hope. Manager of Institutional Advancement. Cleveland Scholarships Program. Personal interview. Cleveland, OH. April 2004.

Love, Karen. Health Industry Liaison. The WorkSource. Telephone interview. Houston, TX. March 2004.

Maloy, Dennis. President/CEO. America's Second Harvest of Coastal Georgia. Telephone interview. Savannah, GA. December 2003.

Manke, Bridget. Manager. (i)Cleveland. Personal interview. Cleveland, OH. April 2004.

Parker, Eric. Executive Director. Wisconsin Regional Training Partnership. Telephone interview. Milwaukee, WI. October 2003.

Polverine, Denise. Editor-in-chief. Cleveland.com. Electronic interview. Cleveland, OH. March 2004.

Porter, Naquetta. Manager of Advisory Services. Cleveland Scholarships Program. Electronic interview. Cleveland, OH. April 2004.

Richmond-Hopes, Shelly. Training Coordinator. Hard-Hatted Women. Telephone interview. September 2003.

Shah, Baiju. President. Bulldogs on the Cuyahoga. Telephone interview. Cleveland, OH. March 2004.

Shingleton, Kathy. Chief Human Resource Officer. University of Texas Medical Branch. Board Representative. The WorkSource. Telephone interview. Houston, TX. March 2004.

Simko, Michelle. Job Developer. Hard-Hatted Women. Telephone interview. Cleveland, OH. September 2003.

Singleton, Margaret. Vice President of Economic and Workforce Development. D.C. Chamber of Commerce. Personal interview. Washington, D.C. January 2002.

Stadler, Marilyn. Workforce Division Manager, Employer Services. The WorkSource. Telephone interview. Houston, TX. March 2004.

Thomas, Chuck. Executive Director. The William Goodling Regional Advanced Skills Center. Telephone interview. York, PA. October 2003.

Tinker, Alton. President. Cleveland Chapter of National Black MBAs. Personal interview. Cleveland, OH. April 2004.

Wood, John E. Principal Investigator. Manufacturing Engineering Program, University of New Mexico. Telephone interview. Albuquerque, NM. September 2003.

Index

Accountability, 39–40, 51
Adelman, Clifford, 68–69, 71
Affinity networks, 93, 98, 106–107
Aging of population, 16–17
America's Second Harvest, 81, 86n
Atkinson, Robert, 16
Autor, David, 48

Baby-boom/bust period, 17
Bell, Diane, 124
Bergholz, David, 98
Brain drain/gain problems, 87, 156
Bread and Butter Café, 81–82, 84–85, 116,
    122, 124, 131, 150, 152
Bridge Programs for low-income students,
    95, 104–105
Bulldogs in the Bluegrass, 101
Bulldogs on the Cuyahoga, 100–102
Business community
    engagement of, 121, 155, 158–159
    people-centered policies and, 148
    skill standards and, 68–71, 84
    talent and, 148
Business consultant strategy, 63
Business intermediaries; see Intermediaries
Business, labor, and representative
    associations, 32
Business-to-business networks, 5
Byrd, Robert, 14

Campus Boulevard Corporation (CBC), 30
Career advancement/pathways, 25, 126,
    150
Career ladders, 24, 135–139
    health-care sector and, 137–139
    obstacles to, 139–140
Carlson, Virginia, 136, 138–140
Case managers, 82
Castilla, Emilio J., 53
Center on Wisconsin Strategy (COWS), 57

Certification, 66–67, 153, 155; see also
    Skill standards
    equity issues, 72
    information technology (IT) credentialing,
    68–71
Chambers of commerce, 32
Charitable organizations, 33
Child care and health care, as employment
    barriers, 54
Clark, Susan, 8
Cleveland Foundation internship program,
    99
Cluster and cluster leadership, 117–121
Community-based organizations (CBOs),
    29–30, 163
Community and technical colleges, 26–28,
    49, 155, 162
    certification, 70, 84–85
Competitiveness, 147
    accelerated innovation and, 3–4
    people and, 3–4, 6, 16
Conway, Carol, 11
Core academic skills, 74
Cortright, Joseph, 4
Council on Competitiveness, 19, 88
Credentials, 149, 156; see also
    Certification
Creticos, Peter, 142–143
Customer choice, 39
Customized intermediaries, 48–49

Davis, Shara, 71
Demographics
    aging of population, 16–17
    changes in, 16–18
    immigration, 16
    minority populations, 16
    racial and ethnic diversity, 16–17
    scenarios for future, 18
    science and technology workforce, 16–17

Department of Education, 30, 35, 74
  National Commission on Excellence in
    Education, 74
Department of Health and Human Services,
  30, 35
Department of Labor, 30, 35, 74
Discrimination, 21, 54

Eastern Idaho Forum for Information
  Technology (EIFIT), 116, 121, 154
Echo boom period, 17
Economic development, 89–95
  core changes in, 10
  decline of jurisdictions, 11
  emerging trends and challenges, 12–13
  federal programs and redistributive
    issues, 7
  globalization effects on, 7–8
  history of, 7
  human capital approach to, 43–46
  models of, 10
  paradigm change in, 3, 21
  resurgence of government role, 10–11
  smokestack chasing model, 7
Education; see also Human capital
    development; Knowledge
    development; Lifelong learning
  community and technical colleges,
    26–28
  core academic skills, 74
  educational divergences, 7
  human capital development strategy, 34–36,
    162
  No Child Left Behind Act, 25
  parents, guidance counselors, 34
  primary schools, 25–26
  public tuition as migration factor, 90
  skill standards, 73–76
  training gap and, 129–130
  universities, 28–29
Emerging workforce, 34
Employer engagement; see also Workforce
    system
  business intermediaries, 121
  challenges to, 111–115
  clusters and cluster leadership, 117–121
  high-road partnerships, 119
  introduction to, 110–111
  multiple information-gathering methods,
    123–124
  personalized relationships, 121–122
  quality issues, 122–123
  strategies for, 115–117
Employer's brand attributes, 55–57

Employment barriers, 53–55
  child care and health care, 54
  employer's brand attributes, 55–57
  finance, 53
  geography, 53–54
  language and culture, 54–55
  race and ethnicity, 54
Employment Policy Foundation (EPF), 14, 19
Empower Baltimore Management
    Corporation (EBMC), 116, 120–121,
    124, 137
Enterprise zones, 8, 120, 137, 140
Entrepreneurial institutions, 47; see also
    Intermediaries
Equality of opportunity, 21, 54
Equity issues, 72, 146

Federal, state, and city agencies, 30–31,
    160–161
Fernandez, Robert M., 53
Financial barriers, 53
Fitzgerald, Joan, 136, 138–140
Flexibility, 40
Florida, Richard, 89, 91
Fogarty, Michael, 15, 73
Food Stamp Employment and Training, 37
Foundations, 33

Gaille, Gary, 8
Gates Foundation, 104
Geographical barriers, 53
George, Pam, 99
Giloth, Robert, 35, 50
Glaeser, Edward, 15
Global labor market, 88, 153
Globalization, 3, 7–8, 19, 24
Goodling Regional Advanced Skills Center
    (ASC), 50–51, 79–80, 84, 116, 123
Gottlieb, Paul, 15–6, 73, 90
Granovetter, Mark, 52–53, 93–94
Greater Cleveland Region case study, 96–109
  attraction strategies
    increasing college enrollments, 102–104
    out-of-state students, 105–106
    outside college graduates, 100–102
    science, engineering, and math
      programs, 106
  bridge programs, 104–105
  degree completion, 104
  embedding young professionals, 106–107
  lessons from, 107–109
  retention strategies
    high-achieving college students, 99–100
    local college students, 98–99

Grubb, W. Norton, 128–130
Guidance counselors, 34
Gulf Coast Workforce Board, 61–64, 116
  business consultant strategy, 63
  industry liaisons, 62
  purpose of industry model, 62

Health care, 54
  career ladder programs, 138
Hickman, Chuck, 103, 106
Hicks, Donald, 12
High-road partnerships, 119
High school graduates, 14–15
Holder, Kim, 105
Holistic training, 81
Holzer, Harry, 68
Human capital development, 5–6, 34–35,
    88; *see also* People-centered policies;
    Talent development, retention, and
    attraction
  economic development, 43–46
  infrastructure for, 151–157
  limitations of WIA, 40

Imai, Ken-ichi, 49
Immigration, 16
Incentives, 111
Income equality gap, 7, 161
Incumbent training, 141–144
  lessons of, 144
  state-financed training programs, 142–143
  variables of, 142
Industrial skill standards, 78–79
Industry groups, 32
Information age, labor market, 3, 23
Information gap, 44
Information-gathering methods, 123–124,
    151
Information technology (IT) certification,
    68–71, 85, 153
Innovation process, acceleration of, 3–4
Intermediaries; *see also* Knowledge-
    economy intermediaries
  career ladder programs and, 136–137
  characteristics of successful, 164–165
  common attributes for success, 152–153
  creating business intermediaries, 121
  customized intermediaries, 48–49
  employer's brand attributes, 55–57
  functional categories of, 48
  Gulf Coast Workforce Board case study,
    61–64
  information management, 64, 151
  knowledge-economy intermediaries, 50–55

Intermediaries *(continued)*
  labor-market negotiators, 49
  one-on-one intermediaries, 48
  ongoing challenges of, 55–57
  overview of, 47–50
  people-centered policies, and, 148
  as system entrepreneurs, 50
  use of, 48
  Wisconsin Regional Training Partnership
    (WRTP) case study, 57–61
International workers, 31
Internships, 98–99
Investing in People, 16

Jacobs, Jim, 70
Jefferson, Mike, 52, 124
Job-finding networks, 52
Job mobility, 24, 94
Job Training Partnership Act (JTPA),
    36–37

Kazis, Richard, 40–41, 112
Klein, Paul, 100
Knowledge
  defined, 4
  tacit knowledge, 4
Knowledge development
  actions for investment in, 5
  human capital development, 5
  new knowledge production, 5
  pace of, 24
  wage inequality, 19
Knowledge economy
  competitiveness and people, 3–4
  as growth driver, 4–6
  intermediaries and, 49
  rich-poor income gap, 18–19
  skill shortages, 13–16
  workforce development and, 3, 6
Knowledge-economy intermediaries, 50–55
  accountability for mission/goals, 51
  characteristics of, 50–51
  employee-employer perspectives on, 50–51
  employment barriers, 53–55
  funding streams, 51
  job-matching function, 53
  local knowledge base, 51
  networking of, 52
  personal relationships of, 52
  social networks and, 52–53
Knowledge Industry Partnership (KIP), 93

Labor market
  changes in organization of, 22–25, 153

Labor market *(continued)*
  competition in, 88
  education and, 23
  industrial economy and, 22
  in information age, 23
  institutional perspective on, 23
  institutions influencing, 23
Labor market negotiators, 49
Labor mobility, 44, 66, 92, 148, 154, 159–160
Labor unions, 32
Language and culture, as employment
    barriers, 54–55
Laufer, Jessica, 55–56, 150
Leete, Laura, 47–48
Life/workplace readiness skills, 75–76
Lifelong learning, 34, 44–45, 72, 157, 159
  advancement programs, 139–141
  career ladders and upward mobility,
    135–139
  defined, 126
  education-training gap, 129–130
  educational entities and, 131–132
  incumbent training, 141–144
  information economy and, 126–127
  instituting a culture of, 126–138
  integrated spectrum of opportunities,
    128–135
  people-centered policies and, 148
Literacy, 15
Local knowledge base, 51

Manke, Bridget, 98–99
Mentoring relationships, 98
Migration patterns, 90
Mills, Jack, 40
Moore, Paul, 52

A Nation At Risk, 74
National Alliance of Business (NAB), 14
National Association of Black MBAs, 101,
  105
National Center on the Education Quality of
  the Workforce, 129
National Center for Health Workforce
  Information and Analysis, 92
National and Community Service Act, 37
National Science Foundation (NSF), 14, 132
National Skill Standards Board (NSSB), 82–83
Neighborhood organizations, 29–30
Networking opportunities, 98
New Horizons Computer Learning Centers, 70
No Child Left Behind Act, 25
Northcoast Consortium for Career
  Advancement (NCCA), 99–100

Northeast Ohio Council on Higher
  Education (NOCHE), 99, 105

Occupational skill standards, 78–79
Ohio College Access Network (OCAN), 102
One-on-one intermediaries, 48
One-stop partner agencies, 38
One-stop service delivery, 37, 112–113
Ong, Paul, 150
Osterman, Paul, 24, 48

Parents, 34
Parker, Eric, 59
People-centered policies, 3, 146–147
  business community and, 148
  as competitive advantage, 6, 16
  credentials, 149, 154
  cultural shift for, 148
  infrastructure for, 151–157
  intermediaries and, 148, 152–153
  labor market mobility and, 148
  leading the change, 160–165
  lifelong learning and, 148
  system to scale, 157–160
  talent expansion strategies, 156
  workforce system for, 147–151
  workforce talent expansion, 148, 151
Performance measures, 39
Personal (soft) skills, 75–76, 85
Personalized relationships, 121–122
Polverine, Denise, 107
Primary schools, 25–26
Prince, Heath, 40–41, 112
Private Investment Councils (PICs), 37
Public institutions
  adaptations of, 11–12
  as learning institutions, 12
Public-private organizations, 32–33

Quality of life issues, 91–92
Quality of workforce issues, 122–123

Race and ethnicity, as employment
  barriers, 54
Racial and ethnic diversity, 16–17
Raphael, Steven, 68
Retail trade, 20
Romer, P. M., 12
Rubin, Jerry, 40–41, 112

Savannah Technical College, 81
School systems, 12
Schorr, Lisbeth, 163–164
Science and technology workforce, 16–17

Secretary's Commission on Achieving
  Necessary Skills (SCANS), 74–75, 78,
  146
Sector/sector focus, 117–118, 158
Service sector dominance, 19–21
Shapiro, Jesse, 15
Sheets, Robert, 142–143
Skill certification, 68
Skill shortages, 13–16
  summary of needs forecasts, 14
Skill standards, 66
  as basis for certification, 67
  Bread and Butter Café, 81–82, 84–85
  business community and, 68–71, 84
  core academic skills, 66, 74
  creating and implementing of, 78–79
  existing standards, 82–84
  general workplace readiness skills, 66
  Goodling Regional Advanced Skill center,
    79–80
  industry core skills, 66
  information technology (IT) credentialing,
    68–71
  insufficient standards, 73
  labor market alignment and, 83
  life/workplace readiness skills, 75–76
  lifelong learning and, 131
  occupational family standards, 66
  occupational/job-specific standards, 67
  personal (soft) skills, 75–76, 85
  prescreening of applications, 81
  schools and educational quality, 73–76
  state level, 83
  STRIVE, 76–78
  support and training, 76–77
Smokestack chasing model, 7
Social networks, 52, 93–94
Social programs, attributes of successful,
  163–164
Southern Technology Council (STC), 89–91
Staffing agents, 33
State-financed training programs, 142–143
Stoll, Michael, 68
Sun MicroSystems, 70
Supply side institutions, 44–45, 150
Support and Training Result in Valuable
  Employees (STRIVE), 76–78, 117
System, defined, 147
System-level strategic planning, 37–38

Tacit knowledge, 4
Talent development, retention, and attraction,
  35, 90, 98
  business community and, 148

Talent development, retention, and attraction
  (continued)
  Greater Cleveland Region case study, 96–109
  attracting out-of-state students,
    105–106
  attraction of outside state college
    graduates, 100–102
  bridge programs for low-incomes,
    104–105
  degree completion strategies, 104
  embedding young professionals,
    106–107
  increasing college enrollment,
    102–104
  retention of high-achieving college
    students, 99–100
  retention of local college students,
    98–99
  science, engineering, and math
    enrollments, 106
  jobs vs. place, 89–95
Talent expansion strategies, 87–89, 156
  comprehensive strategy dimensions,
    94–95
  purpose of, 87
Telecommuting, 11
Temporary Assistance to Needy Families, 37
Temporary firms, 48, 50
Thomas, Chuck, 50, 80, 123
Thomas, Ward, 150
Thurow, Lester, 19
Tournatzky, Louis, 90
Trade associations, 32
Training, 155, 158
  incumbent training, 141–144
  reduction in training opportunities, 41–43
  as screening technique, 48
Training and staffing agents, 33
Transitional workers, 34, 53

Union Mission, 81
Universal access, 38–39
Universities, 28–29, 162
Upward mobility, 126, 135–139
  health-care sector and, 137–139

Vickers, Margaret, 84
Vocational institutions, 155

Wage inequality, 19
Waits, Mary Jo, 9
Welfare-to-work program, 40, 113
"What Work Requires of Schools," 74
Winship, Sian, 55–56, 150

Wisconsin Regional Training Partnership
(WRTP), 49, 51, 57–61, 115–116, 120,
122, 150, 152
benchmark data, 60
firm modernization, 58
incumbent training, 58–59
recruiting, 59
Workforce development, 3, 6, 22; *see also*
Intermediaries; Talent development,
retention, and attraction; Workforce
system
challenges of, 146
in competitive market, 64–65
complexity of, 22
decline of jurisdictions, 11
emerging trends and challenges, 12–13
emerging workforce, 34
lifelong learning, 34–35
talent development, retention, and
attractions, 35
transitional workforce, 34
Workforce Investment Act (WIA), 30–31, 61
accountability, 39–40
customer choice, 39
employers and, 112–114
flexibility, 40
limitations of, 40–43
limited value to business, 40–41
mandatory partner agencies, 38
one-stop service delivery, 37
principles of, 37
promise and limitations of, 36–43
reduction in training opportunities, 41–43
system-level strategic planning, 37–38
universal access, 38–39

Workforce Investment Boards (WIBs), 11,
31–32, 37–39, 112–113, 156
Workforce-related institutions, 25
Workforce system
attributes of successful, 163–164
certification, 72
development of, 24–25
foundations of, 150
governance structure of, 34–36
key players and roles, 23, 25–34
business, labor, and associations, 32
community and technical colleges,
26–28
federal, state, and city agencies,
30–31, 160–161
foundation/charitable organizations,
33
neighborhood/community-based
organizations, 29–30
parents, guidance counselors, 34
primary schools, 25–26
private training/staffing agents, 33
public agencies and, 31
public-private organizations, 32–33
universities, 28–29
workforce investment boards,
31–32
lessons learned in, 147–151
Workforce Investment Boards (WIBs)
and, 32
workforce participation in, 162–163
Workforce training programs, 8
Workplace readiness skills, 78

Yochelson, John, 88

Shari Garmise is assistant professor at the Maxine Goodman Levin College of Urban Affairs at Cleveland State University (CSU). Dr. Garmise received her M.A. in international relations from the Johns Hopkins School of Advanced International Studies and her B.A. from Tufts University.

In 1995, she received her Ph.D. in political science from the London School of Economics, where she specialized in local economic development policy. Prior to her arrival at CSU, Dr. Garmise ran her own economic development consulting business and held the post of vice president for research at the Council for Urban Economic Development, now the International Economic Development Council, the professional association serving economic development practitioners.